STORIES FROM
THE BIG APPLE
AND BEYOND

By

John R. Drake

Stories From the Big Apple and Beyond

By John R. Drake

ISBN– 13:978-1547034017

ISBN–10:1547034017

John R Drake Publications

www.johndrake.gallery

humanitybyjohn@gmail.com

"They call me the seeker

I've been searching low and high

I won't get to get what I'm after

Till the day I die."

THE WHO

STORIES FROM THE BIG APPLE and BEYOND

Stoneleigh Surrey. England

Tuesday 1ˢᵗ June 1976

It was gray when I woke up on my day of departure. My mother was getting ready to go to the coast with her friend from across the road and I felt the worst I had felt in years. Tears were in mother's eyes as I kissed her goodbye once more, and I too broke down and cried. The last couple of months had been a healing time for both of us – the death of my father at sixty years of age had hit my mother hard. A sudden heart attack, and he was gone leaving my mother alone. I had painted the whole house as she was going to get contractors to do it, but I told her to save her money and did it myself, besides it took my mind off my father's death and gave me something concrete to do, but now the time had come to say goodbye. I had finished packing and was waiting for my cousin Sheila to arrive to take me to Heathrow airport. I felt lost and empty, as I waved my mother goodbye from the car, and glanced back to see this little lonely lady of fifty-five standing outside of the house where I had grown up from the age of eleven. The car turned the corner and she was gone and I didn't know when I would see her again.

The flight ended up being three and a half hours late taking off, so I started drinking at the airport bar, and met this American guy who had just come back from Kuwait and seemed like he had already had a drink or two. We were then joined by another American, a woman in her late thirties, who was also flying to New York and then on to her house in Haiti she told us. We had a conversation about Hispaniola and I told her of my experiences in the Dominican Republic. I was beginning to feel like a man of the world again.

1

I boarded the 747 flight 509 to New York and the captain apologized profusely for the lateness of the flight and soon we were high above the Atlantic Ocean flying west to a new world. The film they played was 'The Sunshine Boys' starring Walter Matthau, and I sedated myself in my grief with half a bottle of wine, a quarter bottle of brandy followed by a small vodka and coke. I ate a meal and sank back in my seat as I wondered what I was doing alone in the sky 40,000ft above the Atlantic, heading to a place I knew very little about. I reflected as I was always want to do and turned the pages of my past once again as I thought of Kathy and building swimming pools, thoughts of the cotton mill in North Carolina and how I met and fell in love with Ingrid. I thought of my mother now alone in a house that held so much happiness and pleasure for her and my dear father, who was now just a pile of ashes, and how bizarre and so unpredictable life can be.

After circling over Long Island for forty-five minutes we landed and I got through customs OK and was granted a visa for six months. I rang Ingrid from the airport and told her I had arrived. I caught the bus to 42nd Street in Manhattan, then caught a cab down to Cornelia Street in the village, paid the driver $4.00 and by now it was getting on for ten o'clock at night. I rang the buzzer and suddenly I was once again in Ingrid's arms. She looked as wonderful as ever and we laughed and talked and Ingrid opened a bottle of champagne to celebrate my return. Her apartment was a typical tenement village apartment, with a bathtub in the kitchen. When the tub was not in use it was covered with a board that held cosmetics and smelly stuff. The bedroom was tiny and there were bars on the window, but the place had a nice homey feel to it. There was a couch and a TV set in the living room. The apartment received no direct light as the living room looked down into a courtyard below. We finished the bottle of champagne, and went to bed.

Wednesday June 2nd

Ingrid dressed, then she went off to work and I arranged to see her later in the day in a loft on Broadway where she was working as a secretary to the director. I picked her up and we walked around Manhattan and strolled down Fifth Avenue and I felt like dancing like one of the sailors in 'On The Town' that great musical with Gene Kelly, as New York was becoming more of a reality or maybe it was a movie, and I was now in it. I saw the Empire State building and the Pan Am building and looking downtown the majestic World Trade Towers sparkling in the late afternoon sun. New York – a city I never really thought about visiting, in fact America was not even on the list of countries to visit. I had been put off by American TV with all the violence and shootings and thought that people were killing each other in the streets every day. This was not the case here however, at least not here on Fifth Avenue, in fact it was the hub of modern civilization. There were certainly areas where one had to be careful about going especially at night like Harlem and Alphabet City, but all in all I felt safer here walking around, than I would have in London.

Thursday June 3rd

Lily (Ingrid's friend) called and told me she arranged an interview for me with a known photographer on 22nd St. I spent the day wandering around the village which is easy to do, popping in and out of antique stores on Bleecker Street and in and out of coffee bars like the Figaro and later on in the afternoon I visited a couple of bars whose names I forget. I meandered back to my new temporary home on Cornelia St. Ingrid came home about 7' o clock and we arranged to go dancing with some friends and ended up at Somebody's Steak House where Eighth crosses Fifth. We managed to get in free as it was early, but the drinks were expensive at two dollars a beer. Her friends left early and Ingrid and I danced the night away on an almost empty dance floor, like we had done months earlier in that redneck bar in North Carolina.

3

Friday June 4th.

Went for my interview with Howard the photographer at the studio on 22nd St. He was a really nice guy and seemed to like me, and I him, but he couldn't offer me employment as I didn't have a green card, otherwise he said he would have definitely considered me. I left the studio feeling a little depressed but realized that I had only been in New York a couple of days and I was on a visitor's visa, and was not allowed to work anyway. I walked down Fifth Avenue again until I got to Washington Square Park where I looked up at the hanging tree, and imagined people swinging from a rope there maybe, a hundred years ago. Crazy kids were jumping in and out of the fountain to the sounds of African drums and a familiar smell of marijuana wafted across my nose. It was a hot June afternoon and this was the park where all kinds of people from young to old hung out. Some read books sitting on the benches, hippies sat on the wall strumming guitars facing the fountain, while a couple of preachers were preaching, singers were singing, talkers were talking, walkers were walking, whilst others sat at concrete tables playing chess (like they did years later when they filmed Searching for Bobby Fischer). It was a good show - all of it and I thought how well everyone seemed to interact and just accepted each other.

In the evening, Annie from the film in North Carolina came over - we met at the door and we hugged and kissed – it was good to see her, and memories of North Carolina came streaming back. Later, Roy who was the key grip on the film came over and we all went to get a souvlaki at the local Greek place.

Sunday 6th June

Ingrid left for California, she was about to start work on a documentary down in San Diego to be directed by Robert Young about migrant workers and Mexicans crossing the border illegally looking for a better life in El Norte. Lilly came over and Glenn arrived

4

with a truck filled with equipment and bags of stuff. We all went out for a coffee, and Ingrid and I had a big hug before she got into the truck. Glenn started the engine and off they went leaving a cloud of exhaust fumes behind - California bound, and left me standing, watching as the truck disappeared around the corner. People were coming and going from my life like a turnstile. I turned to Lilly, we both shrugged our shoulders, put on a happy face, then went to get a pizza and a bottle of wine at Emilio's on Sixth Avenue. After we went to the movies to see Missouri Breaks, a western starring the great Marlon Brando and Jack Nicholson, a very bizarre Western, where Brando at one point dresses up as a woman. Lilly left for downtown and I for my new home on Cornelia Street. I walked in the door to number 29 turned on the light, saw a couple of roaches scamper back to their home in the old walls and I went to bed feeling lonely once again.

And so the days went by - a couple of weeks had passed and Monty (who had worked on the film in North Carolina) invited me out to the country in Connecticut to a party at a friend's house, where I had a game of badminton. It was a beautiful house set back from a beautiful lake. There was money in these parts and Connecticut reminded me a little of the countryside of England. There was a girl there who gave me her phone number and insisted that I call her sometime, even though her gentleman friend was standing directly behind her. Well it was the age of free love - a time before aids, a time of love and peace (even though the Haight Ashbury days in San Francisco were over) there was still that feeling in the air. People still wore their hair long and the women dressed in summer cotton dresses.

It was good to get out of Jungleland - to breathe the country fresh air. New York was hot in the summertime and bloody cold in the winter, but the spring and the fall with the leaves on the trees turning from green to explosive colors of rusty browns and reds, yellows and oranges was a sight to behold. I was becoming more and more of a New Yorker each day and understood the need to escape from the Big Apple from time to time. Fortunately work as an electrician at this time enabled me to escape on a couple of films to Connecticut in Westport, another affluent part of New England. So not only did I escape from Manhattan but was also paid to do so. Life was grand.

Sunday 13ᵗʰ June

It was interesting being at Ingi's apartment as it was in a great part of town in between Bleecker Street and West Fourth. A friend of mine knew these two sisters who introduced me to midnight swims at the Carmine Street pool. There was a hole in the wire fence and a few of us would climb through and dive into the pool around midnight for an hour or so, and we would see others who were already there, before us, splashing about, keeping cool. It was the perfect remedy to those steaming hot New York nights in the middle of summer. It was then when I started to feel like a local, as if I had grown up there, as I began to understand the Yin and Yang of the city.

The next few days were spent exploring this magnificent city and I walked around the West Village and the East Village, which really were like villages contained within this huge metropolis. The East Village was fine until you got to Alphabet City, which was the area even east of the East Village. This is where the streets ran in alphabetical order from Avenue A to D. First Avenue was fine and Avenue A began to get a little dodgy at night and usually one wouldn't venture to Avenue B – D especially at night for fear of being mugged. So I walked and walked, as New York is a very walk-able City. I positively walked down Fourth Street, after the name of Dylan's album (Positively Fourth Street) and meandered around all day immersed in the daily hustle and bustle. Things moved a lot faster here than in London. People spoke faster and didn't bother with superfluous words such as 'please' and 'thank you' which to start with I found to be very rude, but later realized that I wasn't in London anymore! This was the new land of America and it was all right - there was no time for 'please' and 'thank you.' Everyone seemed to be on a mission going somewhere, probably to work or a meeting, while I spun around mesmerized by all this human energy. It was an exciting place to be and for the next few days I had to shake my head and tell myself that I was in Manhattan (a word derived from Manna-hatta from the Lenape language of the Lenape Indians. The word was written in the 1609 logbook of an officer who sailed with Henry Hudson an Englishman. In 1626 Manhattan was sold to the Dutch colonists from an unnamed native tribe in exchange for trade for the sum of about $25! Which is about the cost of three pints of beer now! I continued to wander around the city for the next few days thinking what it must have been like to have first sailed in here.

I continued to explore Bob Dylan's village and saw Folk City a bar/club on Fourth Street where Dylan played some of his early songs and The Bitter End, a club I used to go to quite often. I ventured to Midtown, Seventh Avenue in the thirties, the heart of the rag trade and further north to the infamous 42nd St. where all the porno theatres were and sex shops and drug dealers, then over to Broadway – theatre land. Everywhere I went a song entered my head, as the fantasy of New York became a very definite reality. I began to sing to myself 'New York, New York such a wonderful town, the Bronx is up and the Battery's down where people ride in a hole in the ground.' Then at 59th Street I hit the park – Central Park, and at this point the city changed yet again, it opened up and became grand and expensive as I looked up at the apartments on Central Park South, as the horse and carriages disappeared with young lovers into the foliage and greenery of the park. I bought a hot dog from a vender at the entrance to the park. The guy who sold it to me was from Eastern Europe and I realized that this city was built from people from all over the world- it really was a huge melting pot. What does it say at the Statue of Liberty?

"Give me your tired, your poor, your huddled masses yearning to breathe free, the wretched refuse of your teeming share. Send these, the homeless, tempest tossed to me. I lift my lamp beside the golden door."

1976 The Year of the Bi-Centennial

I was still living at Ingi's place on Cornelia Street when July 4th turned up (Independence Day), on which day the Americans, (God bless their souls) celebrate the signing of the Declaration of Independence from people like me - the British, proclaiming their separation from Great Britain. From that day on 'all men were created equal,' but they were soon to realize that some are born more equal than others. However it was a noble gesture and the pursuit of happiness was most paramount in my own personal psychology of life.

So a bunch of people, mostly from the film crew from North Carolina decided to get together to do the loft party scene in Soho and Tribeca. We all met up somewhere or other in Soho and someone dished out some Mickey Mouse blotter acid, which we digested with a drink or two. And so the adventure began! I was still an apprentice to the New York scene and so everything still seemed fresh, exciting and exotic. The streets were alive with people and celebrations had started early for a lot of downtowners, and it seemed as if half the city was on some kind of hallucinogenic or other. Everyone was smiling and there was an incredible feeling of good will and joy in the air. People embraced each other on the streets and wished each other well. It was a red, white and blue day, commercial products appeared in the tri colors and everything seemed to be painted red, white and blue, including mailboxes and fire hydrants. There was a strong feeling of healthy patriotism in the air as New York City grew taller every minute. The Vietnam War had ended a couple of years before and people seemed to have a positive attitude towards the future.

And so the festivities began and our happy band of brothers and sisters scampered from one loft party to the next, ending up on roofs, looking out over the harbor at the sailing ships anchored there. Tall ships from days past had sailed into New York Harbor from all over the world. It was a beautiful sight and I was transported back in time imagining what life was like back in those days, as I remembered my visit to Nelson's ship 'The Victory' in dear Olde England.

Another rickety staircase to a roof appeared before me, as Mickey began to change my perspective of solid matter, as one particular staircase felt like I was stepping into a bucket of jelly. People began to look into each other's eyes and start to laugh - a minute would turn into an hour, or a second, as time had no bearing on the moment and the moment became a moment, like the blink of an eyelid. Then it was off to the next party until the sun went down, when we all made our way to the elevated west side highway, down to Battery Park to watch the firework display that was about to take place at the Statue of Liberty. And so it got dark and fireworks came rocketing out of Chinatown lighting up the sky to the east. Music was playing and the Stars and Stripes were flying everywhere and people were singing the National anthem and I was beginning to shrink like Alice as my 'trip' was nearing my destination and I thought that maybe I shouldn't speak, in case I revealed that I was an Englishman and maybe some of these Yankees around me didn't like the English, (after all these celebrations were to do with kicking the English out!). So I was watching all the fireworks exploding from Chinatown when a man with a broad Brooklyn accent tapped me on the shoulder and said, "Hey buddy the fireworks are over there!" and pointed in the direction of the Statue of Liberty - and there sure enough was this amazing display of the rocket's red glare, and the bombs bursting in air, and then all of a sudden a rocket shot way higher than all the others and a perfect star spangled banner exploded into the air, high into the sky, above the Statue of Liberty, and twinkled and fell as if in slow motion, and the star spangled banner in triumph did wave, over the land of the free and the home of the brave, as it sunk into the dark deep sea. And the show was over and the people cheered and cried and emotions ran high and I think a tear may have trickled from my eye, and it was a spectacle to behold and the atmosphere was electric and I was amazed and felt so lucky to have been a part of this most exciting and extraordinary day, and I don't think that I have experienced anything quite like it since.

I went back to Cornelia Street where I wrote a poem, still high on LSD. I also wrote a screenplay that year about growing up in England

9

in the sixties called 'Hard Knocks.' I wanted to use the Kinks music as a soundtrack as they epitomized the social structure of England at that time with songs like 'Dead End Street,' and 'Dedicated Follower of Fashion.' These were the days of the 'Swinging Sixties.' I sent the script to Lorimar Productions - they liked it, they said, and I got a positive letter back from them, except they were busy with other productions etc. etc. so I didn't pursue it any further.

1976 turned out to be quite the year worldwide. Jimmy Carter was elected President of the United States and James Callaghan became the Prime Minister of England as Harold Wilson resigned. Patty Hearst was arrested and found guilty for her part in a bank robbery, after being abducted by The Symbionese Liberation Army. She was threatened with death, but then became supportive of their cause. She was the Granddaughter of William Randolph Hearst.

There were riots at the Notting Hill carnival in London, which was of no surprise to me, knowing how the English love to get drunk and rowdy, and the world's longest pier in Southend England was destroyed by fire. Paul Kossoff of one of my favorite bands at the time being 'Free' died at the age of twenty six, never even making it to the magic number of twenty seven, the age when all the super rock stars died like Hendrix, Janis Joplin, Jim Morrison and Brian Jones. I will always remember dancing to the 'Free' song 'All Right Now' at a party in Virginia Water, and I could not get the song out of my head for weeks after. Agatha Christie who wrote 'Murder on the Orient Express' and other great novels, died at the age of 86, (the age my mother died) and so did John Paul Getty the billionaire. Isabel Peron who was the first female president in the world was deposed as President of Argentina by a military coup. She sanctioned political murders and was responsible for the disappearance of hundreds of political dissidents. She went to Spain and remained there, despite efforts to extradite her for human rights violations in Argentina.

1976 also saw the first commercial flight of Concorde and NASA unveiled the first space shuttle 'The Enterprise.' Steve Jobs formed the 'Apple Computer Company' in April of that year, which gradually opened up the world to an infinite amount of possibilities, one of them affording me to write down all my madness, and talking of madness 'One Flew Over the Cuckoos Nest' was released starring Jack Nicholson and Brad Dourif, whom I met the year before working on the 'The Gardner's Son' in North Carolina. Other films that were released that year were 'Rocky' and the amazing 'Taxi Driver' starring Robert De Niro. By the end of the year graffiti art was adorning many walls down in Soho and one artist in particular stood out from the rest, and his name was Basquiat. So by the time Christmas rolled around and the year was about to end I counted my blessings that I was living in the best city in the world at that time.

NEW YORK ON THE FOURTH OF JULY 1976

In the dark and dank catacombs of your brain lies a man,

In the wet weary tunnels of your heart lies a woman,

But the two are miles apart.

Although entombed within the frame of one mould

You're fitted out from head to toe like a Goddess or an angel to

behold.

Whilst the noise carries on its endless interruption,

And the clouds drift past your windowpane,

And the badges glint of blatant corruption,

Then you see yourself wading through the conglomeration

Of the beaten brains that squelch in your path,

But you know they're just a shadow of their extinct sophistication.

11

And you talk, but words get in your way
Just around your neck entangled,
With the flags and streamers in the street bespangled,
By a non- existent past, that's grown up much too fast
And a policy for gays to rule the world.
Then you look around and see there's not a single bumble - bee,
Nor a bird in the sky that wants to fly,
And your eyes are open, but you cannot see.

The chariots holding Romans stand undefeated,
As Caesar at the Senate sees the faces of the pirates and jokes
retreated,
And a pizza in the night will soothe your appetite
As a burger in the day will make you pay another way,
But it's there anyway just in spite.

The towers like two rockets stand majestic,
And the other is dwarfed and neglected
As two brothers sprang out the earth, like on elastic.
Meanwhile deeper in your body lies the square,
That's full of hundreds sitting and just talking,
And the sun is shining bright
And there's no one in the park would give a care.

The pimples on your skin secrete pollution,

While the convict and the priest

And the beauty and the beast,

Shrug their shoulders as if to say no solution.

All the same the atmosphere is electric,

And then later in the night, your eyes are shining bright

And you seem to me to act quite paralytic.

Although your friendliness is parasitic,

You feed them tea and lead and then lead them to your bed,

But you know your intercourse is quite synthetic.

There's a part of you that is quite pornographic,

But you wear it with a smile as they hand you a file

To escape into the National Geographic.

The travelers that make up the paraphernalia,

Will stand around all day, as their dreams get swept away

By the sinking British ships of the regalia.

And the whole show's for the sake of history

Red, white and blue, all the colors are for you,

But to me the whole thing's just a mystery.

New York on the Bi- Centennial 1976

The elevated West Side Highway 1976

Bethune Street

So I had moved into a small one-bedroom apartment on Bethune Street above The Bus Stop Coffee Shop. It was on the second floor and the buses would stop right below my fire escape and chug away until they drove off. There was a working fireplace in the living room/kitchen, which was a huge asset, and in the winter I would lay on my captain's bed and watch the Duralogs burn away for the next three hours. The other great thing about my apartment was the rent, which was a walloping $175 a month – this was in 1977. Now I believe it rents for just over $2000 a month. By the way, in these days I was working as a best boy electrician making about $350 a day with some overtime, so my rent added up to half a day's pay!

I had a friend called Duane, (a grip) who I met on a film who drove an Econoline van, who suggested driving me to the Upper East Side where he said I would be able to find furniture for my humble abode. So we drove to the Upper East Side (where the rich people lived), the night before the garbage trucks came around. We drove up one street and down the next and sure enough someone had thrown out onto the sidewalk a captain's bed, single with drawers underneath, which was in great condition. We loaded it into the van then drove a few more blocks – eyes peeled, looking for more free gifts from the doctors and lawyers who inhabited this neighborhood who threw out perfectly good pieces. Somewhere near York Avenue and the seventies I spotted two wooden chairs (they weren't Louis XIV), but good enough for me, and once again there was absolutely nothing wrong with them. We jumped out and loaded them into the van, when I turned around and spotted on the other side of the road a small stereo – turntable unit with two attached speakers, so I thought, "Why not?" We had a good night hunting and the two scavengers carried the spoils of the night up the one flight of stairs to my tiny apartment and voila! It was furnished. The bedroom was tiny, but had a loft bed where underneath I used as an office. I bought a Queen sized mattress for the loft, some plates, cutlery, glasses, coffee mugs etc... and now I had

15

my very own home in The West village in Manhattan, The Big Apple, New York City.

The next day I went out into the village and bought Bruce Springsteen's album "Born To Run" from a record store on Bleecker Street, then went home to play it on my free record player, over and over until I almost wore out the grooves. I was living in the greatest city in the world, in the center of the universe, where life moved at an incredible pace 24 hours a day. There wasn't time to sleep, as an electric energy vibrated on those Manhattan streets. It was now the middle of the summer and temperatures had soared into the high 90's and even hit the low 100's. I sat on my fire escape at night, when it had cooled down to a balmy 80 degrees and listened as Bruce serenaded me from the turntable as he sang about "A town full of losers and suicide machines." I think my favorite track was " Meeting Across the River" – "Hey Eddie can you lend me a few bucks, can you give me a ride – got a meeting with a man on the other side," as I was stranded in the jungle and taking all the heat that it was giving. It was perfect and incredibly relevant and just as I felt like a member of 'Sergeant Pepper's Lonely Hearts Club Band' in London I was now a part of 'The Runaway American Dream.' New York pulsated with an excitement that I had never felt before and quite honestly in this period of time left dear old London Town back in the Dark Ages. There was no comparison. The clubs in New York were cool and stayed open all night and were full of all kinds of people, of course there were always the pretentious ones, but all in all a great bunch of interesting people inhabited these places – artists, poets, musicians most of them struggling to get by, but enjoying every minute of it.

I used to go to the Mudd Club down on White Street in the area called Tribeca, which was a synonym for the triangle below Canal Street. Canal Street separated Soho (the area south of Houston Street) from Tribeca. Tribeca at this time was a strange desolate place that smelt of spices. This was the area along with Soho where the artists lived in commercial spaces that were sometimes as big as 4,000sq.ft. Usually at weekends there would be a party in one of these lofts and I would run into as many as fifty people that I knew. It was a great community and one felt special to be a part of it.

The Summer of Sam 1976

So after Independence Day things sort of went back to normal - whatever that was in The Big Apple, as life had taken a different turn. I was no longer a drifter and after crazy adventures as a young man in London, Greece, India and the Caribbean, I seemed to be involved in some sort of career that turned out to be the film business. I was working on commercials, industrials and low budget films. I started as a second grip to a friend of mine who was a key grip, but after a couple of jobs realized that I wanted to learn how to be a gaffer and so switched to the electric department, where I became a 'best boy' to some of the best gaffers in town. I joined N.A.B.E.T the local union in New York, which was filled with like-minded people as myself, many having studied at film schools in New York and other places, but most of them falling into the business by being at the right place at the right time. The union in New York had a lot of members who were Vietnam Vets, so the film business was a good transition for many, as working on a film needed a certain amount of discipline and hard work and long hours, without the thought of getting one's head blown off! There were many wild and crazy characters in the world of film in New York and almost everyone I met back in those days seemed to be pretty interesting or just stark raving mad. I fitted in there somewhere and had some amazing friends.

So one job lead to the next and working relationships were formed, whereby if you did a good job and kept your mouth shut, then more than likely you would be hired back for the next job. So I decided to take this new career a little more seriously than other jobs I had done in the past, especially as this film world enabled me to travel with work and stay in different places and actually get paid for it.

I got some business cards printed that read: GOLDENHIND PRODUCTIONS. The Gay Gaffer.

With my name and phone number underneath. Needless to say when I handed out my card I received some very strange looks, especially as I was living in the West Village that at the time was known as the gay part of town. Where I came from, that is to say England - gay meant happy, so I thought that people would want a happy person on the set. A friend of mine then explained that the Goldenhind was also not a good idea! The Goldenhind was in fact Sir Francis Drake's ship, that he sailed around the world in, and as I had the same surname as this famous pirate, thought it to be the perfect name for my small production company, but needless to say, I didn't use the cards again.

Then there was the famous meat - packing district, which started up in the early 1800's, and by the turn of the 20th century rows of open air meat markets lined the cobblestone streets, and by the time I lived around the corner on Bethune Street in 1976 there were over 100 businesses handling meat, with sides of beef hanging off hooks, dripping blood everywhere and men with knives in their hands wearing blood soaked white aprons. In the summer flies would be buzzing around their heads and landing on the nice juicy bloody carcasses. But this time in history the meat market had other connotations. It was where the transvestites would sell their wares or maybe just give them away. At night they would saunter up and down the streets in their high-heeled shoes with handbags in hand, wearing some strange clothes as if from Victorian times. Others wore very little and paraded up and down with all the others. It was a strange scene, but one that added to the eccentric nature of Manhattan. Then of course there was the famous Christopher Street, that was laden with gay bars and restaurants and closer to the West Side Highway the area became very seedy and potentially dangerous, where boys and men would cruise the strip there looking for a partner. There were codes that had to do with the wearing of colored handkerchiefs in the back pockets that signified one's preferences as to who would like to do what, to whom, or who would like to be done by. There was a joke or two of course about all this area, but the one I remembered was: "What do you do if you drop your keys on Christopher Street?" and the answer was "Kick them to Seventh Avenue." For those who don't get the joke - too bad as I am not going to explain! There were many strange sadistic and masochistic dive bars - one called The Anvil, which according to legend actually had a rack that one could be stretched out on, and after a long hard day on a film set the crew would crack jokes about going there, and getting their backs put back into place on the rack. Don't know anyone who went there or even if this rack thing was true, but probably was! There was a club called the Mineshaft which became even more popular to the gay population after it was used as a location in Friedkin's film 'Cruising' starring Al Pacino, about the dark seedy world of this neighborhood. In 1985 Mayor Koch closed down the gay bars and bathhouses as AIDS had become an epidemic and hundreds of men were dying of the disease.

I met a girl called Robin who worked as a waitress in a dive on Bleecker Street, she would get off work at about 12, or sometimes 2am, and would usually take a cab to my humble abode, but some nights I would walk there to meet her and pick her up for fear that Sam may be out there stalking young girls. Sam (whose real name was David Berkowitz), also known as the Son of Sam and the .44 Caliber Killer was eventually arrested in August of 77 for killing six victims and wounding seven others - most were young women. The first shooting by the Son of Sam occurred in the Pelham Bay area of the Bronx and other murders in Flushing Queens. Lots of people in New York were freaked out about this serial killer on the loose and as the summer wore on David Berkowitz was becoming somewhat of a celebrity as he eluded a massive police hunt, taunting the police with letters suggesting further crimes, which of course was highly publicized by the New York press. When he was eventually captured he confessed to all the murders and explained that he was obeying the orders of a demon manifested in the form of a dog that belonged to his neighbor Sam. At the time of his arrest he was working for the U.S. postal service, so I don't if that was where the expression 'going postal' came from?

The West Side Highway 1976

It was New Year's Eve - the end of 1976, and the beginning of 1977, and I had been living in New York for just over six months. I had become a New Yorker, and was proud of it! I had been on a non-stop roller coaster ride all this time, and by the time everyone said 'Happy New Year' my head was still spinning. I stood at 42nd Street at Times Square with three or four other friends, as the countdown began, 5 - 4 - 3 - 2 - 1 and the ball came down, and everyone was happy wishing everyone else a Happy New Year! People were hugging and kissing each other that you had never met in your life before, and people were happy, and the noise from those horns that you blow, and the car horns in the street was enough to blow out your eardrums! The streets were packed with people, and you could barely move for fear of stepping on someone's foot, but there was no trouble and people were courteous to each other. I was thinking if this were London there might be a good fight going on right now with a bunch of drunken hooligans! I believe we walked for a few blocks south, to let the crowds die down and then we jumped on a subway back down to the village.

When I awoke it was the beginning of a new year. The shops and the banks were closed and quite a few bars and restaurants, but there was still enough bars open to keep the serious revelers reveling. It was cold and people started to venture out onto the streets more and more as it got close to midday. It was a new year and I couldn't wait to get it going! I still saw Ingrid on and off, but now she had a boyfriend that lived in Seattle and would buzz off there to see him.

Summer arrived and I continued working, and one job I distinctly remember was out on Long Island. Coming home in the van the crew and I were drinking a few beers and Manhattan with all its lights looked like a Christmas tree through the windshield. Suddenly half the cities lights went out in the downtown area and we all looked at each other wondering what had happened. It was the evening of July 13, 1977, and it was the New York City blackout.

We drove back in to the city through the tunnel and entered a mysterious world - a city with no lights - no streetlights, and no lights in the homes. The city was being lit only by car headlights, which created a wonderful sense of mystery. We all got dropped off in our neighborhoods and I went back to Bethune Street and lit some candles. People were still on edge over the Son of Sam murders, and the night was made for another Jack the Ripper to appear. The village seemed pretty calm and people dealt with the situation very well, but looting and vandalism became widespread especially in the poorer neighborhoods, and over four thousand people were arrested for looting, as another four thousand had to be rescued from the subways which had to have been a nerve racking experience. This night was labeled, 'The night of terror' by some. The TV stations were off the

21

air and the city was thrown back into a time before electricity and in that respect was interesting.

I am not sure what caused the blackout, but there was a brutal heat wave going on at the time, so whether the power stations were overloaded or not I can't remember. I sat outside on my fire escape, taking all the heat of the city, as I cracked open a beer and actually enjoyed this strange experience. The power was out for about twenty-four hours, when everything returned back to normal. New York recovered as New York always does.

In the United Kingdom June 7th had been the Queen's jubilee to celebrate her reign so far of twenty-five years, so I drank a toast to Her Majesty with another Englishman at The White Horse Tavern.

Roman Polanski was arrested, charged with a number of offenses including sodomy rape and the use of drugs upon a child. Elvis, 'The King of Rock and Roll' died on August 16th from a massive heart attack at the age of 42. An autopsy found that he had ten times the amount of codeine in his system that had been prescribed. He had been in bad health and was quite overweight. Later in the year Jimmy Carter was elected president and being a good man he granted pardon to the draft dodgers of the Vietnam War. The Clash released their first album called 'The Clash' and The Eagles came out with 'Hotel California' and Saturday Night Fever and Annie Hall were playing at the movie theatres. The great Charlie Chaplin, Bing Crosby, and Vladimir Nabokov who wrote 'Lolita' also died that year along with Elvis. So once again it was the end of yet another year.

New Year's Eve was always a crazy time as there were always so many parties to attend and one tried to jam as many as one could into one night. The streets were jammed with people hailing cabs and once inside they hardly moved, and so it was quicker to walk. There were so many times I wished the turbaned Sikh taxi driver a happy new year as the clock struck midnight as I was in-between parties desperately trying to get to the next one. Cabbies beeped their horns and people yelled out 'happy new year' to strangers.

A Porn Film

One day I get a call from a friend of mine, telling me of a job, for me to work as his 2nd grip, him being the Key. "Are you available from next week for ten days to work on this film?"

"Of course" I answer, "What is it?"

"Well it's another porno," he said a little reluctantly.

"Work's work," he said before I could say another word.

I had already worked on one with a certain director of photography who is now quite well known in the world of TV. Quite a few cameraman cut their teeth so to speak in this line of work usually working under made up names such as Mickey Mole (which is a light) as they didn't want people to know that they had stooped so low as to be working on such smut. These were the early days of porn and many a film had fairly good budgets, which enabled the films to be shot in 35mm using Panavision cameras sometimes, or else on super sixteen, but it was all shot on film as opposed to shooting on video, so that the cum shots could be seen in wonderful slow motion! Ah what a world I had now found myself in!

I had worked with this grip on another film a couple of weeks before and it was during the time a hurricane was blowing in through Manhattan sending garbage cans up into the air, crashing down on to parked cars. People had boarded up their windows so save them being smashed from flying debris. Meanwhile inside of a sleazy hotel, the director was showing the 'lead actor' how to use a bullwhip. As the hurricane progressed we moved down from the mezzanine of the hotel where we were shooting, to the lobby and then ended up in the basement. Needless to say that the hotel had been closed for renovation so we had the use of it while the thunder and lightning was rumbling and crackling outside. I felt like I was in between the pages of 'The Pit and the Pendulum.' I saw things that I had never seen before (being a nice innocent lad from England) and naked women were walking around everywhere, and men too.

There were a couple of teamsters on the job, one who particularly liked me because of my accent, and he would comment from time to time on the performances, not in a Shakespearean tongue, but in a language that I could barely understand, which did fit in with the whole shebang. He used to make me laugh with his crude sense of humor (long before The Sopranos came into being).

So the following week I found myself on the set of another porn film, and of course it was much like the last, not a lot of dialogue (thank God, as these were certainly not actors from the Stella Adler school) their performances were more physically driven shall we say! I remember asking one of the actresses what she does in the evening as she spent all day shagging every Tom Dick and Harry.

"Oh I have a boyfriend."

"And he knows what you do for a living?" I stuttered.

She replied that her boyfriend was cool with it all, as she was keeping him - while he was writing a book. She was from San Francisco, so I decided people were more open to that sort of thing there. She was actually a very beautiful redhead with lilywhite skin and beautiful cheekbones and if you saw this woman in the street on Fifth Avenue your head would turn, especially as she dressed so elegantly.

So the days went by and another day on the set and more rumpy pumpy all around, I saw things that I could never have imagined possible. We were filming in the very heart of the red light district and I believe the Hotel was called 'The Royal Manhattan Hotel,' which was under renovation at the time, but there was nothing very 'Royal' about it and could not imagine the Queen staying there! I could go into more gruesome detail that would probably sell more copies of this book, but I would sooner leave the rest up to the imagination of the reader.

24

I had written a letter home to my dear old Mum telling her that I had got into the film business thinking that she would be very proud of me - needless to say I didn't tell her exactly the type of film I was working on. At one point in the making I was asked to hold an inky (a light of about 200 watts) with the obligatory pink gel attached to add more light to the actresses vagina that was winking right at me - it was a fascinating sight and I thought that maybe I should change my profession to gynecologist, while at the same time thinking about the 'dear mum' letter I had written just a couple of days earlier. Well it was all in a days work, but the worst job on the set was for the make-up girls who walked around with a large box of Kleenex all day - say no more! So after ten days or so of filming in 35mm the film came to an end and I was ready to get me to a monastery!

Manhattan from the top of the Empire State building

I never planned on going to America, and New York was the last place on Earth I ever wanted to visit, but as destiny had it, I ended up in Miami, then North Carolina and eventually New York. I had finally found a place where I belonged. I loved everyone I met (well almost everyone) and loved a lot of women there. They were liberated, free of convention and radical, being in their twenties, and having left home for the Big Apple and were ready for a life of excitement and creativity. They were jazz dancers, ballet dancers and I even met a belly dancer from Connecticut! A couple of girls I met were studying to be lawyers, and I remember one who loved to smoke pot all day, and I often wondered what happened to her? There were songwriters, poets, screenwriters, authors, painters, sculptors and waitresses studying to be actresses and actresses wanting to just be mothers. No matter what people were doing they seemed to be enjoying their life and seemed to be genuinely happy with their lot.

A whole new world had opened up to me. I was living in Greenwich Village and one could still feel the vibes from those times and the days of the beat generation. The Bottom Line (a music venue) and Folk City where Dylan played were still happening and I would walk these streets, bug eyed and in awe of what those days must have been like. There was a good smoky club called The Village Vanguard where Kool jazz musicians played. I was not a huge jazz fan, but enjoyed the atmosphere there, watching these very cool black dudes play their music. Big strong black hands plucking the strings on a stand up base, as trumpets cut through the swirling clouds of toxic blue cigarette smoke. It epitomized New York for me and when I was there I felt like I was in an old black and white 1940's film starring Humphrey Bogart, as I listened to 'some broad' sing seductively into the microphone. I did know who Miles Davis was and Thelonious Monk (because I liked the name) and Charlie Mingus, who I believed all played there at one time or another. I can't remember whom I saw but after leaving the place in the early hours of the next morning, had to shake my head once again to realize where I was living. There was a modern history to Manhattan - it wasn't ancient, like the history of

26

London, but somehow this history of New York of the forties, fifties and sixties seemed more relevant to my life at that moment.

Then there were the film art houses - The Bleecker Street Cinema and not forgetting The Elgin Cinema up on Eighth Avenue, which would show double and triple features, old black and white films from directors such as Bergman and Truffaut, Goddard and Fellini. This was a perfect place to spend a cold wintery afternoon with the latest love of one's life watching flickering images on the big screen and forgetting about the snow piled up outside. After the double feature a nice cappuccino at The Figaro Café or Café Dante on Macdougal Street would be in order, and then a walk back along the snowy streets to my abode. This was definitely another time, another era - it was a romantic time, a black and white time and I for one felt very much as though I were living in a movie. There was a certainty about life that I remember, a feeling of great hope and joy and people that I knew seemed very aware of what was going on. They were intelligent and creative and I felt very much a part of this unique moment in time.

Carl's Visit

Carl came to visit me from South Carolina, where he had been the art director on the 'Gardner's Son,' the film where we first met in Chapel Hill. He was a good - hearted fellow - a real southern gentleman, born in Sumter, South Carolina, which was an important supply route for the Confederacy during the Civil War. He was ten years my senior and was a mentor to me, being quite the expert on Greek mythology, and had even made himself a Trojan helmet, an exact replica of the real thing. He lived in the woods just outside of Columbia S.C. and drove an old Volkswagen bus that had bullet holes in the door from the rednecks shooting at it. They didn't like hippies in that part of the world! Carl was not really a hippie, although he did love to get high and when he did he turned into a naughty teenage boy that was so refreshing to see. He had a great sense of humor and was a bit of a practical joker, always looking on the bright side of life with 'Monty

Python' being his favorite show and very often quoting from John Cleese, Michael Palin and the rest of the gang. He was quite athletic and quite short but stocky at about 5' 7' and many a time you would see him walking around on his hands with his feet in the air - not in New York, but when he was out in the country where he felt more at home. He wore a good thick grey beard with short grey hair and looked like a sage of sorts. One week in the Big Apple was usually enough for Carl as he found the people and the place to be all too much and would look at the eccentrics and laugh his good old southern boy head off! By the end of the week he would get the shakes and would realize it would be time to go back to the woods where the rednecks would take pot shots at his cabin when they drove by in their pickup trucks. I don't think they liked his cow skull that was attached to the front of the van either!

So Carl slept on the futon in the living room and at night we would play my record player and put on LP's from Crosby Stills and Nash, James Taylor, Joni Mitchell and like me he enjoyed 'mellow music' with a folk feel to it. Of course there were many times when Mick and the boys would hop on to the turntable with 'Jumping Jack Flash' and 'Street Fighting Man' depending on how much alcohol we had consumed.

One day we decided to meet up with Ingrid who he hadn't seen for quite a while and the three of us decided to go out for lunch somewhere in Soho (possibly the Prince Street Bar). Now I am not sure how this happened but out came the LSD again - I don't know who procured it, but there it was and before we knew it we had ingested it, and was beginning 'our trip' into the unknown. Suddenly our small party of three turned into six as Ingrid now had a twin sister and Carl a twin brother. We ordered brunch and I had some fries and a burger. For a joke I placed one of the fries in between one of my fingers substituting a finger for a fry and coated the inside of the fry with a large dollop of ketchup. I then held up my hand to Ingrid and bit off the French fry along with the red ketchup. My practical joke worked and Ingrid thought I had bitten my finger off, while Carl was in hysterics Ingrid let out a cry that was heard in Brooklyn and needless to say we were asked to leave the restaurant, which we did, as the rest of the customers looked on. I didn't go back to that bar for quite a while.

So what were we to do now that the three of us had just gone through the looking glass? Well it was obvious of course - take the A train to Harlem. So down the hole in the ground we went and jumped on the rickety rackety A train where we made our way to the front and the three of us screamed like children as the train flew into the darkness around corners at break neck speed. We alighted at 125th street in the heart of Harlem and the three of us came out into the sunlight - three white honkies amass a sea of black faces, but nobody cared we were just other humans having a good time and laughing which I think was appreciated by our brothers and sisters. So nothing bad or crazy happened otherwise I would have remembered and somehow or other we made it back Downtown.

Kiss Me I'm Puerto Rican

After the couple of porno films, I got onto a real film, called 'Kiss Me I'm Puerto Rican.' I was now working as a best boy to the gaffer who was Nancy Schreiber. The best boy or 'sparks' as they are called in England (for obvious reasons) are responsible for getting electrical power from the distribution boxes to the lights, which in turn comes from a generator, or back in those days a "tie in" to a distribution box or breaker box in the basement where the filming was to take place, whether it be in a house or barn or wherever.

The best boy also handles the lights under the direction of the gaffer. The term best boy is an old English term, and would be the master's oldest and most experienced apprentice and usually the second in charge. The gaffer confers with the DP (director of photography) as to the placing of the lights and ultimately 'the look of the film.' Gaffer can also mean the boss or manager back in old England and is also a slang term for Grandfather and was meant as a term of respect. Other definitions include; a mumbling of obscure words, that don't follow any pattern of language and /or a person who has an eccentric personality and dances in public without music, all of which I have been guilty of. Gaffer also means foreman in charge of a gang of workers. Another definition of gaffer was the man who tended the street lamps with a pole and a hook, during the time of Jack the Ripper!

So here I was working now as a crewmember on a 'real movie' with a responsible job. I felt like I was part of a circus. The film was starring Raul Julia and I believe this may have been his very first film. I remember he was working on 'Three Penny Opera' on Broadway at the time also. After a few days of filming or maybe a week I happened to be plugging in a light when the director came up to me and asked me if I wouldn't mind playing Jesus next to Raul Julia in a crazy dream sequence where Raul would sit between Jesus and the Devil. They had a guy to play Jesus but the director didn't like him for some reason, so I was picked for the part as I was sporting long hair and a beard at the time. Next thing I knew I was wearing a robe and walking onto the 'dream scene set,' meanwhile Nancy the gaffer was yelling out for me, but I had already been promoted to Jesus and I apologized for the fact that I had been chosen! I suppose the director could tell that I had a very spiritual quality about me! Luckily I wasn't required to speak in Hebrew or to utter any sounds whatsoever, I merely had to sit in a half lotus position with Raul next to me and the Devil on the other side of him. Obviously it was a dream of great conflict and when the shot was done I was back on the set as the best boy, but from that point on I realized I was made for bigger and better things!

On the second or third week of filming out in Brooklyn the crew arrived first thing of a Monday morning, but the atmosphere felt strange as though something had gone wrong. The leading lady had broken out in a terrible case of acne from the makeup and so it was not possible to film her, no matter how much make up was used to hide it. So it was a wrap on the film and it never got finished.

Many years later I was in a bar Uptown on the West Side, and if my memory serves me well I think it was called Café Central which was known as an actors hang out. I can't remember whom I was with, but there at the bar stood Raul Julia - by now it was about midnight or later, so I plucked up enough courage to approach the man after quite a few drinks and said, "I don't know if you remember me but I was Jesus in 'Kiss Me I'm Puerto Rican." I didn't know what response I was going to get as I suppose the film ended as a bit of a disaster, but he immediately lit up as though I was a long lost friend, put his arm around me and bought me a couple of drinks. We spoke until the early hours of the next day about all kinds of things, from Buddhism I remember, to Greece and the islands until eventually the bar cleared out which left just the two of us and a couple of stragglers looking on, as we danced Zorba's dance together, the dance which Anthony Quinn performed on the beaches of Crete in the film of the same name Zorba the Greek. And that was it - a strange evening with a great actor and individual, very engaging and kind, with a free spirit and a great sense of humor. I never saw him again and was very saddened by his death years later.

The Year of 1978

The year for serial killers, psychos and perverts. It seems that '78 in particular uncovered more than usual, although a lot of good things happened as well, such as the USA stopping production of the neutron bomb that was capable of killing people but would leave buildings standing. In which case we would end up with a lot of empty buildings! On the other hand had that bomb been available during WWII all the beautiful buildings would have been left standing and the wonderful architecture would have been preserved and I am sure there would have been enough humans left to have re-populated Europe. Just a thought! War of course on any level should try to be avoided, but as we all know a lot of people make a lot of money from Wars.

31

In February Roman Polanski fled to France before he was formally sentenced for rape and sodomy and the use of drugs on a child thirteen years of age. A great film director, responsible for films such as Chinatown and Rosemary's Baby - what was he thinking?

On March 6 in a legal battle related to obscenity in Gwinnett County Georgia, Larry Flynt and his lawyer were returning to the courthouse when they were both shot on the sidewalk by a sniper across the street. Flynt was left partially paralyzed and had to spend the rest of his life in a wheelchair. He was known for publishing Hustler magazine in July '74.

The Son of Sam was sentenced to 25 years to life in prison and Ted Bundy another serial killer was captured in Pensicola, Florida. Bundy was a serial killer and confessed to thirty homicides, but some estimates have been as high as one hundred. He assaulted and murdered young girls, during the seventies and possibly earlier. He kidnapped and raped his victims and was a necrophile. He decapitated at least twelve of his victims with a hacksaw and kept some of the severed heads in his apartment. He received three death sentences.

The Hillside Strangler claimed victim number ten in Los Angeles. The Hillside Strangler terrorized Los Angeles much like The Son of Sam had terrorized New York. The Strangler turned out to be two cousins who were committing these murders and got the name from the fact that many of the bodies of females were discovered on the sides of the Hollywood Hills. Most of the murders happened between October '77 and Feb '78. The cousins were Kenneth Bianchi and Angelo Buono. Bianchi was later arrested in '79 for the murder of two more young women in Washington, which then linked him to the Hillside murders. The cousins were convicted of kidnapping, raping, torturing and murdering ten females from the ages of twelve to twenty-eight years old and both received life sentences.

In England Keith Moon, the crazy amazing drummer for the Who, died on September 7th at the age of thirty-two. He supposedly was taking a drug to alleviate his alcohol withdrawal symptoms. He was living at Harry Nilsson's flat in London where Cass Elliot (of the Mamas and Papas) died at thirty-two, four years earlier. Nilsson was concerned about letting the flat to Keith as he felt it was cursed.

Bulgarian defector Georgi Markov was assassinated in London, James Bond style by the secret police (KGB) using a poisoned umbrella tip containing ricin. He was a BBC journalist and was waiting for the bus on Waterloo Bridge when he was assassinated.

Back in New York on October 12th Nancy Spungen, the girlfriend of Sid Vicious was found dead in the bathroom of room 100 at the Chelsea Hotel - she was twenty years old. At fifteen she was diagnosed with schizophrenia. She had worked as a prostitute and a stripper and moved to London in '76 where she met Sid Vicious of The Sex Pistols. Together they moved to New York where they lived in room 100 at The Chelsea Hotel and were registered as Mr. and Mrs. John Simon Ritchie, which was Sid's real name. Sid was charged with stabbing Nancy, but it was also believed that she could have died by one of two other drug dealers that had visited that night. Sid died of a heroin overdose while out on bail in February '79.

Harvey Milk was assassinated in San Francisco along with George Mosconi, the Mayor of San Francisco on November 27th. Harvey Milk was an American politician who became the first gay person to be elected for public office when he secured a seat on the San Francisco board of supervisors. Milk was an icon and a leader in the gay community. He was posthumously awarded the Presidential Medal of Freedom. Diane Feinstein succeeded the murdered George Moscone to become the first woman Mayor of San Francisco.

Pope Paul VI died at the age of eighty and John Paul I became the Pope and mysteriously dies in his bed of a heart attack thirty-three days later, when Cardinal Karol Wojtyla becomes Pope John Paul II.

Just to round up the year for mass murder. In November in Jonestown Guyana, Jim Jones who was a cult leader and had his own church called 'The Peoples Temple Agricultural Project' (which sounds to me like he was going to turn everyone into vegetables) murdered 918 people by forcing most of them to drink Kool Aid laced with cyanide. Over 300 of these were children. He believed he and his followers would all die together and move to another planet where they would live blissfully. He started Jonestown as a means to create a socialist paradise and a sanctuary away from the media. Before the move to Guyana he started to preach that he was the reincarnation of Mahatma Gandhi, Jesus and the Buddha, not forgetting Vladimir Lenin and if this were the case, he would have been one hell of a guy! He also stated that he was an atheist and an agnostic, and so was obviously a very confused individual.

If one wanted to get a cult going anywhere in the world America at this time was the place to do it. For some reason Americans seemed to be the easiest people in the world to brainwash. It was easy to prey on the disenchanted and the poor, and so people looked for direction in their lives, and then these nut jobs would pop up every once in a while and in no time would get huge followings. We have our share of lunatics in England but the US takes the cake. Jones thought the world would end by nuclear apocalypse and so went looking for a safe haven and on his way stopped in Guyana in 1961, which at that time was British Guyana. Now in this day and age he may not have been so wrong about the nuclear apocalypse! He never allowed anyone to leave Jonestown and when some members of the press came down to visit he had them shot. After the mass suicide/murder he shot himself in the head.

Oops! Almost forgot one more serial killer for the year although, most of this chap's killings happened much later. However in the summer of '78 Jeffrey Dahmer, also known as the Milwaukee Cannibal started his killing career at the age of eighteen, three weeks after his graduation. He bludgeoned his victim with a 10lb dumbbell, then strangled him to death. The next day he dissected the body and dissolved the flesh in acid and crushed the bones with a sledgehammer, then scattered them in the woods behind the family home. He only killed boys and young men unlike Ted Bundy. He did not kill again apparently for nine years when he got into a bit of cannibalism and necrophilia and had a reputation for dismembering his victims. He was eventually convicted of sixteen murders and was sentenced to sixteen life imprisonments.

Another tragedy in the year was that Argentina won the World Cup and in Germany the VW Beetle stopped production. The US dollar plunged to record lows against the European currencies, but in England the first test tube baby was born. Space Invaders was invented and the movie 'The Deer Hunter' came out.

However the very best news of the year was that Jimmy Carter signed a bill that made it legal to brew your own beer at home. Now that is what I call good news!

ABBY   New York, 1978.   Summer time, when the living is easy!

The first time I saw Abby was at the Buffalo Roadhouse, a bar on Seventh Avenue near Bleecker Street. It was a hangout for film people when they were out of work. It was a weekday I remember that, at lunchtime, I was there eating a burger and drinking a beer with a good friend of mine who was a Vietnam vet and converted Buddhist called Antonio. I was sitting at the bar eating and drinking and I glanced across at a table where two girls sat, one was English - I heard a northern English accent crack through the sound of Americanisms, the other girl looked like she'd just crossed the desert and would be quite happy sitting in the Kasbah somewhere in the Middle East. She was very exotic looking, voluptuous with big brown eyes and thick black curly hair that hung way over her shoulders. I was totally infatuated with her there and then.

I had to talk to this woman but how do I do it? My friend who was a hopeless romantic at heart and a converted Buddhist, ex-soldier in Vietnam and general bullshit artist suggested I run across the road to the florist and buy her a red rose.

35

"You crazy?" I said,

"No go on do it - it always works," replied the Buddhist.

I was in turmoil but plucked up the courage to do it and ran across Seventh Avenue South and came back with a red rose in hand and gingerly walked up to her table and presented her with this flower.

I stuttered nervously and said, "I just think you should have this as you're so beautiful" or something to that effect, I continued to stand up and stutter nervously but I wasn't looking too good as I was trying to eat and drink off a hangover from the night before. She didn't give me her phone number but I gave her mine.

Abby called me the next night. We went out for a drink somewhere on the Upper West Side. She had a studio apartment and was working at Harlem Hospital. I think we both fell in love that night when I went back to her place and we continued to drink some wine. We were making love - it was about 12 o'clock at night when I heard the sound of a key in the door, I completely froze,

"Who's that" I whispered.

"Oh my God! It's my boyfriend" Abby replied.

"Your boyfriend!" I exclaimed.

"Shhh! Keep still, he's only got one key and I locked the other lock," she said, hoping that would console me.

I completely froze - I didn't know what to do, jump out onto the fire escape naked or what? Anyway we both laid their completely quiet for the next five minutes the boyfriend on the other side of the door tried the key once more, nothing happened the door did not open and he walked away. That's how it all began with Abby. We saw each other a lot in those days whenever we could, she was studying hard for her exams as she was training to be a psychiatrist. Her apartment was full of books on medicine and shrinkage.

36

We went to see 'The Last Waltz' directed by Martin Scorsese, a film about the Band's last concert at the Ziegfeld Theatre. The Band was Bob Dylan's backup band for a long time. I believe it is one of the best music films ever made. I was working as a gaffer then, working on commercials at Mother's studio in the East Village which many years later burnt down I heard. We used to go out to East Quogue on Long Island where her parents owned a house - it was beautiful out there. It was part of the Hamptons minus the pretentious Hamptons scene. I remember we had a party out there and our friends from the city came out and crashed wherever they could on the floor on couches, a couple brought their sleeping bags and slept outside on the lawn.

We went down to the local beach and were sitting there when my friend Jenny opened up her handbag and looked inside. "Look what I've found!" and opened up the palm of her hand. There were three little blotter acid tabs with a picture of Mickey Mouse on them.

"Should we do them?"

There were six of us.

"I can cut them in half," she said

"Why not!" we all agreed and each popped a half of Mickey Mouse under our tongues and waited.

Half an hour later I was sitting on the beach with seaweed covering my head like a long mane, chanting in some unknown African tongue whilst my friends brought me gifts of shells and stones and laid them at my feet. It was at this point I knew I had been reincarnated from a King – we were all laughing hysterically and normal people with their families who were close by, packed up and left us a wide berth to continue our psychedelic activities for the rest of the afternoon. I don't know how we got back to the house but we did and the party continued there into the early hours of the next day.

The following summer Abby went off to San Francisco for her internship as a shrink, I followed her out a few weeks later as I had been booked on a few commercials in the Big Apple. I flew out to San Francisco where I lived with Abby the next six weeks in a cute little apartment on Filbert Street near the corner of Franklin.

My friend Steve came over from England my ex - pool digger buddy and the two of us took off to Big Sur together for a few days leaving Abby on her own. We shoved Steve into the walk-in closet that served as his own little bedroom for the next few days. After another week he went back to England. I'm not sure I ever saw him again. I had to leave San Francisco as I had a job to go to in Miami working on a film starring Julio Iglesias.

 Julio Iglesias was once recruited to play for Real Madrid as their goalkeeper, but was involved in a car accident that put him in hospital for a couple of years. It was there he taught himself to play guitar and wrote songs - the rest is history. He had with him an entourage and his backup singers were these beautiful 18-year-old triplets from Buenas Aires, you couldn't tell them apart, one from the other. I tried to flirt with one of them but they played a game with me and I really couldn't tell one from another. I had to bail from the film as the crew was leaving for Contadora Island off the coast of Panama, as I didn't think my Visa for the US was up-to-date. So I flew back to New York and the rest of the crew went on down to Panama and I probably got a few more jobs working as a gaffer in commercials for the next few months.

Abby came back to New York after her internship in San Francisco a few months later and life very much continued as it did before she went away. She moved to Tribeca and I was living on Bethune Street just off Hudson. We would eat at the Cottonwood café on Bleecker Street get a burger at the Corner Bistro and sometimes have breakfast at the Bus Stop Café that was below where I lived. It was a good old greasy spoon. Not forgetting of course the White Horse Tavern where Dylan Thomas drank himself to death.

Abby and I had lots of arguments as I found her to be far too analytical. Being analytical was part of her job of course being a shrink, but we loved each other a lot and that was the main thing, so we ambled on in a perpetual state of a roller coaster ride. Her analysis of me was that 'I was fucked in the head' and I wondered how many books on Freud and Jung and Kierkegaard she had read to come up with this very wordy analysis.

At this point I was thinking of becoming a shrink myself, after all how difficult could it be?

"Good morning Mr. Jones" I would say, "I believe you are fucked in the head, take two of these tablets every night and come see me next week."

Her shelves were jammed with books on psychoanalysis and the like and I do believe that dear Abby had read them all, but mine was a simple diagnosis - she never gave me any pills and didn't tell me to come back as we were pretty much seeing each other every night as we only lived a few blocks from each other.

ISRAEL

Abby and I took a few adventurous trips together over the years, and one of them was to Israel. She was already there and had been for a couple of weeks. She was renting from an artist friend of hers in the old quarter of Jerusalem. I joined up with her there after an El Al flight from New York. These guys had the security thing locked up way before the advent of terrorist attacks, that later became more the norm in the future. Security at the airline at Kennedy was excellent and everyone was scanned. I felt pretty safe boarding the flight to Tel Aviv. Abby met me at the airport and we took a bus to Jerusalem. On the bus were a few Israeli women soldiers who were young and beautiful with Uzi machine guns hanging off their shoulders. I had never seen women soldiers before and realized that the state of Israel was ready within minutes to defend itself in case of an attack from the Arab countries that surrounded it. I loved the old part of the city, the Arab quarter and the narrow streets and the markets. We rented a small car and drove out to the Sinai Desert and then visited the Dead Sea. There are no fish in the Sea as there is so much saline in the water. I floated on my back and read the newspaper as the salt made it impossible to sink.

We slept on the beach at a beautiful blue lagoon and in the night we were awaked by the Israeli army who told us to be careful and were advised not to sleep on the beach for fear of terrorist attacks from neighboring Arab countries. We thanked them for their advice and they drove off in their jeeps. I enjoyed our trip to Israel and particularly the Sinai desert and I was sorry I didn't take more photographs of the trip. I would like to have stayed longer but had to get back to work in New York.

We rented a car and drove through the Sinai Desert

Sinai Israel

The Lagoon in the Red Sea

New York was beginning to feel more and more like home every day, I wore out Springsteen's 'Born to Run' album, so went out and walked down Bleecker Street to the record store to buy a couple more albums to play on my newly found Upper East Side turntable, one being 'Aftermath' by the Stones, which was one of the first albums I bought as a teenager in England, but missed it so much that I bought another one, and 'Revolver' by those lovely Liverpudlian lads from England, and I sat there on my newly acquired captains bed watching as my Duraflame logs burnt away in the little fireplace to the sounds of The Beatles. It was Revolver that took the Beatles on a new course in music lyrically and instrumentally, introducing the sitar once again into rock music, the first time being on The Rubber Soul album. I was in paradise- I had my own little apartment in one of the best areas in the City, and could pop out at any time for a pint or two at the White Horse Tavern, made famous by the Welsh drunk poet Dylan Thomas, and the ghosts of Hunter S. Thompson and Jack Kerouac who were known to have frequented the place. There were great Italian restaurants all around and if I wanted a burger and fries then off to the Corner Bistro I would go. In the winter, when the snow was on the ground the village was like a little village in any northern town in Europe and there was no need to go anywhere else. It was only when one looked south towards The World Trade Towers or north towards the Empire State building when you would realize that you were living in a great metropolis. There were great little diners where one could eat for peanuts, and 14th Street where one could eat Cuban/Chinese food which was delicious and very filling for a couple of bucks.

Abby and I would eat at The Cotton Wood Café that had just opened by a guy from Texas called Stan and many a time downstairs at The Bus Stop café when she stayed the night. Another good greasy spoon was the Pink Tea Cup further down Bleecker Street. Chumley's was another haunt of ours that was usually full of students, and also served a good burger that was tucked away in the village. There was no lack of good cheap restaurants in those days and the word neuvo - cuisine had not yet been invented. Many a time at The Bus Stop Café I would run into the twins Ted and Jack Churchill, who were both cameramen, Ted being one of the best Steadicam operators around - they were a couple of wild and crazy guys and very often had a good laugh there together.

As time wore on I began to get more work as a Best Boy for a number of Gaffers in the business and would be tying in to electrical distribution boxes all over the City, so as to run power for the lights. The first person to show me how to tie in was this old guy (seemed old to me at the time), but was probably way younger than I now. He had long grey hair and a moustache and very shaky hands - possibly a drinking problem? So to explain the rather dangerous technique of tying in: First one should make sure that they are not grounded, and the best way to do that is to stand on a wooden box, called an apple box, then between the lugs of the hot legs one would place fairly thick pieces of cut up rubber matting so as not to arc out the box. There

43

were clips we used called Alligator or Anderson clips which one would clip onto the lugs of the neutral and ground wires and then - and this was the part where one had to be especially careful, clip on to the positive wires without electrocuting yourself, using only one hand so if one did receive a shock it would go down through one side of your body, and not create a circuit through your heart, which could result in meeting one's maker! So there I was standing there with my mentor, as he was about to show me how to tie in. He gave me a long piece of two by four wood and told me to whack him hard on the arm if perchance he got a shock and was stuck to the breaker box with all this high amperage going through him. So with his wobbly hands he manages to tie in, there were a couple of sparks as he did so and I thought 'should I hit him now,' but he assured me as his hair was standing up like Einstein's that everything was alright, as he had done this a thousand times before. I was relieved that we both got out the basement alive and I started to run the power from the stage box out to the lights. So that was my initiation ceremony as a Best Boy.

So the jobs came and went until I started to get more efficient and tying in to these electrical boxes all over the City become an everyday thing. I started to work on more and more low budget films and we had to pick up the equipment many a time after four or five in the afternoon as lots of films were non-union, which were frowned upon by the New York and Jersey teamsters, and could give the production a very hard time, as obviously the teamsters wanted to drive the trucks, but so many productions could not afford them so went underground so to speak. I had just got another job as the best boy and was given a list by the gaffer as to what to pick up from an equipment house on the west side of Manhattan. The driver and myself sat around the corner till the teamsters left. Then we could load up the truck with the help of a couple of other guys.

On the list was hundreds of feet of cable and I had to get a hundred feet or so of 'horse cock' cable, I didn't know if someone was playing a joke on me or not and I very gingerly asked for the 'horse cock' cable. There was not a blink of an eyelid by the guy who worked there

44

and he dragged this cable out on a dolly, and then I saw why it was called horse cock. It was a very wide heavy cable, capable of taking very large amperage that would connect to the generator that we were going to use. So we loaded the truck with no problem then went on our merry way.

The teamsters had a very strong union and these guys drove all the film trucks in and around the city, and most were good down to earth working class lads, who were a great asset in loading the trucks after a hard long day of work. Many had a great sense of humor and one teamster taught me the teamster alphabet that was: fucking A, fucking B, fucking C, and so on.

I loved the work, it was physically hard but very rewarding and I loved joking around with the rest of the crew. There were great characters, men and women and a few 'charlatans' who came over from England who pulled the wool over everyone's eyes because of their toffee - nosed accents and attitudes, that I thought even back then with my little experience were only mediocre in what they produced. There were also some American DP's like that too, but all in all every job was a learning experience.

There was a lot more respect for Directors of Photography in those days than there are today, as there was a certain mystique and magic to being behind the camera. As time went on I was beginning to learn the difference between a soft light and a hard light and a bounce light. Then there was a front light, a back light, a side light, a top light, a kicker, which didn't take a genius to figure out what was what, but it was where you placed them that counted and knowing when to use a soft light as opposed to a hard light. For instance you would not generally light a woman's face with a hard light, a soft light was more desirable, and at the same time a strong side light to a man's face could add character, depending on the scene and so on.

There was a time when I gaffed for a DP called Michael Butler who insisted on using arc lights for his commercial shoots. An arc light is an old Hollywood type of light and back in the forties they were used most of the time, but usually outside as they gave off a lot of smoke. The light was emitted by two carbons that when struck would create a flame between them that gave off a beautiful light closer to sunlight than any other light and maybe true to this day! I loved working with arcs and each light needed an operator who sat on the top of a ladder and watched the carbons burn, so they needed trimming. There was a knob on the side to turn so as to maintain the consistency of light as the carbons burnt down and to also make sure that they didn't flicker. If I remember rightly, there were two types of carbons one was a white carbon for daylight and the other to match the color temperature of a tungsten light which was a yellow carbon.

One of my first feature films was called 'Here Come the Tigers' - a kids baseball film, shot near Westport Connecticut, which was directed by Sean Cunningham, who later went on to direct 'Friday the Thirteenth'. I was working as the 'best boy' to Denver Collins (brother of Judy) who was the gaffer. It was a hot glorious summer, and a good time was had by all on the crew. So the jobs came and went - a low budget feature film in those days shot for about five or six weeks and the pay relative to the time, pretty reasonable.

The main thing was that crew people were like a band of traveling gypsies, going from one place to the next. A phone call one day could decide your future for the next month or two. There were obviously down times when one would think you were never going to work again, but just when you were feeling desperate, something would pop up, even if it might be a commercial for a supermarket chain or a diaper spot! A job was a job and money was money, but all in all it gave you time to do other things or take a quick trip somewhere, although my trips ended up taking months.

The following year we all went back to Westport which was the home turf of Cunningham and Minor to film a kid's soccer movie called Manny's Orphans much like the last film but this time using a bigger ball that they kicked instead of hitting with a bat! I'm not sure what film was first but either way both were directed by Cunningham. We were all pleased of the work and now had become like a little family and another wonderful summer was spent this time on a soccer field.

My very first job as a gaffer was working on a couple of commercials with Oliver Wood who was and is a fellow Englishman, we hit it off and became good friends and he and his girlfriend came out to Abby's parent's house in East Quogue for the weekend. East Quogue was out on Long Island, but not really part of the 'Hamptons' scene. People from the City would have shares in houses out there, only being able to visit every two or even three weeks as the rents for the summer where so high.

It was a 'scene' and not one that I cared for, people watching in East and West Hampton and Southampton. Sag Harbor was a place I liked which was further out on the island and sometimes I would go out there on my own and stay at the American Hotel, which to me was more interesting than the Hamptons. A friend of mine had a boat that he had moored in Sag Harbor and every year we would do the booze cruise along with another boatload of sailors, sailing to Martha's Vineyard, anchoring at Block Island, and mooring at Newport Rhode Island on the way. It was a fun trip, but once the fog came in so bad it was hard to see your hand in front of your face. A couple of blasts on the foghorn made sure we didn't run into anyone. Getting out to Long Island in the summer was too much of a big deal, although the beaches there were beautiful, so I opted for going upstate, away from the crowds, which is what I thought the whole point of getting out of New York was all about.

The first film I gaffed was with Oliver Wood (who went on to fame and fortune shooting The Bourne Series starring Matt Damon). The film was called 'Feedback' and I have no idea what happened to it, but it was a real art film although I can't remember the storyline at all. A friend of mine said he saw it in a box, along with a bunch of Chinese films on Canal Street. Oliver then went on to shoot Alphabet City, which was about that area of the East Side of New York, from Avenue A to D. The film starred Vincent Spano who was an unknown actor at the time and was directed by Amos Poe. I didn't work on it as I had a film to shoot (my first) as a Director of Photography in Osh Gosh - be gosh in Wisconsin. The Film was called 'Dreams Come True' about a couple of kids who could astral travel. It was really a kid's film, but I think it was aimed at a higher age range. I went to Osh Gosh with the director and producer and a soundman.

The production placed one add in the local paper for people who would be interested working as crew on a film and 'yours truly' was going to train them all in different categories such as a gaffer and a grip. So not only was this my first venture out as a DP, but I also had to train everyone. My gaffer ended up being an ex-prison guard and the grip was an ex Vietnam Veteran or vice versa. Others came from the film school attached to Madison University such as script supervisor and make-up etc.

In the evenings I would be loading my own 400ft magazines for the Arri BLIII ready for the next day of filming till after a day or so I managed to get a real Assistant Cameraman. After a week or so I had my crew whipped into shape and when we arrived on location early in the morning the ex-vets in the crew would be playing Wagner's flight of the Valkyrie full blast from the speakers in their van that was used as a soundtrack in the helicopter sequence in Apocalypse Now, and my boys were off to do battle using lights and flags and grip stands and film equipment instead of M16's! We screened the dailies on a big screen at the local movie theatre in town and the whole crew came to watch with six packs of beer.

So there I was watching my very first frame of film that I ever shot that was on 35mm film projected on to a screen, like a real movie, and the whole crew clapped afterwards, and I felt like a hero and it was exciting, and I had become a Director of Photography!

At the weekend a few of us went to the outlet store and I bought the Osh Gosh overalls and hat so that if the Cinematography thing didn't work out, then I was at least kitted out to be a train driver! There is no more to be said, except it got me out in the field as a

Cinematographer and I realized that I had learnt quite a lot about lighting by working as a gaffer. My experience as a photographer in London taught me about lenses and composition and framing so the transition for me from gaffer to DP was not too difficult.

My first film as Director of Photography
on the set of 'Dreams Come True'

Before this film I worked on a few more jobs with Oliver Wood, a couple of after school specials and some industrials. There was one commercial that I gaffed uptown which was a chocolate cookie commercial, and after the shoot was over we were all given half a dozen packs of cookies to take home with us if we wanted. I took my share being a chocoholic and walking to the subway to take the train downtown passed a homeless man. I stopped and offered him a pack of cookies. He took them from my hand and after reading the ingredients, said, "I'm not eating this crap," and threw them back at me. He then stood up, and in an upper class English accent started to quote from Shakespeare's Macbeth as I continued on down the road.

In 1981, MTV was launched on August 1st and this lead to lots of work for everyone in the film business. New styles of filming were invented and a 'new look' was required for every video. The word 'stylized' was thrown around a lot by directors wanting a different look, that no one had seen before and this went for the commercial business as well. In fact the top music video DP's went on to shoot high end commercials and feature films where producers were looking for 'something new'. We want a 'European look' was another buzz phrase that was on the lips of money hungry producers. That term ultimately meant nothing, as there were as many different styles from DP's in Europe as in the States.

It was The Beatles who first introduced music with film when they or someone produced their zany 'Magical Mystery Tour' back when the band was altogether. However the music video world opened its doors to sex drugs and rock n' roll where almost anything went. I worked on a dozen or so as a gaffer and also shot some lesser - known bands myself, such as The John Hall Band in Woodstock and some others, whose names I can't remember.

I gaffed a number of music videos working with a number of bands such as Little Stevie (of Springsteen's band) and Michael Bolton. Other bands I worked with were Cheap Trick, and in Atlantic City I gaffed a job with Jon Bon Jovi, which was one of their early songs. "Such was the world of music videos."

Regina Bell was another artist I worked with and one day I got a call to work on a Madonna video filming her song 'True Blue' that was shot by Michael Ballhaus. I do remember a lot of cocaine being dished out in this world but I never indulged when I was working, as it clouded my view and I didn't want to get a heart attack as the work was very physical and hard physical labor and cocaine don't mix, although many of my comrades did indulge whilst working. The worst offenders of the drug were usually the directors themselves who after sniffing half a kilo up their nose thought they became the Michelangelo's of the video world, and with noses running and eyes red and chewing on their own lips like a cow chews on the cud, would say things like, "I've got a better idea, let's shoot from that roof top" and after the crew had spent all morning lighting a set would have to break it down, much to the chagrin of the producers who looked on horrified as this hip new director would come up with another world shattering idea, which is why the days sometimes went sixteen hours to twenty if you were lucky, and one would go home and sleep all the next day. On awakening you would shake your head and say to yourself "What the fuck was that all about" as you looked over and saw an up and coming young starlet next to you and wondered where she came from. Such was the world of music videos and as I said many a cameraman cut their teeth on them to go on to shoot some big features.

When I wasn't working on music videos I would gaff for an eccentric director who shot his own work, which was another area of commercials called 'Table Top.' As the term suggests, it was cinematography shot on a table or rigs that involved a lot of macro and close - up photography and Elbert Budin was the King of tabletop in the city in those days. Others may disagree, but it wasn't just his work that made him the 'King,' in my eyes it was his Zen like personality, where he would sit like the Buddha in front of a product such as a MacDonald's burger or film a pizza very close with the lens of the camera almost scraping the cheese off the surface, making it look like a National Geographic special as if filming the plains of the Serengeti. He would take the pin out of the lens, which meant one could focus as close to a subject as necessary whilst keeping it in focus, which is not an easy thing to do. He was probably in his fifties when I worked with him and had a nice round belly like the Laughing Buddha and long grey hair over his shoulders and many times wore a kind of wrap around Kimono or an outfit that looked like a pair of pajamas. He had a great dry sense of humor and would enjoy my Mick Jagger impersonations that I did using a grip stand as the microphone, but only when the agency and clients were not around. This may have been one of the reasons why he hired me as a little light entertainment! His company was called Ampersand and was located in the thirties off Ninth Avenue in a large commercial loft space.

I loved working there, one reason was because it was fun, and the other because we would knock up the overtime and many a morning I spent having breakfast down in the village at six in the morning after an all-night shoot, feeling tired and wired at the same time. It was a class outfit and lunchtime he had his own chef to prepare food for the crew and clients. There was also a pool table in a separate room where one could pocket a few balls when not working.

There was one particular commercial, which always stuck in my mind that personified Elbert's dry wit and sense of humor. The product was some kind of Texas barbecue sauce and the client was this obnoxious Texan who wore a ten - gallon or maybe five - gallon hat, who was large and loud and overbearing. The time was about three in the morning and the crew was getting a little sleepy until the second wind would take over. The food stylists were working away on the sauce trying to make it look delicious, when the Texan looked over Elbert's shoulder and in that delightful Texan drawl said, "How much you got in the budget for me to get laid Elbert?" Elbert replied, without taking his eyes off the product he was filming, "For the money you spent on this commercial you've already been fucked." This was a classic

Elbert response to people he had contempt for and got away with it because of his charm.

Another commercial that I gaffed was for the great Vilmos Zsigmund who was the cinematographer on 'McCabe and Mrs. Miller' starring the lovely Julie Christie and Warren Beatty. He also filmed 'Close Encounters of the Third Kind,' 'The Deer Hunter' and many more. I had worked with him one time before, but this particular commercial was in Jersey City and was for an insurance company. I had to light a street at nighttime. Vilmos went off with the agency and client somewhere and left me with my crew to light the street and homes in it. After a couple of h

ours he returned, looked at the street, told me to drop a scrim in one light that was lighting a room and he was ready to shoot. I was flattered by the fact that he had the confidence in me to be left alone to light the street and so from that day on I knew I was ready to be a director of photography.

Many years later when I went out to California I hooked up with a director and I shot his food commercials as he switched from being a stills photographer into the moving images of the commercial world. It was not what I had in mind, as I wanted to shoot films but I realized I had gained enough knowledge from the master, as to light and shoot food flying through the air in slow motion, at 120 frames per second and being able to make the product look edible along with the help of the food stylist, so I said why not, and a few years later, I became a director/cameraman myself, shooting for companies such as Pizza Hut, CiCi's pizza out of Dallas and a host of other clients including Kellogg's and the like. I could not compete however with the established directors who had their own studios and established clientele, but I made a fairly good living, as a day rate for a director was a substantial amount, and because of this was a highly competitive field to be in.

Sometime in the year Abby and I went to see the Simon and Garfunkel reunion in Central Park. The two didn't really get along, but they were asked by the city to perform so as to raise funds to give the park a bit of a facelift and renovation. The Mayor at the time was Ed Koch and introduced the duo to a crowd of about half a million that were crammed into The Great Lawn. Abby and I were way at the back but managed to hear the music quite well and absorb the atmosphere. They started the performance with 'Mrs. Robinson' that was made even more famous by the film 'The Graduate.' They went on to sing a lot of their great songs including 'Homeward Bound' which I often sang to myself whilst traveling. "Let us be lovers we'll marry our fortunes together," I said to Abbey as they sang America. I think it is my favorite song of theirs, with lines such as 'counting the cars on the New Jersey Turnpike,' as I walked off to look for America now six years ago and had been enjoying every minute of it! It was a great concert and to me at that time the songs seemed to epitomize the wonder and the diversity and the opportunities that this 'great land that was made for you and me' had to offer.

So that was the end of my sixth year in New York and that year our lad from England Prince Charles married Lady Diana, Ronald Reagan became president, Muhammed Ali retired from boxing, the great king of reggae Bob Marley died so did William Holden and Natalie Wood. 'Chariots of Fire' was released and Mark David Chapman was sentenced to twenty years to life in prison for the murder of John Lennon. The TGV high-speed train from Paris to Lyon goes into service, whilst American trains still chug along at a pathetic pace thirty-five years later. How great it would be to have a high speed train from Los Angeles to San Francisco and another from New York to Boston, but the government are too busy putting the money into wars!

CLUBS

There was a great club called The World that was on Second Avenue that was a fun venue with lots of great music and dancing and beautiful women that I would frequent once in a while. Artists such as Prince and Bowie and Neil Young and even The Pink Floyd appeared there, none of which I saw unfortunately.

All these clubs were great venues to see bands as they were all very cozy and it was as if they were playing to you in your own living room. Back in those days there were a lot of interesting clubs around, some that open and closed and others that lasted a couple of years including Area that was downtown on Hudson Street. This was probably my favorite as it was one of the closest to me. It had a castle like stone entrance and a long stone hallway with performance art going on along both sides. There was always some weird theme that would change from week to week like mime artists and the like. It was a hangout for the rich 'Euro Trash,' as we called them, and the beautiful people, to which I was not! The bathrooms were unisex and the sound of people snorting cocaine could very often be heard from outside.

However, Area did not have a long life span and closed in 1987 after opening just four years before as the growing AIDS epidemic made people more weary about who they went home with, which really changed the New York club scene forever. There was also the famous Mudd Club and the Peppermint Lounge, then Limelight that was a converted church on Sixth Avenue, but was more for 'The Bridge and Tunnel' crowd. Max's Kansas City was a restaurant and nightclub on Park Avenue South and was a hot spot for musicians to gather and was re - opened by a guy called Tony Dean Hills in 1975. I believe Mickey Ruskin was the original owner who went on to open The Lower Manhattan Ocean Club. Andy Warhol also was a patron there along with other venues such as Studio 54.

The Velvet Underground played at Max's as well as Iggy Pop and Alice Cooper. I was fortunate to see Blondie play there, she had a great act where she had a tee shirt that was pre - cut where she pulled the sleeves off and other parts almost revealing her breasts, she was a hot act and her music was unique for the time. She used to work as a waitress at the club so I guess someone or other gave her a break there? Max's also became one of the birthplaces for punk and featured acts such as The New York Dolls, Patti Smith, The Ramones, Talking Heads and even Sid Vicious performed there after breaking with the Sex Pistols. The club closed in 1981 and I felt fortunate to have experienced Max's and a few of the other great venues at that time. I feel like I missed out on a lot of great bands as well, but I did get a chance to see John Cale and Lou Reed, from The Velvet Underground along with Patti Smith, not long after I had just arrived in New York sometime back in the summer of '76. I only once went to Studio54 as I must have been with 'someone special' as it was a hard place to get past the purple ropes outside. It was a different crowd to the clubs downtown and I much preferred the downtown crowd. 'We built this City on Rock and Roll' as the song goes and The Big Apple was rocking 24 hours a day and I loved it as long as you could keep up with it!

The summers were steamy hot and the winters were bloody cold, but the Spring and the Autumn were moments to behold, especially the Autumn upstate and even in Central Park where the trees turned yellow and orange and even bright red, it was a palette of color fit for an artist to paint. There were times where I felt very lonely also and took solace at the Buddhist monastery outside of Woodstock. I would drive up there before I rented a place in that area and sleep on a mat in a small basic room in the Buddhist Temple that was at the top of Mead Mountain Road. The Buddhists built a temple there as they felt the spiritual energy of the area was in keeping with their spiritual practice. The top of the mountain was the perfect place for it as it looked out in a certain direction, which fulfilled certain Buddhist requirements. For a while I practiced Shinay Meditation and teachings in the Karma Kagya tradition of Tibetan Buddhism, the head of the Kagya lineage being the Karmapa. In the morning I would sit in front of the shrine and meditate for an hour and then visit some friends in town. Other times I would stay in one of about twenty little cabins that my friend's boyfriend owned in Woodstock for a couple of nights, until I found my own little cabin in the woods. I would then drive back to New York feeling refreshed and ready once more to do battle with The Big Apple. Living in New York was always a love/hate relationship, the energy of the city being so over - powering at times that an escape was necessary. I know that I was not the only one that felt this way as many people I knew made the same escape north and some had second homes up there in the country.

THE UPPER EAST SIDE CLINIC

Another job I got in the early days of New York was as a Best Boy on a documentary about men who had had or were about to have the surgery that would transform them into a woman. It was in a clinic on the Upper East Side, a part of town that seemed way too normal for the rest of New York. It was where the doctors and lawyers lived and seemed to me to have little personality unlike downtown.

The documentary I was working on was anything but normal. Between the gaffer and myself we had lit a small office and waiting room ready for a set of interviews about all kinds of men from all walks of life and of different ages who had never felt right about their sexuality, that they were women living in a man's body, and so were here to talk about their experiences. The potential interviewees were sitting in the waiting room and as I was also working as a sort of PA (production assistant) and I had to go into the room and ask for Edna who was the next in line for an interview. I cautiously opened the door to the waiting room poked my head in an asked for Edna.

 "Is there an Edna here?" I asked.

"Yes, I'm Edna," came the reply from the back of the room in a rather deep baritone voice,

"Are you ready for your interview?" I chirped up, my voice a higher octave than Edna's.

"I'm ready," said Edna as she stood up, a powerful looking individual with big hands that grasped the handbag next to her. I noticed a large tattoo on her rather flabby upper arm as she followed me into the interview office. The director welcomed Edna and Edna sat down in between two tungsten lights and proceeded to tell the story of Edna the tugboat captain.

Edna was once Edward, shortened to Ed, who was once a tugboat captain on the River Hudson. Every Sunday, which was the day off for the rest of the crew Ed would dress up in women's clothes and sit on his boat hidden from the view of passing sailors. For years Ed felt like he was a woman living in a rather large man's body. In his day Ed was the quintessential tugboat captain, tough with large hands and big arms and a square face that would have passed any casting call for that character. Now Edna sat in front of the camera with fingernails painted a bright red, her left hand resting on her handbag and the right in the lap of her paisley summer dress. Her arms that were probably quite muscular at one time, hung like pieces of flabby meat with some kind of worn out sea-faring tattoo etched into the old sea dog. I was standing off to the side, but managed to hear most of Edna's story. Edna was now sixty-two years old, was married with two beautiful daughters she said and a boyfriend on the side. The boyfriend wanted Ed to get the sex change, which he did and after a while the boyfriend left him leaving Edna even more confused than before. I felt sorry for Edna and for all these people in the world who feel like they are living in the wrong body. It must be an on-going nightmare…

Antonio

I was a friend of Antonio in New York City for quite a few years. We met on a television commercial. He was working as the production manager at the time and I was the gaffer. He was a strange man, an ex-Vietnam vet, born in Sicily and a converted Buddhist. He served in Vietnam when he was only 19 years old and he told me about when he was in the jungle, fighting the Vietcong. They were on maneuvers and Antonio came face-to-face with a Vietcong soldier. They pointed their guns at each other as though they were kids playing in the back yard. But this wasn't the backyard and they were not kids anymore and not really adults either. Their guns pointed at each other - his so-called enemy was the same age as himself. They stared into each other's eyes recognizing themselves in the other person. They were part of the same wondrous world. They were the same person, but they were at War, because someone in an office told them so. Antonio fired first and shot the young Vietcong boy in the heart. He fell to his knees and died. Antonio knelt down next to his dead body, and took the dog tag from around his neck and placed it around his own, then picked up the Lugar that lay by his side. He never took that dog tag off from around his neck. And from that day on half of him died, the other half lay rotting in a Vietnam jungle. The Lugar he kept in a drawer in his loft on 23rd Street.

Antonio had a bounty on his head from the Vietcong at $10,000. He had become one of the top artillery spotters and would go into the jungle alone and spot the Vietcong gun placements. He would radio back to base and minutes later bombers would fly over and drop napalm into the jungle which incinerated the Vietcong turning them into charcoal within a few seconds. Antonio was a Sicilian and hard core and hated being called Tony, so I never did. He told me that he had once hid underground for four days in a leper colony trying to avoid the Vietcong that were after him. Antonio was good at his job, but by now he was already beginning to hate himself.

So I was the gaffer on a Jeans commercial that we filmed in Martha's Vineyard on Cape Cod. The European version required a topless woman on a white horse, like Lady Godiva. We shot as the sun was going down so the warm golden glow would add a feeling of sexuality to the already topless woman on the white horse. After two days of shooting the crew went home and I stayed there with Antonio using the production money.

The next morning we had breakfast on a deck overlooking the Atlantic Ocean and drank champagne. He reminded me of the Samoan from Hunter S. Thomson's book 'Fear and Loathing in Las Vegas.' Antonio came armed on the job with cocaine, Quaaludes and marijuana. He gave me a Quaalude that evening to take as I had met this skinny Jewish girl from Brooklyn. I took her to an Italian restaurant where I ordered a plate of Spaghetti, but before I had a chance to taste it, my face fell into the bowl. I was out cold from the Quaalude. My date left me on the spot and I was escorted out the front door by two Italian gentlemen. They obviously thought I was drunk. I was asked not to return to the restaurant again and my date was never to be seen again either. So that was life with Antonio. He was a good influence on my life! By the way, this was before I met Abby.

Antonio was a little like myself, or maybe I was a little like him as he was older than me, which is why we became good friends. I had many strange psychic and out of body experiences with him, as he was a bit of a shaman and wizard and although was by no means a handsome man, he had something about him that attracted him to women. He played on his mystical persona quite a bit and laid traps for many a fair maiden who would be fascinated by this unusual man. Under his layer of skin lay a man who was haunted by his experiences in Vietnam and would bury his dark thoughts in a concoction of drugs and booze. His pain and guilt I'm sure came from the killing of the Vietcong soldier the young boy who was a reflection of himself. He found some kind of solace in Buddhism and he took me to an initiation ceremony in Uptown New York.

The Karmapa was visiting New York from Tibet or should I say northern India, which is where the Tibetans have made their new home, as the Chinese drove them from Tibet in the early fifties. We spent two days at the Buddhist ceremony where there was a banging of drums and blowing of trumpets … large Tibetan horns strange mystical sounds that would scare any demon away. I received a blessing from the Karmapa himself and he gave me a Tibetan name that I still keep next to my Buddha in Santa Monica. Antonio was always talking about good and evil and the forces that are out there that we cannot see. He told me there are such things as demons, and they walk amongst us every day and he pointed out a demon to me on the way back downtown on the A train. I must say I was feeling like I had been cleansed of all the garbage that we carry inside of our mind and heart. At 42nd Street the doors opened and a tall devilish looking man wearing a black trench coat and wearing a trilby hat stepped into our carriage. Antonio noticed him right away and pointed him out to me. "There's a demon there" he said to me "hold on this is going to be a ride, you can always tell them, because their feet swell up, like a cloven hoof of a goat," he explained to me. The devilish man spotted us immediately and in an instant I felt this triangle of power between this entity and us and some strange kind of force field that seemed to accelerate through all three of us. Antonio told me to hang on and to remember the teachings. I had a red ribbon around my neck that was given to me by the Karmapa and I felt protected from all evil forces. I could feel the hatred in this tall man that entered our carriage and the anger in his heart. The energy between the three of us became intense. Antonio told me to hang on again. There were two of us against him. I saw the man's sneaker swell up from inside, until his foot became the hoof of a goat, I got a little afraid and excited when I saw this and realized that there are strange occurrences out there. The train pulled into 34th Street Penn Station, and by now the triangle of mixed energy came to a head, when the devilish man let out a high - pitched scream and stamped his foot down hard on the carriage floor. The doors opened and the devil ran out of the carriage onto the station in an incredible rage, his trench coat flapping behind him as he flew out. Antonio and I were victorious and looked at each other as if to say 'We did it.' I had never had an experience as intense as this concerning the dark side and haven't had one since. Whatever it was, it was powerful, and I realized that everything is not always what it appeared to be. The two of us laughed a little as a sigh of relief. It felt good to know that we had some kind of power that was born out of an inherent goodness. We knew that we had overcome some kind of evil force. It was strange that this incident happened after a couple of days of

61

intense Buddhist teaching. Maybe this was our test. Antonio and I looked at each other and he gave me a knowing nod of the head as if to say, 'see I told you.'

Wayne

Wayne was another good friend of mine he was also another Vietnam vet he was about six foot two slim with wild red curly hair a good old boy from Knoxville Tennessee he'd been a captain in the Marine Corps and had a heart of gold and a crazy streak right down the middle. He was another tormented soldier and these guys rarely spoke about the war, but Wayne did tell me a story once when he was in Saigon and a rocket came through the window where he was with five of his mates. He was knocked unconscious by the blast and when he came to, he was the only one left alive - all his friends were dead around him.

'Angelo My Love'

After only four years in the business I received a phone call from a production manager to come in for an interview to gaff a docu/drama about a couple of gypsy kids living in Manhattan. The film was to be directed by Robert Duvall. I got the job, and for the next few weeks were lighting locations all over the City, usually in homes, a school classroom and out in Queens a couple of times where we filmed a 'Kris,' which is a gypsy trial. The film was based around a folklore story about a ring and in this case one that was stolen from Angelo the boy, which is the driving force in the film as they try to get the ring back.

Duvall met Angelo on the streets of New York when he was eight years old in 1977 and three years later started filming the story when Angelo was eleven. Angelo could not read nor write at this age and like a lot of the gypsies were very superstitious. There were some great real life characters in the film - Steve Tsigonoff who played Patalay being one, and his sister in real life Millie, being another. They are Russian gypsies.

It was an interesting experience for me as it was a look into the lives of gypsies that were living in New York. There were many ethnicities, Russian gypsies, Greek, Rumanian, Italian, but the film dealt basically with two families, the Russian and the Greeks. The gypsies lived by their own laws and pretty much lived outside of society's norm. They horded gold, which was their main currency and the women worked as Tarot card readers. There was one on every second street almost, especially in the village. I never realized how many until I started work on this film. The men usually had some car body workshop out in the boroughs. At one time when filming the 'Kris' (a trial) in Jamaica Queens tensions got to run a bit high and a huge fight broke out - tables and chairs went flying and the crew went hurrying for the door onto the street.

I drove the equipment truck along with a guy called Brad up to Quebec City as we were about to film at the Basilica of Sainte Anne de Beaupre, a basilica along the Saint Lawrence river a few miles outside of Quebec City. It has been credited with many miracles having cured hundreds of sick and disabled. At the entrance I remember seeing racks of crutches, canes and braces that had been left there after certain miracles had been performed. The basilica is Quebec's equivalent to Lourdes in France where people make a pilgrimage to be cured of their ailments. Quebec is a beautiful city and most people only speak French there and it feels like you are in France for a while.

Robert Duvall and I on the set of 'Angelo My Love'

Eventually 'wrap' was called and I ended up with a Lighting Director credit. I took a photo of Duvall and Angelo that was published in New Yorker magazine and Bob and I became friends. One time Bob invited me to a screening of Francis Ford Coppola's 'One From The Heart,' which was shown at Radio City Music Hall. We all arrived in a limo that is to say myself, Ellen Barkin, Tess Harper and Robert Duvall. Ellen Barkin had played Duvall's daughter and Tess Harper his wife in a film called 'Tender Mercies' which had been recently completed where Robert Duvall played a washed up Country singer. As the limo pulled up outside Radio City Music Hall all the cameras were there to greet us and I could hear the reporters yelling "Look there's Bob Duvall"- "Look Ellen Barkin and Tess Harper" and then I thought I bet they were wondering who the hell I was!

After the screening there was a party at the Rainbow Room in Rockefeller Plaza. I sat with Bob and he introduced me to Francis Coppola who of course had worked with Duvall on 'The Godfather' and 'Apocalypse Now' two of the greatest films ever made in my opinion.

Another time Bob invited me to Meryl Streep's husband's art opening on West Broadway and after we went to eat and drink at the Greene Street bar in Soho. I sat at a table with Bob Duvall, Robert De Niro, Matt Dillon, Mickey Rourke and of course Meryl Streep and husband. Ulu Grosbard was directing 'Falling in Love' with De Niro and Streep at the time and he may have been at the table as well. And so once again people in the bar pointed and nodded at the celebrities and at one point I heard someone say "Who the fucks that guy" in their best New York accent. I had an idea that they may have been talking about yours truly. I don't remember any of the conversations around the table.

One day, months later, I got a message on my answering machine from Duvall asking me to get a hold of a camera so as to shoot some research footage for a film he wanted to make about TV evangelists in the south, which much later was to become 'The Apostle.' For some reason or other I never returned his phone call, whether, I was out of town, or had some crazy relationship going on at the time, or whether I didn't want to film a bunch of hypocrites and bigots, I don't know. My problem was that I didn't do anything that I didn't want to do, but at times you end up doing things that you thought you wanted to do, but end up realizing that you shouldn't have done it! But it's the things that one doesn't do, that lays the road to regret. To all intents and purposes I snubbed him, which was not my intention by any means. He was a good friend to me and for my thirty-second birthday bought me a gold watch, when I had a party at Heartbreak a bar on Seventh Avenue. As a friend and professionally I let him down, and to this day do not really know why. I could have gone on to have had a great career in the business, but gave it all away.

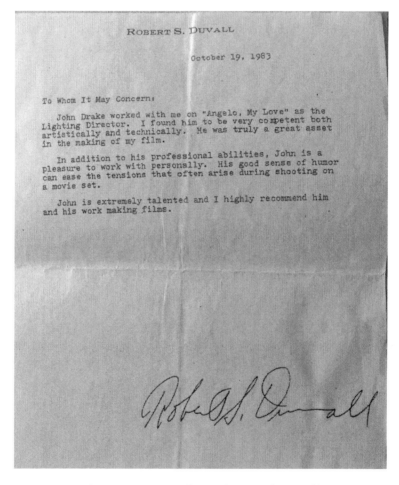

A nice recommendation from Bob Duvall

Abby and I went to see Elton John play on The Great Lawn in Central Park. It was the middle of September and the leaves were beginning to change colors. We got there fairly early in the afternoon hoping to get a good view somewhere near the stage. However we were not the first ones there as about 300,000 fans had beaten us to it. We were quite far back, but I had brought a good pair of binoculars with me. We sat for a couple of hours drinking the beers we had bought at a local deli and eating our sandwiches. I looked behind me and the whole lawn had filled up with another quarter million people behind us. There was no way out, so it felt a bit claustrophobic until the Maestro himself came on stage. I had seen Elton John before at Epsom Baths in Surrey England, of all places soon after he wrote 'Your Song, and now here I was in The Big Apple to see him again.' He walked on stage and a cheer went up as he seated himself in front of a white Grand piano. Just like 'Liberace' he was a showman and had a few costume changes one of them being a Donald Duck outfit, when he sang 'Your Song' which was a bit strange, but that's Elton. He sang a few songs from the 'Madman Across the Water' album including 'Tiny Dancer.' which I always thought was his best album. A woman managed to get up on stage and sat next to Elton actually on his piano stool. Nobody dragged her off the stage - she was waving to the audience and was ecstatic to have had the experience. She left after the song finished and that was that. Elton sang 'Imagine' written by John Lennon of course and he mentioned that Lennon lived across the way there, pointing to the Dakota building. Nobody could have for-seen the tragedy that would happen outside that building in just three months.

It was the Fall again in The Big Apple and a chill crept in through the cracks between the window panes. I slipped out of bed and jumped into my sweat pants that I always wore around the house. The heating had not come on yet, so I threw a wooly jumper over my head and shivered for an instant as I threw my arms around myself, as there was no one else there to do it. There were some days I loved myself more than others! I walked into the kitchen and heated some water for a nice cup of tea, then walked back into the living room with a cup of

Darjeeling. As I sat down on my futon by the window, the fairly quiet morning was broken by the sound of sirens as I watched a paramedic van pull up across the street. Two men jumped out and unloaded a stretcher. An old Italian woman held the door open as they made their way up the stairs. A small crowd began to gather outside in the street as curious onlookers gossiped amongst themselves. About five minutes later, the same two men that went up the stairs, came out the door with a body on the stretcher. I couldn't see who it was and wouldn't have known them anyway- such is the anonymity of New York. The paramedics slid the stretcher into the back of the van closed the doors and drove off, leaving the crowd to gossip amongst themselves. I found out that it was an old man that had died in the bathtub and three days later someone had found him. I had an idea of who it was as one sees people come and go. I think he was an Eastern European from Poland or Hungary and had lived in the neighborhood forever. Some said he was in his eighties when he died. I was not even thirty at this point in time, but I began to imagine if that could happen to me as an old man, that I would be alone and one day be found dead days later, and who would know and who would care.

THE BATH

He opened the door to emptiness
The key now fit the lock
The room was filled with useless things
He didn't want to look.

He sat upon a pillow and tried to understand
What had made the difference
He was in a foreign land.

He tried to think of living
But death was in his path
Nothing seemed to matter
So he went to take a bath.

He was found just three days later
And no one knew his name
There was no one he could talk to
There was no one he could blame.

He had lived there all his life they said
They'd seen him come and go
No one ever talked to him
I wondered, did they know.

Manhattan 1980

December came around and Christmas was on the horizon again. The stores already had the Christmas decorations up and people were walking around wrapped up against the cold, wearing woolen gloves and wooly hats. It was a good time of year to be in New York with all the approaching festivities and on a couple of occasions it snowed but didn't settle. Abby and I were getting along just fine and I was spending more and more time with her at her loft in Tribeca and the weekend of the sixth and seventh of December, I stayed over for the weekend and went back home early Monday morning as Abby had to work. I climbed the four flights of stairs back to my humble abode on Sullivan Street and put on Double Fantasy that Abby had just bought. I can't say that it was my favorite Lennon album, but she really liked it. We were both big fans of The Beatles of course and John Lennon. I called around for work but things were slowing down because of the holiday season and some companies closed their doors for a month as the owners went off to exotic locations in the sun. I think I may have gone off to Fanellis Bar for a burger and fries along with a mad conversation with one of the locals. I went to bed early and so I never got the news about the tragedy that happened that night, until the next morning.

New Yorkers making good use of the winter,
enjoying themselves on the ice

Manhattan circa 1980

Tuesday December 9th 1980

I woke up bright and early after going to bed at a reasonable time, took a shower as I usually do, then made myself a bowl of cereal with milk. I walked back into the living room and turned on the radio only to hear that John Lennon had been shot and killed outside of the Dakota building where he lived with Yoko. Apparently Howard Cosell was the first to announce the news as he was commentating on ABC's Monday Night Football. John Lennon was shot down in cold blood, by Mark David Chapman in the archway of the Dakota building after John and Yoko had just returned from the recording studio. It was almost 11pm. Lennon was rushed to Roosevelt Hospital where he was pronounced dead on arrival. He had received four gunshot wounds from the gun of Mark Chapman. Chapman was a security guard and was twenty - five years old at the time of the shooting. John Lennon had signed a copy of Double Fantasy for Chapman earlier in the day and later Chapman came back and shot him.

The Big Apple stopped. Manhattan became filled with grief. I heard people wailing from outside in the street. The radio kept repeating the news and Beatles music was played all day. Abby called me in tears and I probably started crying myself. She told me there was to be a wake in Central Park, so we should get on the subway and go up there, which we did. There were thousands of mourning fans there, from the very young to the very old, from all walks of life and those that were able to sing who were not crying sang 'All You Need Is Love' and many more. The sadness was overwhelming. John was loved by all New Yorkers, just as he loved New York, and the people looked to the heavens and asked why? The world had lost a great man, a unique artist who spoke his mind, now dead, shot down in his prime at the age of forty. Yoko issued a statement the next day, saying there will be no funeral for John. Yoko asked for the people to pray for John as John loved and prayed for the human race. New York dedicated an area in Central Park to John directly across from The Dakota, that became known as Strawberry Fields and the City of Naples Italy donated the 'Imagine' mosaic centerpiece. John Lennon was admired and loved throughout the world and on December 8, 2000, Fidel Castro unveiled a bronze statue of Lennon in a park in Havana. John touched the whole world with his love of humanity and his pacifist views and involvement with political activism and not forgetting the wonderful songs he gave the world and I know that there are still a lot of us who still miss him.

1980 also saw the start of the Iran - Iraq war when Saddam Hussein invaded Western Iran. The fighting went on for eight years after which time they signed a ceasefire, after a million people had lost their lives.

Zimbabwe gained Independence from Britain, which was formerly known as Rhodesia, and Ronald Reagan was elected President. Killer Clown (John Wayne Gacy Jnr) was sentenced to death for the murder of thirty-three boys and young men and Mount St. Helens erupted back in May killing fifty-seven people. 'Raging Bull' about the boxer Jake LaMotta was released which was a masterpiece shot in black and white. John Lennon's death ended the year of 1980!

The Cabin in Willow

'New York, New York, such a wonderful town, the Bronx is up and the Battery's down,' - so the song goes, though I would sooner go down to Battery Park and look out at the Statue of Liberty or Statue of Bigotry as Lou Reed called it in one of his songs. Even on a hot summer's day the breeze would blow in off the bay cooling down the heat of the City, by a few degrees and in the middle of the summer every little bit helped. I remember summers where the temperatures soared to a staggering 108 degrees and would stay that way for a week or two when it would drop down to a mild 90 or so. I was still living on Bethune Street at the time and didn't even have an air conditioner, but would sweat the nights away and probably woke up a couple of pounds lighter in the morning with the sheets soaking wet. The Spring and Fall were the best times to be in the Big Apple and even in the early years I realized the importance of being able to escape from New York to the country, and so I rented a little cabin in the woods in a place called Willow just out of town from Woodstock. It was a pretty basic handmade job with a pot - bellied stove on the ground floor and a propane powered cooker with a tiny bedroom upstairs where I had a futon on the floor to rest my weary head. There was also a small deck to sit on that looked out over a small stream a few yards away. It was cool there even in the summer, as the cabin was shaded by tall pine trees. At night, it was very quiet, with just the sound of a few barking dogs to break the silence from other houses nearby. There were times where I would scare myself to death out there in the woods, as the imagination would run wild, fearing an attack from Zombies or Vampires so I kept an axe near the bed just in case.

One time I was there alone except for some magic mushrooms, it was the end of the summer and the leaves were changing color and I felt like I was living in a page from a Carlos Castaneda novel and was searching for the Yaqui Indians. I prepared myself a nice chewy cup of tea from the mushrooms and walked down to the stream where I spoke to the rocks - they didn't say too much, but as I looked up to the hill above the stream I saw an Indian hunting party, maybe a dozen or so warriors wearing war paint, some were on horseback and others were walking, some had feathered headdresses and most had bows and quivers. I ducked down behind a large rock for fear they might see me as they silently drifted by into the fading light, and as I peered out once again to see them they were gone. It was the land of the Mohicans and Munsee tribes and they used these mountains mostly for their rituals and usually passed through this area to other parts. At that point I sat there expecting to see more, but no more came, so I dangled my feet in the stream and listened to the birds singing high up in the trees and realized that I time traveled for a few minutes or else those Indians were really there, or that I was going stark raving mad! But no! They were as real as real could be, and I have not had an experience quite like it since. I told Abby about it the following weekend and she just gave me the raised eyebrow and yet she could not deny my experience or disprove what I had seen.

The Morning After The Night Before

For very shame I blamed myself for my death
Possessed by the very Devil himself
I saw his reflection when I stared into the silky silver pond
And shaking my head violently to lose this image
Shook loose the very sense that I was born with
Till the wind took heed and blew delicate ripples across the pond

Releasing me from my own reflection.

I turned to loose myself
And on so doing faced an old man with eyes like mine
And naked as the day was young
Except for leaves to hide his private parts, said,
"Good day young man," in a quiet knowing voice.
"I've been following and watching you for years."

He had tears in his eyes and wisdom in his head
I stood alone
The question, why?
Lingered in the mist that he left behind.

Woodstock Winter

I kept my place in Willow through the winter and managed to get there a few times, but with only the pot-bellied stove to keep me from freezing to death, the trips in the winter became fewer and fewer, but I imagined and did experience what life must have been like decades before. I kept warm by chopping wood and keeping the stove burning and with one good pile of wood in there before going to sleep, I managed to keep fairly warm through the night as the heat rose up to the bedroom as I was tucked up in my sleeping bag feeling like an early pioneer.

The Catskill mountain range was home to many Jewish New Yorkers in the mid twentieth century who also used to escape from the big city and spend a few days or a week or more in one of the many resorts there. The Borscht Belt was the name used for the resorts in this area, and the term comes from the soup that was a standard dish in Eastern Europe made from beets. Lots of the Jewish descendants from Eastern Europe escaped the Nazi persecution of Jews and made New York their home.

Even though I had my little retreat in Willow in the woods, I would still go to the Karma Triyana Dharmachakra Monastery at the top of Mead Mountain Road and sit and collect my thoughts in front of the Buddha there. The Karmapa Rangjung Rigpe Dorje was the sixteenth in the Kagya lineage in the tradition of Tibetan Buddhism and became head of the Kagyu School and is thought to be a manifestation of an enlightened being. He came to the United States in 1981 to teach the way of the Kagya lineage and felt that America was dying of spiritual poverty. He taught his followers to seek guidance from wise and compassionate people and to listen to them in earnest. He died in America on November 5, 1981 (Guy Fawkes Day in England) in a hospital in Zion Illinois. He refused pain medication and felt no signs of profound pain that other patients with his condition would feel. Upon his death and in keeping with Tibetan beliefs, he was left in the hospital for three days where his heart remained warm. The chief doctor had no explanation for this. Apparently during the seven weeks between his death and cremation the Karmapa's body shrunk to the size of a small child. He was taken to Rumtek Monastery where he was cremated and on that day his two dogs died. While his body burnt on the funeral pyre his eyes, tongue and heart rolled from the flames, which was taken to indicate that the body, speech and mind came together to be saved as relics for the future. The same thing had happened during the cremation of other Karmapas. During his cremation a triple rainbow appeared above the monastery even though there was a clear blue sky. How does a normal person have an explanation for any of these extraordinary events that take place, like miracles performed at Lourdes in France and other occurrences around the world?

There is another world that revolves around us that is hard to understand, but the Tibetan monks and other religious sects seem to have an everyday understanding of something that cannot be touched and seems intangible to the average person. I have dabbled in various schools of spirituality throughout my life, always searching for answers, but the answers are not out there- they are within, and all the teachings are there to try to make us understand this magical mystical world.

I realize that we don't necessarily do the things we want to do - we get diverted in one direction or another and end up down a path we never planned on, sometimes it's a good path, and sometimes the path ends with only a precipice to greet us. Do we jump into the raging torrent below, risking life and limb, but at the same time if we jumped and survived be taken down stream to a beautiful village and a land like Shangri- La? Most of us would turn around and go back down the same path from whence we came, unless being chased by a gang of gun wielding thugs or a hostile tribe of cannibals - then there is no choice but to jump, and there lies the rub, sometimes when we don't have a choice, then a leap of faith is needed and in this extreme example to take that leap is the only way.

My Cabin in Willow

The Joyous Lake

The Joyous Lake was a great little music venue right in the middle of
the town of Woodstock and was founded by a guy called Ron Merians,
who chose the name from the mystical traditions of the 'I Ching,' that
is the 'Chinese Book of Changes'. It was the book that every hippie
traveler had with them when traveling through Europe and India in the
sixties and seventies. One made their traveling decisions based on the
I Ching by throwing down the yarrow sticks, which mystically gave
one advice as to where their next destination or decision in life might
take them. I knew a couple of people back in the day, that wouldn't
even make a cup of tea without first consulting this mystical book. I
also consulted the book for a while, but found that one message could
have a couple of different meanings according to who was interpreting

it. I think I preferred Mrs. Brown's tea - house in Jamaica for some real decision - making! Anyway 'The Joyous Lake' was my hangout for when I had escaped the big city and I used to drive into town from a house I was renting that was about ten miles out of town that overlooked the Ashokan reservoir. Saturday nights was when one could be surprised by local musicians just turning up and playing. One particular night I saw Levon Helm (from 'The Band') and Paul Butterfield perform together and I think Rick Danko was also there from 'The Band.' There were a lot of famous and not so famous musicians that lived in and around Woodstock, including Todd Rundgren and Pat Metheny and a host of others who were tucked away in the woods. I know the whole Band who was Dylan's band all lived there at one time and Dylan composed two albums 'Another Side of Bob Dylan' and 'Bringing it all Back Home' whilst sitting at the Tinker Street Café in town.

There was a lot of dancing at The Joyous Lake and after Abby and I broke up I met a lovely girl called Debbie there, whilst dancing who became my girlfriend for the next few months. She had a beautiful old cottage with a screened in porch and a beautiful view overlooking a valley. It seemed like an idyllic place to live and I wished that I was a musician and could live that life there. But life was good and I really enjoyed country living with fruit and veggie stalls along the sides of the road and the local markets selling their fresh produce. Autumn was the most beautiful time of the year when the leaves changed into vibrant reds and oranges and yellows that seemed not real.

In the winter Debbie and I would cross country ski right off from my doorstep as my house was about a thousand feet high up in the Catskills and the snow would be a couple of feet deep. I would throw a bottle of wine and some bread and cheese into my little pack throw it over my shoulder and we would lose ourselves in the woods, then sit down on a log and have a French snack of bread, cheese and wine. After getting a little tipsy, ski back to the house to throw some logs into the large fireplace and sit back and watch as the flames got higher and warmer as we snuggled up together out of the cold as the night came upon us, usually around five in the afternoon.

The Hermit

He wondered who would know him there

So he never went

He never went anywhere

Because he didn't know anyone

He didn't know anyone

Because he never went anywhere

You don't meet people when you stay at home

But sometimes you learn more.

Woodstock, NY

Sri Lanka

Abby and I decided to take a trip to Sri Lanka. We flew from New York via Amsterdam where we spent the day, and then on to Colombo. Colombo was like an Indian city, but not as frantic. People seemed less hurried. Not sure if that was true or not, but that was my perspective at the time. I didn't know if it had to do with the fact that the majority of the population of India are of the Hindu religion, and the majority of Sri Lanka are Buddhists. Whether it was to do with the fact that the Hindus worshipped many deities and felt like they had to rush around and worship a lot of them - I don't know. In Buddhism there was only one, and that was the Buddha, so that made things a little simpler, just like the Christians in the western world go off to church on a Sunday to worship Jesus nailed to the cross. So it was suffering in the west, and as Buddha said, life is suffering, so then it was suffering in the east as well. I wondered where people weren't suffering. Abby and I were not suffering at this particular moment in time as after a couple of days in Colombo I managed to score a little opium, which we smoked in our hotel room. Abby lay on the bed and I walked out onto the balcony to watch as the day wound down. The black and yellow three wheeler taxis screeched down the street as they do in every Indian city as well, as the bullock carts slowly meandered into the traffic as motorbikes and bicycles weaved in and out as though it were some kind of vehicle dance, chaotic yet organized. Buses spewed out thick black smoke from their exhausts adding to the already polluted atmosphere. The golden light was low and backlit the smoke, as dust and fumes created some kind of abstract canvass as the numerous fires twirled and danced into the heavens. On the street an orchestra was tuning up its instruments of car horns and clanging bells, the hammer and rattle and the relentless chatter and yelling as the city was ready to explode, as I imagined into a crescendo not unlike Tchaikovsky's 1812 Overture. This then was yet another Asian city, full of life and death, decay and rebirth that lived together on the streets, of sounds deafening to the ears, relentless stimulation of the senses, whilst a concoction of smells unknown in the west wafted into the nasal passages to the brain. The senses of sight and smell and hearing were bombarded all day and into the night, as the western sensibilities had to adapt, otherwise madness could set in. Mothers with children on their backs also weaved their way in and out of the traffic whilst whole families rode scooters with mum dad and two kids aboard, all involved in this dance of humans and machines. Children begged with outstretched palms to tourists carrying backpacks or to white women wearing saris, who were trying so hard to be a part of this Asian culture.

The smoke from the opium pipe danced around inside also, as we had our own show inside our hotel room, the smell reminiscent of my life in India six years before. Once again I was back in Asia, this time on a pearl of an island once called Ceylon off the tip of the great sub-continent of India. Here I was now with my girlfriend from New York. I smiled as I looked back at her and thought how wonderful life can be. I inhaled the smoke of the poppy as I handed the pipe back to Abby who was now naked on the bed, her large breasts hanging down on her torso, whilst her thick black gypsy hair curled across her shoulders. Once again I felt like I had stepped back in time as I looked at my exotic Abby sitting there crossed legged as the fan lazily spun above her, keeping the heat of the room circulating. She looked like a princess from the time of Cleopatra or maybe she was a reincarnation of Cleopatra herself. Was I then a reincarnation of Mark Anthony? It was fun playing games with history. We were now light years from New York. This was another world within the world and yet I was removed from myself. I was experiencing this world, this exotic crazy world, from another perspective as though I were a fly on the wall. I loved to travel and I loved my Abby and here we were in this hotel room in our own little dream world. I smiled at Abby and she smiled back, and then it was night, and the noise from the street subsided a little as the hand of God had lowered the volume, and I lit a candle and we curled up like two lion cubs under the mosquito net, as reality and dreams became one.

After three days or so we took a train south down to Hikkaduwa, then Galle that was a fortified city that was occupied by the Portuguese and then the Dutch in the Seventeenth century. In 1796 it was ceded to Great Britain by Holland and the island became a crown colony in 1802. Ceylon declared independence in 1948 soon after India had declared their independence from the British, and in 1972 the island changed its name to Sri Lanka. We found a lovely little hotel that looked out across the sea and in the evening we went out for a curry. From Galle we took another train further south to Unawatuna and rented a little house on the beach a couple of houses down from Arthur C. Clark's house. Clark had lived on the island for years. He was a scientist and wrote 2001 A Space Odyssey that Kubrick made into a very successful film. We stayed for about a week here and then traveled further south to lovely Weligama Bay.

The Buddha at Matara

From there we visited Matara where a huge Buddha stood as high as five floors. We met some young monks there and sat down with them to talk and take some photos. One of them explained the meaning of the moonstones that were in front of a lot of temples.

A Moonstone

We visited many little Buddhist temples and usually at the entrance was a carved piece of stone called a moonstone. It was like a welcoming mat. On the outer circle of the moonstone is a depiction of fire that represents attachment - the clinging to life, the suffering and pains of passion, of greed, hatred and delusion that keeps us in Samsara, the cycle of rebirth. In the next circle are carvings of different animals, an elephant, lion a bull and a horse. To me it seemed strange that a lion was represented here, as there are no lions in Sri Lanka, but used to be many tigers, as in India, but who am I to argue? It looked like the animals were chasing each other. So the animals represent the four noble truths or four stages in life, I have heard different interpretations, but the elephant symbolizes the endless reincarnation, as disease is depicted by the lion, aging by the bull, and death is the horse. According to Buddhist belief whoever sees through this endless chain of suffering is the first of the four noble truths and has therefore taken the first step to salvation. The geese in the next circle represent the distinction between good and evil. In the centre of the moonstone is carved the lotus, with petals encircling it, and that is Nirvana, when we cease the endless reincarnations. The four noble truths are right view, right thought, right speech and right action, which in the end comes down to a basic respect for our fellow human beings and common sense that should be inherent in all of us, but unfortunately it isn't, as we wouldn't have all these wars in the world.

We traveled to Kandy a beautiful little town on a lake where we stayed at The Queen's Hotel an old British Colonial style building, which was once the former governor's residence. The room had an oak four-poster bed and the usual mosquito net that we draped over it at night. In the evening we popped down to the Lord Mountbatten Bar where I had to have a gin and tonic to celebrate forgotten ghosts of the British Empire. Mountbatten frequented the hotel quite often when he was the supreme allied commander during WWII.

We visited the Temple of the Tooth in Kandy where a tooth from the Buddha was held in a gold casket, shaped like a stupa. Only during puja can one enter the room where the casket is housed. Unfortunately one cannot actually see the tooth. In the evening we went to see a 'Devil Dance' where men worked themselves into a trance like state, and then walked across burning coals to the sounds of wild tom toms and high pitched bagpipes played by dark skinned mountain men, that were probably Tamils. It was all very dreamlike as half naked men as black as the night, wearing only a loin cloth danced and sang as we watched this sacred ceremony in the depths of a hot sweaty Asian night. Coconut torches of fire and flame lit up the darkness as they flickered and spat under the moonlight. It was wild and savage and spiritual and even sensual as beautiful young women in colorful saris of red and green and gold looked on at this ancient spectacle as Abby and I were transported back in time once again.

The Temple of the Tooth in Kandy

After a few days relaxing in Kandy we decided to do the pilgrimage to the top of Adam's Peak, also called Sri Prada a holy mountain over 7,000ft in height in the centre of the island. It was known for the 'sacred footprint' of the Buddha that was a rock formation at the summit. The mountain was also known as a holy place for that of the Hindu god Shiva, and the mountain was also a pilgrimage centre for Christians and Muslims alike thinking it to have been the place where Adam landed after being expelled from the Garden of Eden. (Ouch must have hurt!) So it was a holy site for all religions for Christians, Buddhists, Muslims and Hindus alike and Sri Pada is the only mountain in the world that is venerated by four different faiths. The footprint is under a boulder on a blue sapphire to prevent it from sacrilegious tampering, so the god Sakra covered it with a boulder.

Apparently it bears some resemblance to a human foot but the size is gigantic. So once again these mythological discoveries are open to interpretation. Marco Polo on his travels of 1298 gave credit to Adam's Peak as an important place for pilgrimage. So the mountain had been a part of adventurers and pilgrim's lives for centuries past. Sri Pada literally translated means 'Sacred Foot.'

Abby and I arrived by bus to the foot of the mountain sometime in the evening as the best time to climb to the top was at night as it was cooler. Also it was important to see the sun rise at dawn from the top of Sri Pada, as the sun produced a perfect triangular shadow of the mountain on the plains below that was a rather magical and spectacular sight. We each had our own sweater and a little backpack for snacks on the way up. There were many chai places on the path where one could get a nice cup of Ceylon tea. The stairs to climb the mountain ahead were lit by lights on poles, and as one looked up it seemed like it could be the 'stairway to heaven' as the stairs and lights disappeared into the clouds. I mentioned to Abby that that is what it looked like and on cue we started to sing the Led Zeppelin song of the same name and I wondered if they got the inspiration from this magical mountain. So we started to ascend the holy mountain and as we got closer to the top we put on our sweaters as the air got colder and colder into the night. We got to the top after a five or six hour hike with over 10,000 steps just before dawn, and sure enough as the sun came up we saw the triangular shadow laid out on the plains below.

So now it was time to descend the holy mountain and we couldn't decide on what path we took, not realizing that there was more than one way up and down. We had a little argument and I can't remember who decided what, but we took the long way down and once at the bottom didn't have a clue where we were. I can't remember how we got back to Kandy but we did.

Half way up Sri Pada (Adams Peak)

JIMMY DEAN AND THE FALKLANDS

On Friday, April 2, 1982 Argentina invaded and occupied the Falkland Islands that had been a Crown Colony and flew the Union Jack since 1841. How us Brits got there or were doing there in the first place I'm not sure, nevertheless they were subjects of the Queen that needed protecting from these foreign invaders. Not forgetting the sheep that could not remain neutral, as British sheep were the best in the world - ask any Scotsman? So on the 5th April Britain dispatched the SAS, certain Commando Brigades and The Gurkha Rifles, (who carried those curly knives and could lop your head off in a second) to engage the Argentine Navy and Air Force in battle. The British made an amphibious attack on the island and in 74 days the Argentines surrendered on 14th June. It also solidified Margaret Thatcher's term in office for the next few years as The Iron Lady with a lot of flag waving and Rule Britannia rules the waves!

I was working on "Come back to the Five and Dime Jimmy Dean Jimmy Dean" at the time as third electrician. The film was directed by the great Robert Altman of 'McCabe and Mrs. Miller' fame that was shot in British Columbia many years before starring Warren Beatty and the beautiful Julie Christie.

The Story

Jimmy Dean's disciples meet up on an anniversary of his death and basically mull over lives in present and in flashbacks by use of a two - way mirror. A two-way mirror separated the two identical sets, so that when the audience was taken back into the past, the lights on the 'now set' would dim and the lights on the 'then set' would come up allowing the audience to see through the mirror into the past. All the effects were therefore 'done in camera' and may have been one of the most interesting lighting situations I had seen.

The film starred Cher, Karen Black and Sandy Dennis with an appearance from Kathy Bates. 'Come Back to the Five and Dime' was originally a play on Broadway also directed by Altman with the same cast. It was supposed to be set in a Woolworth's Five and Dime in Texas.

So every day arriving on the set with my New York Times newspaper would see how the Brits were doing restoring the Crown Colony to Britain. The Queen Elizabeth was decked - out to be used as a troop ship along with the SS Canberra with three brigades of commandos aboard, and they sailed off to the other side of the world to return 'The Malvinas' back to the Falkland Islands. The whole task force comprised of 127 ships that included 62 merchant ships. The nuclear submarine Conqueror set sail from France and two aircraft carriers, The Invincible and The Hermes set sail from Portsmouth. The United

States Navy considered a successful invasion by the British to be a military impossibility. They obviously didn't consider the history of wars that were conducted by the British Navy over the past 500 years! The elite SAS troops went in as well as other commando units. The Harrier jet that was the vertical takeoff plane, was also put to good use. The Argentine warship The General Belgrano was sank by HMS Conqueror and 323 men on board lost their lives, although about another 700 men were rescued from the freezing sea. In total there were 907 casualties 255 being British servicemen. After 74 days the Union Jack was once again raised to flap in the winds from the South Atlantic.

The film was shot at Phoenix Stage in Manhattan and like a lot of the studios from those days the roofs were covered in asbestos in case of fires, but after years the asbestos would turn to dust and many a time focusing a light on the catwalk I would brush against the ceiling and a pile of asbestos dust would fall onto my head and down the back of my shirt, which itched like mad as it stuck to the sweat on my back. The temperatures in the catwalks were probably in the 90's as there were a lot of hot lights being used, and as we all know heat rises. It was not till a few years later that they realized how dangerous asbestos could be, especially to the lungs.

Can She Bake a Cherry Pie?

The following year I gaffed a film called 'Can She Bake A Cherry Pie" starring Karen Black again, when on meeting me said, "Oh no not you again?" I apologized for being me, and she had a good sense of humor. The film was about a relationship between two lost souls and was a bit of an art film directed by Henry Jaglom. Francis Fisher and Larry David also acted in it. I don't remember too much more about it, but I don't think the shooting schedule was too long. The locations were all in and around New York.

June 1982

It was time for Abby and I to take our yearly trip to Central Park to listen to music. This time however was a little different. To get to the park we joined in with all the demonstrations that were being held in mid-town and in the park. They were peaceful demonstrations to stop the proliferation of nuclear weapons. People had been bused in from all over the country to try to make their voices heard. The marches were three miles long and there were placards in many languages saying NO to Nuclear weapons. All kinds of people were demonstrating in this hub of democracy where freedom of speech was allowed and accepted and even encouraged. There were anarchists and pacifists, Buddhists and Catholic bishops, communists and students and union leaders and delegations from around the world. There were jugglers and musicians and dancers, and mime artists who didn't say much. There was the sound of bagpipes mixed in with the sound of Tibetan drums and people were singing and chanting for their lives and others. It was all very profound and very necessary and the spectacle of thousands of people coming together as one was very inspiring. There were religious groups and scientists and people from all denominations. There were children and old people, some being pushed in wheelchairs, Vietnam Vets, young people and even the disabled, and they were all there for the same reason, and it was fantastic to be amongst this good sense of humanity, amongst people who cared about the world and others. I teared up as the atmosphere was overwhelming and felt so positive that almost one million people wanted their voices heard. There were banners and signs that read "No Nukes' 'Bread not Bombs' 'Save the Humans' 'US out of El Salvador' and people chanted "No nukes, no nukes, no nukes" as they held up their 'Ban the Bomb' signs as the procession weaved its way like a human snake into the park. An old woman held up a sign that read 'Grandmother Earth Has Had Enough' and so had she, as she joined the throng. There were races from all over the world, people of every ethnicity, joined together to pray to their own gods, or to the heavens and to mankind, for hope and peace for the future of our beautiful planet. A lot of the avenues had been closed off as people walked and sang up sixth and eighth avenues.

By the time Abby and I got to the park the music was in full swing. I know we saw Bruce Springsteen with Jackson Browne and Linda Ronstadt and I think James Taylor played and of course Joan Baez a voice from the sixties. The rally for the abolition of nuclear weapons turned out to be the largest political demonstration in US history and by the time Abby and I got back to the village we felt like we had become a part of it.

Meanwhile back in England, Henry VIII's flagship The Mary Rose is raised from The Solent in October after laying at the bottom of the sea for over four hundred years. Channel Four was launched, Gandhi and Chariots of Fire played in cinemas, and Roxy Music released Avalon, an album that every girl in New York seemed to own. Tottenham Hotspur (my team that I used to see in London as a kid) won the F.A. Cup, beating Queens Park Rangers 1 - 0. Italy won the World Cup, Prince William is born and The Times Man of the Year is The Computer!

THE SHRINK

We are drifting apart, and I can't help it - two souls swept away by chaos in a chaotic world - of the desert that isn't a desert.

He dreamt of far - away places, desert like places, but the real desert, the desert of camels and nomads.

He drove her crazy, just like he had done with all the others. A highway of broken hearts lay behind him. His conscience, heavy with his own confusion played on his mind as he took another sip of tequila. He was tired of America with its irreverence for the truth as lies seemed to be the order of the day, spoken by people who we are supposed to trust.

He went back home where she screamed from the top of her lungs before she threw herself into the pit of worldly delights. The dogs looked on choking on their leash, their fangs bared for the kill. Drums were heard somewhere - he wanted to be a savage. "I'm sick of you" she screamed out from her nightmare as she danced around the Kasbah. The air was heavy with sweat and body odor - sex was oozing down the walls, dripping like candle wax in the heat of the night.

He heard the castratos singing - it was beautiful, the voice of a boy with no balls. She swirled the sword above her head, cutting an arc in the humid heavy air.

"Off with his head" the Queen yelled and off it came, and Henry went on hunting.

He looked and saw nothing, just a looking glass that he had stepped through light years before. He heard the drums beneath an African sky, black hands beating on stretched animal skin echoing sounds of their ancestors. She picked up the scissors and cut off all her hair. "Now how do I look" she had a devilish look in her eyes that flickered when she spoke. "You know I will only kill you with kindness" she muttered to herself as she left him there bathing in his own self-pity.

It was a time of black roll neck sweaters, black berets and the smell of reefer on Eel Pie Island. I told her I used to give the old woman a penny every time I crossed over the bridge into Hades over the river Styx and the ferryman waved as if he knew me.

"You're really fucked in the head," she said in a matter of fact kind of way, these were words from a psychiatrist! It reverberated in his head as he walked along the Bowery. Bums appeared from beneath their cardboard shelters as they rubbed their eyes to greet a cold yet sunny winter's day. The cops took a body away in the morning, frozen like a popsicle. Life was cheap then and there on the Bowery as he realized he was still in the land of the living as he thought about his Eastern teachings. He went back to his little abode and lit a candle that burnt a hole in his thoughts and flickered like a moment in time. He thought

94

about the actress he had just met. She covered herself in stories and fantasies and why not? "Do you know the answer then," she said as she threw a stack of holy books off the mountain only to create valleys of despair. There was no answer. She had one question for him and he gave the wrong answer, her wild Russian red hair covered the sun as she turned to leave him sitting there at Lindos waiting for the Moon to rise. He heard the Goans singing as they pulled in their nets. "How many lives have you had," she asked him as she unzipped his jeans. She smiled at her own reflection as she rode the camel home.

'Zeisters' aka 'Fat Boys Go Nutsoid'

Leonard Maltin the film critic called it "A tasteless comedy about two nerds, who befriend a big fat, retarded fellow and his antics, while on the loose in NYC."

I started on this film as the gaffer, sometime in 1983, but after the first week of filming the producer and director fired the director of photography as they didn't like his work. I realized that he was trying to do something different, but it didn't really pay off. They approached me and told me that they were getting rid of the DP. My film 'Dreams Come True' that I had shot was being edited at the time and told them if they wanted to look at my work they could go with me to the editing bay. Fortunately they liked what they saw and the next day myself, and my best boy became DP and assistant cameraman. The AC who was John Herron had worked with me as an AC on the previous film. So the next day I stepped onto the dolly with John on focus and the dolly grip said, "The king is dead, long live the king." I shall always remember that.

The film was produced and directed by two brothers - John and Roger Golden, John was the director and Roger was the producer who would get up early every morning and do his Tai Chi workout. It was a crazy story about a retarded man called the 'Mouka' whom a couple of friends help escape from a mental institution and accompany him on his adventures around New York. The music was composed by Leo Kotke and was released by Troma Entertainment. This was the height of crazy independent film making in New York.

'Zeisters' Shooting in the Peppermint Lounge

1984

George Orwell wrote this novel in 1948 about the year 1984, but the book is more relevant now than it has ever been. It was Orwell's prophecy of a government that will do anything to control the people. The story is set in Airstrip One, which was formerly known as Great Britain, a province of Oceania in a world of continuous war. The people are under control of the regime that has invented its own language. England has become a police state where individuality and free speech has become a crime and is punished by 'The Thought Police.' It is a story about 'Big Brother,' and for power and control for the sake of it and for no other reason. Newspapers are re-written and 'The Ministry of Truth' makes up its own idea of the 'truth' from its own propaganda machine. Meanwhile people are brainwashed and tortured and the government re-writes history to serve its own end.

Big Brother is watching you! Does any of this sound familiar? And just like Clockwork Orange the book was way ahead of its time. Meanwhile back in the USA Ronald Reagan won a second term in office winning 49 out of 50 states, the only blue state being Minnesota. 'Money for Nothing' was released by Dire Straits, which caused a little controversy because of its lyrics:

'See the little faggot with the earring and the make up

That little faggot got his own jetplane' - and

'Look at that mama, she got it sticking on the camera'

'We gotta move those refrigerators - we gotta move those color TV's'

And so on - I thought it was a great song and so did lots of people as I believe it won an award or two, and was top of the hit parade, but there were some radio stations that wouldn't play it, because of the lyrics. The Canadian Broadcast Standards Council claimed that the unedited version was not acceptable to play on the air. There were also objections from a gay newspaper in London. Apparently Mark Knopfler overheard a couple of shop assistants talking as they were watching Motley Crew in an electronics store that I was told was Crazy Eddie's on Sixth Avenue, New York. Knopfler grabbed a pen and paper and wrote down what these guys were saying and the next thing you know it was a smash hit! A few people have claimed that it was in another store, one being in Arkansas and a couple of other places. Now of course we hear rap songs where the 'F' word is repeated over and over and guys call their girlfriends 'bitches' and as Dylan said, 'The Times They Are A Changing.'

Marvin Gaye was shot to death by his father, before his 45th birthday for intervening in an argument between his parents, and a man in California sprayed a McDonalds with gunfire killing 21 people, before being shot and killed himself.

Indira Gandhi was assassinated by her two Sikh bodyguards in New Delhi, after which anti-Sikh riots break out leaving over 10,000 sikhs dead. Rajiv Gandhi her son took over at the age of forty to become India's youngest Prime Minister. He was later assassinated in 1991. Indira Gandhi was the daughter of India's first Prime Minister Nehru.

The IRA attempted to assassinate Margaret Thatcher with a bomb at The Grand Hotel in Brighton and Hezbollah car bombed the Embassy in Beirut killing 24 people, meanwhile in North Korea Kim Jong - Un is born as the new Supreme Leader of that country. So it was quite the year for assassinations, meanwhile back in the USA The Boss, Bruce Springsteen released 'Born in the USA' and the Summer Olympics are held in Los Angeles.

Johnny Weissmuller who played Tarzan died, as did James Mason who starred in Lolita and North by Northwest and so to the writer Truman Capote. The great Richard Burton also passed away after a lifetime of drinking and smoking at the age of 58. He was married to Elizabeth Taylor twice and starred in 'Who's Afraid of Virginia Woolf' with her. He also was in 'The Spy Who Came In From The Cold,' 'Becket,' The Taming Of The Shrew' and a host of other films. He started his career as a Shakespearian actor. And last but not least the very funny Tommy Cooper a comedian and member of the Magic Circle died of a heart attack on stage whilst giving a performance. He collapsed on national TV and people believed it was part of the act as they were laughing hysterically. What better way for a comedian to die and he died "Just like that!" And so ended the year of 1984.

SULLIVAN STREET

Around about 1980 I moved from Bethune St. into a bigger apartment on Sullivan Street in Soho, between Prince Street and Houston Street. It was diagonally across from Saint Anthony's Church that was featured in Godfather II. Sullivan Street also played host to St. Anthony's feast that sold all kinds of Italian food and had stalls like in a fair where one could win a fluffy doll for knocking over some skittles and the usual rifle range and things like that. The fair stretched for two blocks over Prince St. down to Spring St. It lasted about ten days and I would sit on my fire escape and watch the parade go by below me. I ate enough spicy Italian sausages in those ten days to last me the year. The smell of greasy fried foods would envelope my apartment even days after the Feast closed. It smelt holy like the incense burning in the church across the street. It was a great event as I watched the hoards below, with people stuffing their faces with as much food as their mouths could hold - it was as if these people hadn't eaten for weeks. It was a feeding frenzy and was fun to observe from four floors above. I always looked forward to it when the time got close. On the same side of the street as I lived was a social club where all the old Italian men would congregate to play cards and smoke their cigars, and I believe that once or twice a year some of the Dons from around the country would meet there to discuss business.

The street when I lived there, still had an old world charm to it and one could easily imagine what it was like back in the early nineteen hundreds, when it was a market place for all the Italian and Jewish immigrants to do business. The scene in the Godfather, where Robert De Niro walks down the street, meeting his friends and the Mafia boss, were all filmed there. The Breakstone butter commercials were also filmed on Sullivan Street and the crew would cover the road in soil and sawdust to make it look like the turn of the century, with horse and carts moving through the scene with people dressed in the clothes of that period. On the corner of Sullivan and Houston was and maybe still is a cheese shop that dated back to those times. When I lived there, there were four or five old stores from those days and when I walked down the street I could feel the ambience from those days and wondered what it must have been like back then, although Godfather II depicted that era extremely well. I'm sure there must have been other films that used Sullivan Street as a location.

The Bakery on Prince Street around the corner

My apartment was on the fourth floor that looked out onto the street and the stairs leading to it were well worn with dips in the middle of each step where thousands of feet had climbed over the past one hundred years. My bedroom was in the back that looked out into a courtyard where washing lines were strung from one building to the next, where bloomers were hung out to dry in the hot New York summers.

Women would yell across to one another in Italian and it always seemed like they were arguing and then maybe a man's voice would interrupt very loudly, and then it would be quiet for a while, only to start again later. I felt like I could have been living in Naples Italy. There was no lack of atmosphere on Sullivan St. and I felt like I was living inside of a movie in a foreign land that indeed I was.

A few doors down there lived a lovely Brazilian woman who was a jazz dancer and performed in various loft spaces around Soho and Tribeca. She was a part of the 'Performance Art Scene' downtown. I used to see her walking up and down the street and one day introduced myself as a neighbor and after a few polite conversations we became lovers. Sometimes I would be on my fire escape and she on hers, just three or four buildings down and we would wave to each other and if neither of us were busy, which if we were on the fire escape would normally signify a lack of employment, would get together for a cocktail at her place or mine and spend the rest of the afternoon having fun.

The Girl Next Door

Morning came around once again

Sunlight glowed gold on the windowpanes

A car back - fired in the street, which sounded like a gun.

It was the time after Christmas, just before the New Year

And a cold December breeze slipped through a crack

In the mind of the human that rolled over in the bed.

He scratched his head and purred like a cat

As he thought about the woman he had dinner with the night before.

She wasn't in his bed and wished she was

There was an empty space between having

And not having

A moment in time, a fragment, like a precious scent

An accent or word, or a smile, that lingers deep in the mind.

It was not late in the morning as he rolled over

And thought about her beauty.

He couldn't stay in bed a moment longer without her.

He walked into the kitchen

And danced on the red and white checkered floor.

Brazilian coffee flowed down his throat

As the porridge boiled in a pot

He looked into the mirror

And wondered where the time had gone.

He thought that maybe someone had stolen it.

But this morning had turned into a beautiful woman,

He saw her smile as he began to shave away the night

He lit some incense to purify the living room

He thought about becoming holy once again

Or maybe just a little bit religious

Everyone needs a little religion once in a while.

The work in the film business was inconsistent, but it seemed to arrive just when I needed it, and so managed to keep a decent amount of money in the bank for eating and drinking and to take the occasional trip somewhere. The street where I lived was very safe as the local Italians would keep an eye on things, and the old women would sit outside their front doors, chatting away to each other in Italian.

Very often I would have to shake my head in disbelief that I was living here, in New York City as America was the last place on Earth that I wanted to visit, probably because of its violent reputation and harshness that was portrayed in American TV shows that I would see on English television growing up. Watching those shows as a kid from my parent's home in suburban Surrey, American seemed like another world, another planet far from the safety of the rolling hills of Surrey. However after a trip to India, my mind began to broaden and more adventure was calling me. I left England months after my return from India with a friend headed for South America.

The rest is history as they say and you have to read 'The Laughing Man' as a prelude to my time in 'The Big Apple.' So needless to say I did not regret coming to America and especially my time living in New York, but sometimes do regret career wise heading out to the west coast, even though the weather was better and life easier. Someone said, New York makes you too hard, and LA too soft or something to that effect, which I think is true, although I would say LA makes one more ambivalent and less focused, which was always my problem anyway. New York dragged you along with its own brand of energy, whether you liked it or not, so you had to respond.

Around about 1979 I got a job as a gaffer on a small documentary. It was to do with promoting football (the real game of football, the one that most of the world plays, where one uses their feet to kick the ball). I could not stand to watch American style football, where men ran around in tight pants wearing crash helmets and high fived each other, every seven or eight seconds after falling down. Followed by a TV commercial, or a replay of a guy running for a few yards in slow motion. I found the game to be boring and full of hype! The actual playing time is about 18 minutes, the rest is filled in with TV commercials, back slapping and self - congratulatory nonsense. I probably just lost a lot of fans, (if I had any) but that's my humble opinion.

So this little doc was hoping to promote 'real' football where kids didn't have to have all that gear of padding and helmets, plus the chance of possible concussion and subsequent brain damage. Restricting them then to become either politicians or ready - made burnt out punk rock stars like our lad Sid from England. So off we went to film kids and adults playing football around the country. We filmed a game at the Astrodome in Houston and then another game in San Francisco and a couple of other cities that evades my memory. However we ended up in Vancouver, a beautiful city, where I was to work and live for a number of years in the future. The Vancouver Whitecaps had won the Soccer Bowl and had an international player called Alan Ball with them. Ball had played for Arsenal and Everton in England and was on the 1966 World Cup team when England beat Germany.

After my break-up with Abby I had a number of girlfriends, usually that I met working on film sets. They were usually other crew - members or else actresses or extras, so the film world became quite incestuous. The women in New York were very out-going and intelligent and free spirited (especially before the AIDS epidemic) and I suppose if you wanted to call that time anything then the age of 'free love' is what it was, that had carried over from the 'sixties' and days of 'Haight Ashbury' in San Francisco.

Fanellis Bar was a bar that I frequented most often that was located on the corner of Prince and Mercer Street and was home to a bunch of painters, writers, poets, bullshit artists and the like. Bullshit art had its own place in a bar and some of the most entertaining of people were bullshit artists and if they had a good story to tell and one was amused and the story was told with conviction and humor then who cared if it was true or not? After all I was living in a world of fantasy, living in a story, either you're own or others. Films were invented from scripts that were invented from minds that were invented from an idea and it was a fine line between fantasy and real life that is what I loved about living in 'The Big Apple' where everybody could take a bite.

Fanellis is the second oldest bar in New York, the Bridge Café being the oldest dating back to 1794. Other old bars and landmarks are Pete's tavern from 1851 and McSorleys Ale House a hangout for students more, dating back to 1862. In 1847 Fanellis was originally a grocery store, became a bar, reverted back to a grocery store, then became a bar again in 1867 and stayed that way till present times. The interior had black and white photos of famous boxers hanging on the walls as Fanelli's played host to Rocky Graciano who had a few drinks there, and whose photo is also on the wall, along with Sonny Liston and Joe Frazier and Sugar Ray and Larry Holmes. Bob Dylan was also known to have inhabited the place. There was never a lack of conversation at the bar with the locals, not always coherent but conversations nonetheless. An art gallery on West Broadway had an art opening for all the painters that drank at Fanellis.

Some of the work was great and some of it not so great, but the idea was generous and warm hearted. This was when West Broadway had art galleries and character, before the designer stores moved in for the upwardly mobile yuppie shopper! Later the rogues of Fanelli's were replaced by trust fund babies, although it did still maintain a certain roguish feel to it. The art scene subsequently moved to Chelsea on the west side.

Unfortunately Soho became a shopper's paradise for Europeans with lots of dosh and anyone with money to spend. The times are changing and always will - sometimes for the better and sometimes for the worse. Although I do hate to see the gentrification of areas that had so much history and character demoralized into a homogenized hodge-podge of shopping mall mentality that services tourists, therefore turning every neighborhood into a bus tour holiday, where the locals are like monkeys in cages to be ogled at by hundreds of Japanese tourists all taking the same photo from the same point of view.

I bought an Opel hatch back car from a woman I knew and parked it sometimes outside my door if possible or else on the Westside Highway at an outdoor parking lot at the end of Houston Street for a walloping $2 a night. There were cheap places to eat all around the neighborhood and a fine little café around the corner where one went down the stairs to enter. One of my favorite places to have a hearty breakfast was 'The Cupping Room' on West Broadway, and I would usually meet a good friend of mine there where we would usually have the same thing, which was a waffle, covered in thick yogurt sprinkled with a good dollop of fruit and nuts with lots of maple syrup. After that I didn't need to eat again until the evening.

I shared a place in Woodstock with a friend ten miles out of town that overlooked the Ashokan reservoir. It was an old carriage house that had been moved there. It had three bedrooms and was about a hundred years old with a large deep fireplace that I very often sat in front of for hours watching as the fire licked the logs, as the smoke rose up the chimney, and pine cones crackled, and produced an exotic scent that wafted throughout the house. The rent was five hundred a month, which included about thirty-five acres of land where one could cross country ski in the winter. So all in all I had a car I kept in the city, a country house that I paid half the rent being $250 a month and an apartment in one of the most interesting parts of New York for $325, so life was grand and easy.

Outside My House in Woodstock reading about the Celts

Keeping warm inside   Woodstock Winter 1985

November In Woodstock

Dogs bark in the chill November air,
Their breath lit by the full moon.
Leaves crunch and crack under foot
Their autumn colors, kind and warm,
The trees bare and stark like skeletons
Now dead after summer's skin has shed.
The fire flickers stories to those that wish to listen
As the smell of pinecones caress the chilly air.
Blue smoke rises up the chimney
Not long after Halloween
As I sit by the fire glow
Reading tales of ancient Celts
Feeling that blood stir inside my veins
And knowing of that life.

Woodstock, NY 1985

I had a friend who had a loft on Grand Street and every couple of weeks or so would have a party with people she knew from all over the world. Her father was a diplomat and so she had lived in many different countries with him and so met many people in that world of government and finance and god knows what else. On most occasions she would call and let me know when she was having a bash. The parties were a good place to meet interesting people and I dated some exotic women from all parts of the world that were usually very well off and usually quite spoilt having been brought up in places like South East Asia, India, Singapore, Jakarta and sometimes the Middle East. All had been brought up with servants and cooks and good food. They never went short of anything. Many learnt to ride horses, water-ski, scuba dive, and one woman I met loved sky - diving. Some of the girls reminded me of the ones that I used to meet at Harrods when I was a photographer. They would drop by from Lucy Clayton Finishing School to usually just flirt, but I did take a couple out from time to time.

The parties on Grand Street were often very decadent as the upper class indulged in lots of drugs and at one time after an evening of drinking and smoking a girl got me to try smoking some heroin. I took a few good drags then passed it back to her. After a minute or so I thought I was going to throw up and so went to the bathroom, where I placed my hands on the sink, and looked at myself in the mirror. My face had turned an ashen grey, and I looked ten years older. I looked like a corpse that had been dug up from the grave. The experience was not a pleasant one - I managed not to throw up, but felt quite sick and knew that I wouldn't be doing that again. So being a heroin addict was not in the future for me, and could not imagine sticking a needle in my arm to get high!

Some of the older women I met were usually more interesting than the younger ones being more old school, and had been living in these old Colonial places since after WWII and had a certain eloquence about them, refined, brought about by good breeding. Many had gone to finishing schools and carried a kind, sincere warmth about them,

111

usually with a good sense of humor. Their husbands however were usually more stuck up and seemed very over-protective of their wives, although usually the husbands were not even around. However my relationships with these women who were usually in their thirties did not last long as most returned to their homes on the other side of the world, and I had not the income nor inheritance to keep up with them. I did hear through the grapevine that a girlfriend of mine who was from Colombia, married a prince and bounced around with him between Bali and Goa - what can I say, but c'est la vie.

The Lion's Head Pub

A friend of mine had come over from England and was staying with a woman whom he had met during a drunken tour of Majorca. Apparently she was a journalist of sorts and wrote for a few rags around the world. She had just left town and also left the keys of her place with my friend. He was staying on the Upper East Side somewhere, which to me might just as well have been the Arctic Circle. He told me that he wanted to come down to the village anyway as his 'friend' had told him about this great little pub on Christopher Street where he should get a drink. The pub was called 'The Lions Head' and it was at Sheridan Square. We arranged to meet at 3pm. I made my way over there and realized that I had passed this place many times but never thought about going in for some reason or other. So in I went, and it was about a quarter to three when I got there, as I had finished whatever it was I was doing, and just wanted to get out of my apartment. The walls of the bar were full of book jackets and I immediately realized that I had entered a literary, intellectual drinking establishment. The people in the bar seemed a little different from the average New York watering hole as there seemed to be a club like elitist feel to the place, and I felt a little intimidated as I first walked in, and a wee bit unwelcome for the first few minutes. This was not a place for the weak of heart. I ordered a beer at the bar from a thick set jovial fella and sitting next to me was this wild looking sailor type who happened to have been a wild sailor. He seemed to be as much out of place as myself, but for different reasons, which I was soon to find out. His name, he told me was Tristan Jones as we shook hands. He had circumvented the world a couple of times he told me in his boat and had lost a leg on his travels. This bloke was the real thing. He looked like a pirate and spoke like a pirate, and in our short but entertaining conversation told me he had been a smuggler amongst other things. He told me that he had a Ph.d in drinking, and that everything he knew about the world was from his travels, and I whole-heartedly agreed with a lot of his philosophy on life. After chatting for about an hour, other interesting characters surrounded him, and the chatter became louder and the Irish brogue floated over the harsher New York accents, and I was again reminded that I was in the melting pot of humanity. Tristan was a Welshman, I was English and still am, and an Irishman stood behind me, as a Jew told some Jewish jokes to the left of me. It was like a drunken festival at the United Nations, but it was Tristan who held everyone's attention as he rambled on about his adventures. I had never heard of Tristan before this meeting, but apparently had written a number of books about his exploits. Now on writing this I must go out and buy at least one of them. My friend was an hour late, which didn't matter, as he was always late. I wasn't bored while waiting for him. Just as my friend arrived Tristan Jones decided to leave and I continued to drink with a sympathizer of the IRA and an ex-cop from Brooklyn. My friend's eyes were popping out of his head, as he was still sober and hadn't had time to catch up with all the verbal banter, as we were now surrounded by some harsh, tough individuals, but as we continued to talk, I realized that they all had a great sense of humor and although hard on the outside they were soft in the middle. My friend who was a funny guy had them laughing after he had warmed up to them and the alcohol had smoothed his troubled brow. After about four or five hours we stumbled out of the pub, which actually felt more like a pub than a bar, and I realized that I had undergone my initiation ceremony to an elite club, and that I had met one of the most interesting characters of my life that being the Welshman Tristan Jones.

I had an Aunt called Lilly who lived with my Uncle Alex a Scotsman in the town of Chester that was close to the Welsh border. My Uncle told me about this ancient law whereby Welshman were prohibited from entering the city of Chester before the sun rises, and then would have to leave before sunset. Apparently it is still OK to shoot a Welshman on a Sunday inside of the city walls as long as it is after midnight, which I suppose would make it early Monday morning, but only with a crossbow. I am sure that makes a lot of Welshman feel better, as people probably own more guns now than crossbows. However I have never heard of anyone from Wales being shot with a crossbow, but maybe it's because not many people know of this law. I wondered if Tristan Jones had heard of it.

Tristan was born in Liverpool and died on the island of Phuket (pronounced - Poo - ket, not Fuck it!) in Thailand at the age of 71. And for the short amount of time I spent with this old sea dog I realized that I had met a re-incarnation of Blackbeard or Captain Morgan or any of those rogues who had sailed the Caribbean back in the day and it was an honor and a privilege to have toasted him and drank a pint or two with him at The Lion's Head Pub in New York City.

Miss Jones

I went to visit some friends in Norwalk Connecticut for the weekend
and on the Monday morning I caught the train back to Grand Central
Station. The rush hour was over and the train I caught was around 10
am. It was still quite full however and the only couple of seats that
were available were next to a grouchy looking old man or an attractive
looking young woman who looked like she may have been in her mid-
thirties, about the same age as myself. I chose the empty seat next to
the woman, after throwing my weekend bag onto the luggage rack
above her head. She had the window seat and seemed quite settled in.
I sat down and said, "Good morning," and she replied with "Morning"
without taking her eyes from The New York Times.

The train pulled out of the station as I watched the trees pass the
window faster and faster as the train gathered speed. I had nothing to
read and sat there feeling a little awkward. The woman next to me was
wearing a black two-piece business suit and looked like she may have
been an accountant of sorts, or a high ranking executive in the business
world, maybe working on Wall Street. I kept looking at her,
pretending to be glancing out of the window. She was wearing
spectacles that she kept re-arranging on the end of her nose, as though
she was not used to them. I saw she was reading the obituaries as I
sometimes did - reading about how ordinary people had done so many
un-ordinary things in their lives. As we pulled into the next station she
put the paper down and I thought she was going to get off, as she
wiggled around a little, but she didn't. More people got on than off at
this station, as this was the commuter train to New York and now
some people were even standing near the doors as the compartment
began to fill up again. There was an awkward silence now between

115

myself, and my traveling companion, and I felt the need to break the ice.

"You like to read the obituaries?" I asked her. She looked at me through her spectacles, her secretarial sexy spectacles and took them off while replying,

"Yes."

Then she looked at me for a second or two as if examining this specimen that had the nerve to sit next to her, then glanced out of the window. Did I feel snubbed? And with that one word 'yes' she made me feel like I was that English schoolboy who had just spoken out of turn. I was done, demoralized and humiliated by that one word. She then turned her head from the window back to me and spoke.

"Are you on vacation," she asked, picking up on my English accent. My inner voice responded non - verbally - she spoke, to me.

"No", I replied, "I live here, in New York - downtown."

"Really," she replied, as she now folded her glasses and slipped them into a pink velvet case.

"And what do you do there?" she said in such a manner that I felt like that schoolboy again, that she was my headmistress even though we were about the same age.

This woman had control and power, and the more we spoke the more I believed that she must be head of some huge multi-million dollar corporation.

"Are you head of some multi-million dollar corporation?" I asked like an enquiring schoolboy.

"No, no" she replied as she shook her head.

This woman had powers maybe she was a witch doctor- a high-class sexy witch doctor. She extended her hand to me so politely and smiled

116

as well - (yes she smiled at me). I responded by holding her hand for a second or two in a firm handshake and her harsh façade was instantly lifted as she said,

"My name's Deborah, not Debbie," - she was still in control by this statement, obviously not in a million years wanting to be called Debbie.

"I'm John, not Jonathon," I replied as I still had a hold of her hand. 'Touche', I parried, being a fencer that I had been at school. Aha, perhaps she had met her match.

I was in love with this woman and wanted to marry her on the spot, and started to splutter and mutter as she told me about herself, a little, but not revealing all, in fact I believe she had only scraped the surface as regards the history of her being. She came from money that was obvious, a wealthy New England family I began to figure out as the train pulled in to Grand Central Station.

I reached over her to grab my bag from the luggage rack and I wanted to kiss her right there without saying another word, but I didn't.

"Well it was nice chatting with you," I said, then immediately followed by, "Would you like to get a coffee, or a glass of wine sometime?" expecting in return a comment like sorry but I have a boyfriend, or I'm married or engaged –

"I would like that," came the reply as I felt like dropping to my knees and kissing her feet. We swopped phone numbers when we got off the train,

"I have to rush off now," which she did, leaving me with her phone number in my hand. I saw her disappear into the crowds at Grand Central, as I looked down at her phone number in disbelief.

I called Deborah two days later on the phone. I wanted to call her the next day, but didn't want to appear too pushy. We arranged to meet three days later as she said she was rather tied up for the next two days, and that the third night would be perfect, and she wanted to eat at Odeon which was on West Broadway in Tribeca. Who was I to argue, and the next 72 hours felt like an eternity. I got dressed in my best attire and put on one of my many nice shirts - I was known for my nice shirts, by my friends. It was summer time, so a jacket was not needed and I put on a pair of shoes, not sneakers and I left my shirt to hang over my jeans that by 1985 was quite acceptable attire. I arrived at seven thirty as planned and Deborah was already at the bar with a Martini in her hand. I walked up to the bar feeling a little nervous and thinking that I may have got the time wrong and said,

"Sorry am I late?" after giving her a quick peck on the cheek as all good Europeans do when greeting each other, and didn't think that was too out of place.

"No not at all - I was in Soho earlier than I thought, so thought I may as well nip in and have one before you arrived."

She looked wonderful, much like she did on the train the day we met, wearing just a light jacket and a white low cut blouse underneath which showed off her cleavage between her breasts. Around her neck hung the eye of Horus, which I instantly recognized from Egyptian mythology and mentioned it, which she seemed pleased about. I ordered a beer as it was hot, and I liked a beer in the summertime, as it was the drink that I found most refreshing to quench the thirst. We hadn't booked a table, as it was still fairly early and there was no need to. A waiter walked by and asked how she was, and the bartender seemed quite well acquainted also.

"I have a feeling that you may have been here before," said I.

"Yes," she replied, "it's one of my favorite restaurants and I like the atmosphere here, and the food of course."

"I've been here a couple of times myself," I said, but nobody acknowledged me with a smile or a handshake.

118

"Where shall we sit?" I asked her, trying so hard to be a gentleman. No sooner had I spoken these words, when the waiter approached and said,

"The usual table Miss Jones?"

Deborah replied. "Yes thanks, Richard,"

Richard led the way with a wave of his arm that cut through the air. We arrived at the table and Richard pulled out the chair for Miss Jones and then for me, as he said,

"There we are sir."

"Thanks,"

Richard handed us the menus, one for Miss Jones and the other for myself. We both decided on the same dish. It was to be the salmon and Deborah ordered another couple of Martinis as she was becoming more and more flirtatious. I ordered another beer. Deborah Jones, if that was her real name was obviously much more accustomed to fine dining and expensive cocktails than I, whereby a pint of bitter and a plate of greasy fish n' chips would have done me just fine, as I was beginning to add up the bill in my head as the sweat ran down my back.

We chatted about this and that, but I still couldn't figure out what Miss Jones really did for a living, if anything at all. It was obvious that she came from big bucks and also had gone to the right schools, Wellesley being one of them. She was very refined when she wanted to be, but also had an edge to her, a rebellious edge. I didn't know why, because I didn't know who this mysterious woman was at all, in fact the more we talked the more mysterious she became, as I once again asked what she did for a living. She would become indignant in reply to my pedantic questioning as though it were bad manners to talk about such things, and especially over dinner, and she was quite right of course.

"I'm not so interesting, let's talk about you," as she deflected the conversation away from herself.

So off I went, talking about my travels after switching to a margarita, and tales of India and ganja nights in Jamaica dribbled from my mouth. Her eyes seemed to light up from my stories, and the indignation that she had a minute or so before was replaced by a sincere fascination about my adventures. Suddenly, I felt like I may have now found the key to her heart, and so babbled on with all kinds of nonsense, until she broke into the sexiest laugh I had ever heard, after she finished off her fourth martini, and I my third margarita. The ice had finally been broken and Miss Jones was laughing hysterically after a couple of my jokes. I had now gone into top gear and the finishing line lay ahead, when an elderly gentleman passed by our table, recognizing Deborah. He approached the table very gingerly and said,

"Rebecca, how lovely to see you, I didn't know you came here?" The gentleman seemed as though he may have been gay.

"Yes, I love this place."

Then she introduced me to Rupert. Rupert gave Rebecca, alias Miss Jones a peck on the cheek, then Rupert shook my hand very limply and disappeared for the rest of the night. Before I had a chance to open my mouth,

"Rebecca is my middle name, and Rupert is a friend of the family."

"Deborah Rebecca Jones, you are becoming more mysterious by the minute."

She was definitely flustered for a second, but recovered well with professional confidence and we were back on track, as Miss Jones said,

"Nothing to worry about darling, I'm not with the CIA or anything like that."

It was a strange comment to make as though she really was trying to cover up something or other. There was a lull in conversation as Rebecca broke it with,

"Let's have desert, and by the way this is all on my tab."

I suddenly felt a sense of relief as I said a long

"Noo, I asked you out," but she stopped me there in mid conversation.

"I love your company, and I have money, and it's my treat, and I don't want to hear another word," as she was beginning to slur her speech a little. This woman was used to handling her liquor and was used to the good life.

"We-ell (a long drawn out well) if you insist, thank you, let me at least get the desert and one more for the road."

We agreed and we both had one more drink each, and a desert. Richard came over and Deborah Rebecca Jones paid with a credit card and we left and walked out onto West Broadway, kissed on the lips briefly and Deborah hailed a checker cab, she was back in control again and had a purpose in life as though she was in a hurry. It was now almost eleven-thirty and a cab pulled up immediately and I had little time to say anything except,

"Can I see you again?"

I was back in schoolboy mode, and she was already in the cab as she wound down the window and said,

"Call me!" as the cab drove off, leaving me by the side of the road just as she left me at Grand Central Station looking at her phone number in my hand.

Two or three days went by and all I thought about was Deborah Rebecca Jones if that indeed was her real name. I hadn't seen her driver's license to disprove that that was her real name. So why was I so suspicious? I had never met a woman quite like this before and it seemed that the more I got to know her, the more mysterious she became. I kept going over in my mind the evening that we spent at the restaurant and the waiter Richard, and the chance meeting with Rupert the family friend. Maybe I was being suspicious for no reason, after all it's not like she took me for a ride, on the contrary she paid for the meal, but it was the way she ran off so fast, as if on a mission - maybe she was secret service after all? She had my number, but hadn't called me, so I gave it a couple more days, not wanting to be too enthusiastic, but I felt like the mystery had to be unfolded.

The next night at about nine in the evening she called from a call box and said that she was in my neighborhood and wondered if I wanted to pop out for a quick drink. So I met her at La Gamelle, a French restaurant on Grand Street and a place that I frequented from time to time. She was already there at the bar when I arrived and was talking in French to the barman. I approached her and kissed her on the cheek and then the other cheek as people do in France. She introduced me to Phillipe, the barman and we shook hands. 'Enchante,' said Phillipe and I repeated the welcome back, then he went about his business of serving other customers. Once again she caught me off guard and I was beginning to feel a little out of my depth with this 'bon vivant' who seemed to know everyone in New York."

"Where did you learn to speak French?"

"At the Sorbonne" was her reply.

Then she went on to tell me that her father was a diplomat and that they lived in Paris for a few years and that she knew a fair bit of French even before going to France, and so the language became a second language to her that she spoke fluently like a Parisian. It all seemed like a mystery to me, but this was the life of the privileged and was the complete opposite of how I grew up.

I began to wonder what she saw in me and whether we would just be friends as long as I kept making her laugh. She seemed pleased to see me and I her. She played with her glass of French wine and swished it around the glass like a mini tsunami. She had all the moves down and I felt like I had been shaken and not stirred.

Phillipe came back to the bar and poured me a glass of the same wine that Deborah was drinking.

"Bon santé, it's on the house." Said Phillipe.

"Merci bien," I replied in my schoolboy French.

"That was very nice of him."

"He is a good friend" she replied.

I wondered how many more good friends Miss Jones had. We talked at the bar till just past midnight, when the bar was beginning to get the late night crowd and was filling up. The bars in New York usually stayed open until 4am, so the night for many was still young. We talked and the talking was easier and more relaxed than at the restaurant a few days ago and she revealed a lot more about herself and her childhood and her older sister who was still living in Paris whom she wanted me to meet. Our faces got a little closer and I felt her silky black hair, but she pulled away a little and said that she didn't like to be too amorous in public, even though she felt half French and the French did that sort of thing in public all the time, but she was still a New England girl at heart and was quite proper which indeed she was. Plus she added that we didn't know each other well enough yet. I agreed, because I had to, then realized that maybe we were just going to be friends after all. I didn't mind either way as I did enjoy her company and she told me she enjoyed mine and there wasn't any hurry anyway.

We had a couple more glasses of wine and now it was half an hour after midnight and she told me that she wanted to go home. I paid the bill this time although Phillipe only let me pay for two drinks so I left a good tip and I grabbed a taxi outside. We both jumped in and I told her that I only lived about five blocks away and that she could spend the night if she wanted. She told me that she was very tired and just wanted to go home to her place, wherever that was. I didn't argue and kissed her on the lips as I jumped out at 146 Sullivan Street. She turned and blew me a kiss as the cab drove off, and I felt like that schoolboy again except a more confident and excitable one.

A week went by, this time quite quickly as I was working on a commercial, so the days were long and after work I just went home to bed. After about four days I received a message from Deborah saying that she missed my face, and for me to call her, which I did as soon as I got the message. We decided to meet at the weekend and by now it was Friday, so there wasn't much left of the week. I never had that 'Thank god it's Friday feeling' as I always enjoyed the work. There were times when some jobs were not so good but you always knew that if it was a commercial it would end in a day or two. Most commercials shot for one, two, three or four days.

Before I knew it, it was Saturday morning, and I was awoken by a woman screaming in Italian to another woman who screamed back in Italian. This was not an unusual event. Sometimes I felt like shouting back in my best British accent like, "Ladies please try to keep your charming voices down," but I didn't say a 'dickie bird' as I knew what the response would be. So I just imagined once again as I did on so many occasions that I was living in Napoli and then the noise and the shouting and the music all became a part of living on Sullivan Street. After taking a shower, which was in the kitchen I dried off and called Miss Jones, and by now it was close to midday. There was no answer on the end of the line, not even an answering machine, so I got dressed and jumped down the four flights of stairs out onto the street that was already baking in the midday sun. The temperatures had been in the high nineties all week and immediately sweat began to run down my back. There was nowhere to go to escape the humidity except to a bar or restaurant.

Most of my friends lived in small apartments, but most people didn't spend a lot of time in them. My friends that lived in lofts tended to stay in more as they didn't feel so claustrophobic and would tend to have dinner parties as they had the space to do so. I ended up at Fanelli's Bar on Mercer and Prince Street - my walk had got me four blocks or so. The air conditioning was on and the place was already filling up, but there was space at the bar and I grabbed it and ordered a pint of Guinness for breakfast. A guy I knew was already at the bar and already had a few drinks in him, and when he saw me decided to plop himself down on the bar stool next to me and proceeded to dribble incoherently about this sci-fi zombie movie that he was writing called 'Canal Street,' which as he informed me was where the 'Undead' lived for real, as there was a canal under Canal Street and he had seen them, the 'Undead' that is. He ordered another vodka, as he asked me if I would film his story, to which I replied "Of course" knowing that it would never happen - but never say never!

The strange thing about Fanelli's and bars like it in New York is that one accepted these characters, even though they were off their noodles, but were actually more interesting and entertaining than some suit from Wall Street bragging about how much money they had made all week. I managed to listen to my acquaintance at the bar babbling on in all his madness and confused creativity, but many years later films were made about the 'Undead' and Zombies that did have a cult following. Maybe it was my friend at the bar that got his crazy script to someone who gave it to someone who got it made, and now my drunken friend at the bar is living in Beverly Hills in a multi-million dollar mansion. Such is the way in the world of film.

After being exhausted by the ramblings of a madman, I exited the bar and walked down West Broadway to weave my way through the changing crowd of shoppers and high end designer stores that seemed to have little or nothing in them, like some kind of existential performance art as people examined 'The Emperor's New Clothes' and paid huge sums of money on things that would evaporate into thin air. I was realizing that downtown was being sucked up by the rest of

125

New York, that 'Downtown' was no longer what it was and that I was beginning to feel sad at these monetary changes that were happening, that once again boring people wanted to live where the artists live, thereby forcing the artists out to look for new pastures where they could chew on the cud, and regurgitate their art in another place and were kicked out like lepers. This was a pattern that had been going on for a while around the world. The hippies went to Ibiza in Spain and to Goa in India, to Mykonos in Greece originally, and so on till the word gets out and tourism and shoppers move in destroying all the culture in their path.

It was madness out there on the streets and I decided that walking the streets of Bombay was a lot more interesting than passing yuppie after yuppie on the streets of Soho. I felt trapped in my own neighborhood that had been invaded by a marauding tribe of tourists from New Jersey and Euro-trash from across the seas. Sullivan Street was remaining a stronghold from the past and I felt relieved as I turned the corner and looked up at the green fire escape to my humble home with the strange shower in the kitchen and the long dark hallway that lead to it and the occasional cockroach to welcome me home. I went out for breakfast and came home with three pints of Guinness in me and no food, but I was told that Guinness had iron in it and that was supposed to be good for you and even the advertising which we all know is true is that 'Guinness is Good for You''- at least that is what it used to say on the tube trains in London. So I convinced myself that I had a sustainable breakfast and that eating was for the birds. I was now as level headed as my comrade at the bar and so decided to light up a happy stick and turn on the AC which I had recently acquired after all these years in the Big Apple. I had got out of bed close to midday and by four in the afternoon felt like the day was winding down and that soon I would be ready for bed again. I didn't feel too guilty after all I had worked four days of the week, so I deserved to do whatever I wanted.

Soho

I called Miss Jones again and this time she picked up. It was consoling to hear her refined Wellesley College voice and thought that maybe she could save me from the riff raff that roamed Soho at the weekends. The first thing she asked was if I had been drinking, she obviously had caught the slur in my voice, plus I was still a little tired from working. She told me that I was 'a naughty boy' and that I should be punished. Once again I reverted back to schoolboy mode, she just had this headmistress way about her that I found to be very sexy. I asked her if she wanted to do something later on and she suggested meeting for a drink somewhere in the village. We threw suggestions back and forth to each other on the phone and settled on a bar on Sixth Avenue.

I arrived at the bar at eight o'clock and Miss Jones was already there before me once again and once again she seemed to know the barman and once again had already digested a couple of martinis and was in high spirits. I tapped her on the shoulder when I got up to the bar and was about to give her a kiss, when she turned the other way and immediately introduced me to Patrick the Irish barman, whom she also seemed to know quite well. I shook hands with Patrick who was a big strapping fella with wild red curly hair and quite a good-sized beer belly and a freckly face with a nose that looked like it had been broken once or twice. He had character and looked like he had been in a few bar room brawls, and yet seemed to have the manners of a gentleman of days past.

Although Deborah and I seemed to have difficulty on deciding on what bar to go to on the phone, it appeared that she had already decided that this was the place. I wondered if this was yet another of her mysterious games that she played so well. This bar was the opposite of Odeon and the clientele were down and dirty. It seemed like Deborah Rebecca Jones was capable of mixing with all sorts and once again added even more to the mysterious façade that she had shrouded herself in.

127

On the other hand maybe this was all real and there was no façade and that Miss Jones was the real thing, a woman who was confident in any surrounding and could talk to anyone from a Longshoreman to the Queen of England. She had breeding and could speak three languages fluently and could hold court with the best of them. I was once again dumbfounded because at this particular moment she was being a little cold towards me and I wondered if it had anything to do with Patrick the Irish barkeep.

Patrick asked me what my poison was, and I could have replied that it was Deborah, but ordered a margarita as I realized that I had some catching up to do. "Cheers darling" she said, as we clinked our glasses together as I was now on the barstool next to her. I must admit I was feeling a little jealous of Patrick, but as time wore on it was revealed that he had a wife and three kids and that there was absolutely no amorous connection between them. Three margaritas later I didn't give a shit and was just enjoying the evening and I even told Patrick a few good Irish jokes and he retaliated with some good ones about the English.

"I like this Englishman," he said to Deborah as he towered over me.

"I like him too," replied Miss Jones.

I was rewarded with a kiss on the cheek. Patrick told Deborah that maybe she should hang on to me, as if to say there had been many others who did not last too long. Maybe this woman was the Black Widow Spider that devoured her men and spat them out on a weekly basis. Just as I held that thought a man in his late fifties was now at the very crowded bar and was ordering a drink when he saw my date.

"Deborah, darling!" he yelled from the other side of the bar, as he held up his drink, which looked like a glass of whisky - "Martini?"

Deborah smiled and nodded and then the man fought his way through the crowd and came up behind us.

"Where have you been?" enquired the man.

"Everywhere and nowhere" came the reply.

"Ah, the mystery woman" said the man.

That was an understatement I thought to myself, and before he could say another word we were both introduced to each other. His name was Benjamin, "Not Ben," he interjected, as he gave me a wink. He was yet another character and seemed quite effeminate and out of place in this bar, although this was the Big Apple and everyone was welcome to take a bite. He seemed quite frail and wore an Ascot scarf around his neck and a trilby hat on his head to hide his receding hairline. He was very charming, as it seemed that most of Deborah's acquaintances were, and before I knew it, he had bought me a margarita. By now I was feeling rather blurry eyed and I suggested that perhaps Deborah and I should get a bite to eat somewhere.

She then told me that she had a little surprise for me, as if this woman didn't keep surprising me every time I saw her, and my head started to spin as to what she may have in store for me. The bill was paid and Miss Jones and I took a taxi to Deborah's abode that was only a few blocks away off Sixth Avenue.

We entered through an old wooden door into a hallway and Deborah Rebecca Jones pressed the button for the elevator to the sixth floor and when inside turned the key so that only those with a key could get off on that floor. This was standard procedure for loft spaces in Manhattan, as the elevators opened directly into one's living space.

Deborah led the way off the elevator into an Aladdin's Cave, the space seemed huge as mirrors placed strategically reflected huge murals of Middle Eastern scenes, which gave the illusion that we were in Arabia somewhere and at any minute I was expecting to be greeted by Lawrence.

There were muslin drapes hanging from the ceiling to the floor and Persian rugs scattered around between the seating areas. It was like a Kasbah and once again this mysterious woman had led me into another world. Deborah disappeared behind a gossamer wall of willowing batik fabric. I stood and smelt the incense that gave off a twirling blue smoke.

I turned slowly to absorb my quick transformation to the Middle East, when a gentleman appeared from behind a flowing pillar of lace that was swirling like a snake from a fan that was keeping the air cool. I jumped back startled at the magical appearance of this man who was dressed like a Sufi, but without the fez. Before I could let out a scream, Deborah grabbed my arm from behind and introduced me to Raffy who had been cooking up a meal for us.

"So how do you like my little surprise?"

I was speechless as I looked around the loft that had been flown off on a magic carpet to North Africa. Miss Jones held my hand and led me to a table big enough for eight people. The table had been set for two and was lit by half a dozen huge candles.

"I thought it was time you saw my home, so I had Raffy prepare some couscous and lamb - I hope you eat lamb?"

I nodded, then looked at this unusual woman and bombarded her with questions that she wasn't interested in answering, so as to keep this veil of mystery about her. She told me Raffy was a friend (of course) who was a professional chef from Morocco who was now living in Manhattan and she would pay him to come and cook for her sometimes and that there was nothing else for me to know or even be concerned about. Raffy served the meal and Deborah thanked him with a hug and said that she could do the rest on her own. It was now very late and Raffy had other engagements in this twenty-four hour metropolis and she walked him to the loft gate and watched him descend to the real world below.

Deborah walked back to the table and lent over me from behind and kissed my head. This was the first time that I felt real affection from her. She then sat down and said, "Let's eat!" as she raised a glass of wine as a toast. The lamb melted in the mouth, which was washed down by glass after glass of fine French wine and a desert made from honey and almonds and a flaky pastry similar to the Greek Baklava, but lighter.

After the meal was over I sat back in the upholstered chair feeling like a chapter from 'A Thousand and One Nights' or a page ripped from Paul Bowles' 'Sheltering Sky.' Miss Jones, the mysterious woman from New England, Wellesley College and The Sorbonne just sat back, smiled and said, "Are you happy?"

I walked home from Deborah's place the next morning feeling very happy. I had traveled half way around the world without leaving New York, and felt like I had been on an adventure away from the Big Apple for years, and walking the streets of New York again also felt like a dream. The woman I had spent the night with was a magician of sorts that had the means of transporting her cargo to another dimension and time.

I don't think my feet hit the ground until I took the first step up to my humble abode back on Sullivan Street. I turned the key to my door and entered the hallway that was lined with my photographs from foreign lands. I made myself a cup of tea, sat on the futon by the window and tried to assess what had happened over the last twelve hours or so. I felt like I had been re-born and looked out onto the street with a big grin on my face.

Soho

A couple of nights later

I saw her in the middle of the night. It was on a path in the country - it was Thomas Hardy country and it was from Thomas Hardy times. I was riding a horse slowly down this path. I had just shot a friend of mine who was flirting with my true love to an extent that he took her love from me. I shot him three times. I had the gun inside my leather satchel that hung over my shoulder. Further down the path I saw a young peasant girl with the most beautiful green eyes - big and round. I stopped to talk to her and I think I may have known her from somewhere, and we talked as though we knew each other. She was about to join a convent in a few weeks and take her vows as a nun. She seemed to be floating about six inches off the ground as I began to wonder if she was an apparition. I immediately fell in love with this girl and asked her to marry me then and there.

She was not of this Universe - in fact she was like an angel, untouched by the ills of the world. She exuded love and purity and innocence, which enveloped me so, that I wanted to be a part of her. I needed her - and couldn't live without her. She told me that she couldn't marry me, as she wanted to remain the way she was - holy and pure and untouched by the evils of mankind. I got closer to her face so that our breath mingled in the crisp autumn air. Her breath was warm and her eyes were almost transparent as though I were looking through them to a beautiful life, rich in love. Our lips grew closer and closer until I tasted the wetness and plumpness of her whole mouth and we kissed deeply and immediately her vows were taken by the wind and I felt her with my hand and she was dripping like the dew off a rose petal and I could smell her scent and I entered her body there and then. There was no hesitation as we joined as one, and I was finally home after centuries of a lonely life as I was wandering and searching for this moment with this beautiful young woman of pure spirit. After we made love I told her that I had to hide the gun that I had in my satchel. There was an old wooden desk under an old oak tree with a draw at the front. She told me to put it in there and asked me no questions. She was no longer pure and had entered the world with all its impurities.

133

We got married and nine months later we had a beautiful baby girl, with big green eyes, just like her mother and we lived in a little thatched roof cottage and it seemed like there was always blue smoke escaping from the chimney to join the clouds in an English sky. But it was just a dream I had. I awoke to find myself not in the country, but in Manhattan, under its choking sky's and the solitude and sweet air had been replaced by the reality of car horns and people yelling to each other on the street outside.

I was in a dream state, as I walked into the bathroom to relieve myself. I then made myself a cup of tea in the kitchen and walked with it to my futon couch as I listened to the sounds of Sullivan Street awakening from 'it's dreams.' I was convinced that I had lived before, that I had lived in the country in a cottage under a thatched roof with my beautiful wife, and that it was from that time in my dream in England. I wanted to be there so very much, but I wasn't - I was in the heart of Soho, which was nothing like the English countryside. How strange that some dreams can feel so real, and how disappointing it is to awaken from a good one.

On the other hand, it's a relief to awaken from a terrible dream or nightmare, when the sounds on Sullivan Street would be like music to one's ears. I could not function for the next hour or so, but just kept replaying this dream over and over in my head as it was so strong and therefore was trying to tell me something or maybe it was my spirit from a previous life reminding me what true beauty is. I began to disassemble the dream and wondered if I had shot a man in a past life. In my dream I felt justified of the act of murder and felt no remorse, in fact I was pleased and had satisfaction.

I called Deborah on the phone to tell her about my dream - after all she was the closest I had come to being in a dream state when I was with her, especially after the meal and everything else from the other night. The phone rang and rang and once again there was no message, so I hung up. I wasn't ready for the street just yet and needed more time to recover from my dream or maybe it was because I wanted to savor it in my mind and replay it over and over, but as I did so those big green eyes began to fade into obscurity and I began to feel sad. I enjoyed feelings of melancholy, as they were moments of deep thought for me and at times like these I might pick up a pen to write. I shook my head and told myself to get over it, so I put on a pair of jeans and a t-shirt and ventured out onto those New York streets that would shake any man from his dream state. I didn't have a place in mind where to go, but just wandered around the corner past the Elephant and Castle, then south into deepest Soho where I looked up to see the World Trade Towers reflecting a hazy lazy sun also not truly awakened from its night. I walked across Canal Street and into the territory known as Tribeca and kept on walking and walking until I found myself at the South Street Seaport where the sailing ship is moored. I sat on a capstan and dreamt about old sailing ships sailing across the Atlantic.

Weeks went by before I saw Deborah again as she went off to Paris to stay with her sister, and I went off to Mexico to shoot a film. It was a strange relationship that we had as regards relationships. This was something different. We were both very ethereal and very similar in ways - both of us only had one foot on the ground whilst the other was somewhere in the spirit world. Both of us were dreamers and felt more at home in our own fantasy worlds as the real world to us seemed like a bit of a disaster. It was easier for Deborah than me to live this way, as she had the money to create this freedom and fantasy world, whereas I had to come back down to earth which was fine, as I enjoyed being a cinematographer and I was about to go off to Mexico. Although I had not seen a lot of the mysterious Miss Jones I knew that I would miss her as I had the closest connection with Deborah than I had ever had with anyone else, and yet I hardly knew her. I also did not know what her situation in Paris was or if I would ever see her again.

The Russians

I got a call from my friend Carlisle telling me about this film that he just got hired on as an assistant director. The film was called Osa, and the director was still looking for a DP. So I contacted the production manager and arranged for an interview with the director and producer. The director was Oleg Egorov and the producer was Constantin Alexandrov, they were both Russians and had met in Paris. Oleg had a script that he showed to Constantin and Constantin decided to produce it. I went along for my interview somewhere in Manhattan, met the Russians and showed Oleg my reel, which he liked, and I was hired on the spot.

A few weeks later we all flew down to Mexico City, that is to say the two Russians, Carlisle and myself. I went to Charabusca Studios where I ordered the equipment, and met some of my Mexican crew. I was pretty much given a Moviecam as I didn't think they had any Arriflex cameras. Constantin had many connections in Mexico and we stayed at his friend's penthouse apartment in the centre of the city. We all had our own little bedroom that looked down onto the sprawling metropolis below with choking fumes and honking horns and traffic like I had not seen since India. It was an exciting city and we drank a lot of tequila when we were there. Most of the actors came from New York and some extras and production assistants from Mexico. The living room of the apartment was being used as the production office and people came and went for interviews. One particular day this beautiful Mexican model walked in for a position of some sort and I was sitting in the room on the couch looking at a list of equipment. I couldn't take my eyes off her and we made eye contact a couple of times, although we never spoke. She gave her details in Spanish to the production staff and I managed to overhear some of the details including her phone number that luckily for me the assistant asked her to repeat as he wrote it down. My Spanish at the time was very basic, but I could count from one to ten and I jotted down her phone number on my equipment list. As she left she smiled at me. The following day I called the number and she answered. Her English was a little better than my Spanish, so between the two of us I arranged to see her. She came to the apartment and we were driven to a nightclub by one of the Federalis (police officers) who was assigned to us for our safety for the night. We sat at a table together - the three of us and then the Mexican model and myself got up to dance. I do not remember her name at this moment in time, but at the end of the evening she stayed with me.

After a few days in Mexico City and a trip to the amazing Anthropological Museum with my Mexican girlfriend, we all flew off to Guaymas in the state of Sonora minus my new girlfriend who did come out a little later. We filmed on the old sets and runway that was built for the film Catch 22, which was a black comedy made in 1970 set during WWII and the location was used as a Mediterranean base. One B-25 was burned and destroyed in a landing crash scene and the wreck was buried in the ground by the runway. It was here where most of the filming was to take place, actually in the desert that seemed ideal for the story that was about a world destroyed in an apocalyptic nuclear war where radiation free water was at a premium $200 a gallon. A gang of thugs had the monopoly of the water that worked for a company called Hammond Industries. The film was like Road Warrior but with no road and no warrior! The film starred Kelly Lynch in her acting debut. It was January and New York was cold, but now we were here on the west coast of Mexico and it was hot. Constantin had worked for Club Med in the past and so had connections with the company. We stayed at the Club Med in Guaymas and my room was practically on the beach facing The Sea of Cortez. The next few days were spent finding locations to film and one in particular was high up above the bay at a house that was owned by an American man. The view was stunning looking out over the ocean and mountains. I was outside by the pool with Oleg the director, and Carlisle was inside trying to secure the locations for us to film there the following week. I was standing close to Oleg when he pushed me in the pool with all my clothes on and when I got out Carlisle had come down to introduce the owner to us and I had to make the excuse that I had tripped and fallen into the pool. Such was the sense of humor of the Russians.

137

They called us (myself and Carlisle) the British Bulldogs as the two of us were English, and we called them the Russian Bear. So this was how the tone of the film was set up and it was fun with games and tricks throughout. After scouting locations we would be at the bar in the evening, none of the actors had come down yet from New York and Constantin proceeded to show us some of his Club Med antics. One of his tricks was to get you to stand still and he would throw a ping pong ball at your head expecting you to catch it on the top of your nose where it meets your forehead - of course this was not possible to do but you went along with the joke. After two throws of the ping pong ball and not being able to catch it, Constantin would switch the ball behind his back for a white egg, which he would throw at your face. Well you did not know that was an egg until it was about two inches from your face and splat! There you were with a face full of raw egg splattered all over your face. Another trick that Constantin showed us was to guess how much somebody weighed within ten pounds or so and the joke was usually played on some unsuspecting female. The trick was to lift someone up and then place them on the bar. When the victim was in the air, the barman would place a wet sponge on the bar and that person would sit on it and after a few seconds would feel the wetness seep through to their bum! It was all very infantile, but of course when we were all at the bar having had a few drinks, the juvenile would come out in us, and the tricks would be played on unsuspecting females that were holiday makers. One night I picked up this women, after telling her I could guess her weight and placed her on the wet sponge, she was laughing until she felt her arse get wet and her face changed immediately to anger and she chased me out of the bar until I had to run into the men's room and lock the door. Security had to come and drag her out of the men's room, as she was ready to kill me. Needless to say I never tried that again and left all the tricks to the actors when they came down from New York.

Once we started filming the days were relatively easy as most of the film was shot in daylight except for a couple of night scenes at a church. The days were short as the sun went down around five thirty or six as it was winter in Mexico and then it was time for the Club

Med disco when a lot of tequila was drunk by all of us. I dated the French make-up lady who had flown in from France. She also lived in a world similar to Deborah's world and would reference Fellini when something strange or unusual happened. She told me once after a few tequilas that she wanted to live in a Fellini film. She also lived as an outsider and thought the world to be an absurd place. I suppose one could call her an existentialist, although isn't that the case with a lot of French people? It certainly is with the French women that I have met in my life and I enjoyed their view of the world. I wrote a poem called 'The Make Up Artist' that was about her. Other crew - members and a couple of actors also came in from Paris, so it became a pretty international bunch of wild and crazy people! To this day it was the most fun I had ever had on a film due to the location, the people involved, and the hot sun in the Sonora desert.

Filming with a Moviecam in the Sonora Desert

When the filming was done Carlisle, myself and a couple of other people flew to Cancun then rented a car and drove around the Yucatan visiting the Mayan ruins of Chichen Itza and Tulum. We drove to Merida a lovely old colonial town where we stayed for a couple of nights.

The Make Up Artist

A warm wind blew from the desert
She blinked for an instant
And he was gone.
She had called him Drakie
And spoke to him in French.
He called her a funny little frog
But he loved to hear her talk.
It just sounded so romantic
Though he didn't say a word.

To Me, to You
You are alone too she said
We are all alone, it's funny, listen,
We are born alone
We die alone
And in between, we are just stuff
We must make a good choice for ourselves.

You are a poet, when you talk, you talk of poetry.
After this, there is a big kiss.
Do you have a cigarette?
"I don't smoke," he said.
All my sentences are awkward and full of emptiness.

But I don't know what you want?"

And then she turned the page,

Because she didn't want anyone to see.

What are you waiting for?

Just death, it's tragic.

She smiled and I caught the reflection of myself in her sunglasses.

"What are you doing with all this writing?' she asked.

I put it in a box, with all the others, just to remember.

"Do you write too – I mean seriously?" I asked.

"I like to write," she said.

"I hear the sound of the world, because I need it."

The translation interests me, it becomes romantic.

She laughed all the time and wiped her hand across her mouth.

There was a silence, but it was an angel flying between us.

I said she was an inspiration, a muse.

"You don't make love to a muse," she said.

"Sometimes all I want to do is watch the sun go down,

What's the difference?"

"I miss them all most of the time," I said.

We should go to India.

One day we will, but first I want to go to a house of women, it's

Fellini.

Not to do anything, just to watch.

We kissed, and she bit my tongue hard, so hard that it bled.

She said, "I want to drink your blood."

"You're crazy!"

"You can bite my tongue back if you want."

We were working on a movie

I was the cinematographer,

And she was the French make up artist, from Paris.

She had just taught me a few French words

When someone called wrap.

She went to Paris   And I went back to New York

FIN   THE END

Sonora Desert, Mexico   March 1985

143

The Gran Hotel, Merida, Yucatan

It seemed like a long time since he had been on the road. He had just checked in to an old Spanish hotel in Merida in the Yucatan. The Gran Hotel. It was very grand at one time and had been even grander about 100 years ago. His room looked like so many other rooms he'd frequented on his travels. He sat in front of the chest of drawers and examined his face in the mirror. He didn't look much older than the last time he glanced in the mirror, except for a few more grey hairs and a few more lines around his eyes, but the lines were from laughing in the sun. Beyond his own reflection lay the room – his room. The fan licked away the humidity and flicked back memories into the looking glass. The plaster was falling off the walls, the varnish was peeling off the doors and the dream was fading from his head. He took another swig of Superior beer and walked over to the shutters that hid the light from his room. A shaft of light caressed his cheek as his pupils stopped down to receive the midday Mexican sun. Was it midday already? He rubbed his eyes, scratched his head, yawned then took a step back. Something was not quite right. He walked over to the sink naked and poked out his tongue, like a Maori. The color wasn't too bad – a slight shade of yellow, but nothing that a dab of toothpaste couldn't remedy. The taste was sharp and the day had begun.

He glanced over to the bed – it was empty. He wished it wasn't. He tried to fill it the previous night, in fact the woman he had met had come back to his room – this fellow traveler, with a beer in her hand. They talked and they laughed on the balcony of his room. He had started to bend the conversation a little. He paid her a compliment or two, not that he remembered, but he did remember leaning towards her, after all they had been on the balcony for two hours and thought the time was right to lean towards her, like an animal stalking it's prey. Then like a gun from it's holster came a photo of the boyfriend from her wallet. She was fast and wounded him, but he managed to scramble for a color photo from his wallet of the French make –up

144

artist whom he had had an affair with on his last movie – touché! He thought he saw her flinch.

"I know what I want now in life," she said, looking at the black and white photo of her boyfriend, soon to be her husband. He hated to hear when people were so sure of themselves - so sure of their lives. He thought it inhuman. Wasn't that the mystery of life - the not knowing? He began to realize that he had had this conversation before, in another room, in another country with another girl. He remembered the girl - she had dark brown eyes and was very beautiful. He loved her a lot, but he hated her as well. He hated everything he loved, because he thought they would take his precious freedom away from him, so he became the enemy of himself. He had no enemies now, because he had no loves. He did love hotel rooms with a fan, somewhere too hot.

She saw that he was drifting off into another place and took her cue. "Well" she said. "It's time for bed," as she glanced at her watch, that hung loosely on her thin wrist. There was no time for another word, and she was merely a blur as she exited the room. Like a dream she was gone and he stood there a little saddened and a little relieved. The wind started to pick up and rattled the palm leaves outside his window.

The day before was stormy at Chichen Itza when he screamed at the Gods from the top of the pyramid. Bolts of lightning penetrated the jungle all around him and he thought that maybe this would be a good day to die. He tempted the Gods, but they ignored him and he carefully walked back down the steep steps to the bottom. He threw coins to the long dead virgins that had been drowned at the bottom of a pit as some kind of Mayan sacrifice.

He was back in the room – what a difference a day makes. He thought about human sacrifices and wondered what it would be like to cut open someone's chest and rip out their heart while it was still beating and eat it. He couldn't imagine - then remembered eating his Uncle's haggis in Scotland, which was made of sheep's stomach and was cooked. He didn't need to eat anything raw like a beating heart and decided to stick to cooked Cumberland sausages.

145

He liked his room – no. 29 The Gran Hotel Merida, Yucatan, Mexico. Now the secret was out, his affair with the room was now made public. Rooms were like people, each one had its own personality. Rooms could be mad or sane, comforting or sad. He knew this room held many secrets. He took a swig of Tequila from the bottle next to the bed and a few drops dribbled down his chin and onto his chest. It was now early in the afternoon and the sun was over the mainsail. He placed the bottle carefully back onto the table. It was noisy in the room, the window was open which let in the sounds of the street below him. High pitched two - stroke motorcycles drilled a hole into his tormented mind as he lay back onto the bed and watched as the fan rotated above his head. It was hot outside and the fan diluted the polluted air now sticky and hot that was visiting his room from outside. There was no need to go anywhere, so he stayed in the room and just stared up at the ceiling...

The Gran Hotel Merida

On top of the pyramid in Chichen Itza

I came back to New York from Mexico tanned and thinner than when I left. I was feeling good, and had made some money and was feeling pretty healthy. I had thought about Deborah Rebecca Jones a few times whilst I was away, but I was busy working and had a couple of different girlfriends whilst I was there. I also knew in my heart that Miss Jones was probably not thinking too much about me, especially with her life there in Paris, where she could have been practicing her magic. There was a lovely Mexican girl who worked as staff at Club Med and when she finished work she would sneak into my room late at night where she would spend the night. I remember her skin felt like silk and we would hold each other tight all night long. Early in the morning she would sneak out of the door after I made sure that the coast was clear for her to do so, making sure there were no other employees around. A quick kiss at the door and she would be off to work after we had had a shower together. It was perfect, I would get dressed for a day's shooting out in the Sonora desert. Of course this was not allowed by the rules of Club Med that their workers should have relations with the guests, but what's a nice girl to do working in a place like that? When the film crew left and we got on the bus there were a few Mexican girls blowing kisses to a couple of other crew members, as they looked up to the bus and we looked down to these girls standing there.

My girl was crying and I was tearing up and wondered if I just shouldn't jump off the bus and declare my love for her, as she was very lovable and simple and caring. I was leaving innocence and simplicity for the reality of the real world. It would not have been feasible for me to stay there and I suppose we both accepted it as a holiday romance. We never swooped addresses, so I suppose it was understood. The bus pulled away and I ran to the back of the bus to see her waving goodbye, knowing that I would never see this person again, and then she was gone. I was choked up for the next hour or so and realized that I actually did love this woman even though we didn't know each other that well, but she was soft and kind and I loved looking into her dark Mexican eyes. She was very dark skinned and was a Mexican Indian.

As I think back on these times I know that I never really appreciated these moments as I should have, but just wanted to eat up more and more of life, and my wanderlust made it almost impossible to maintain a normal relationship, which is why I had strange affairs with women like Deborah, which in the back of my mind I knew would not last.

Life picked up from where it left off, before my trip to Mexico. I was back in the Big Apple and ready to take another bite. I never had an agent in New York, so my work that I got was by reputation and word of mouth that seemed to be working out just fine. I called around to my usual contacts and told them I was back in town and went out for a few drinks establishing older connections. The trouble with shooting low budget films was that they were usually a one off deal and a lot of the directors were never heard of again, of course there were many that also went on to do bigger and better films and if they didn't they got lost somewhere in the ozone. I waited a couple of days before I called Miss Jones. It was a Sunday and the bells were clanging across the road at St Anthony's Church, and as I looked out the window there was a Catholic procession walking towards the church from Prince Street. The Statue of the Virgin Mary was being carried on a platform by four tough looking Italian men wearing suits and the women following behind were singing prayers. It was a spectacle to behold and a good welcoming back to Sullivan Street. I watched with a cup of tea in my hand as the procession made its way up the steps and into the church. Once again as I looked out onto the street I thought that I could have been in a small town in Italy. I felt inspired, and so I called Deborah. We had not been in touch for at least three months now and I wondered if she was back from Paris, or whether she had run off with a Greek as a couple of my ex's had done, only to have left two of them holding the baby as they scarpered off back to Greece.

The phone was ringing and I was feeling a little apprehensive and nervous about calling, as I always felt like I was under her spell. The church bells started clanging again really loud and I could barely hear the ringing tone at the other end of the phone. It rang and rang and once again there was no answer, so I put the phone down, only to have my imagination run wild as to what Deborah Rebecca Jones was up to, and in what country she was practicing her magic. I walked over to the stereo and put on Harvest, by Neil Young, then took a puff of mother - nature, as I was feeling relaxed and excited at the same time to be back in Manhattan.

Life continued, and I was dragged along with it, as I never really felt in control of my destiny, having to rely on where my next job was coming from. The only time I felt like I was in control was when I was traveling, which is why I did it so often. At the same time I could not have handled a normal nine to five existence either. I was becoming more and more like a fish out of water, which is why I felt more comfortable around the Deborah's of the world.

149

A couple of weeks went by and Miss Jones was slipping from my memory when out of the blue at about 10pm on a Thursday night the phone rang. I picked it up while I was lying on the couch in a state of semi-consciousness as I had been napping whilst listening to The Dark Side of the Moon. "Hello," said I, and a voice at the end of the phone mumbled something in French and then hung up. I assumed it was the wrong number or maybe it was Frenchie, the make-up artist calling from Paris, which would have made it four in the morning there. Maybe it was Miss Jones? I didn't know if I was dreaming or not, so I couldn't be bothered to figure who it could have been. The phone never rang again and I fell back to sleep on the couch.

It was Summer time again and it was hot. I thought about the phone call from the other night and so I decided to call Deborah. I realized that it was once again the weekend and also realized that it had been about three months or so since I had seen her. A lot had happened in those three months. I had shot a film in Mexico, met a couple of beautiful interesting women and traveled around the Yucatan with a few of the crew. Now back in New York I had to shake my head to figure out what was real and what was not. After a cup of Darjeeling tea I realized that it was all real, and as I sat back on my faithful futon I actually laughed out loud, remembering the adventures of the past three months or so. How wonderful life is, I thought to myself, and jumped up to call my mysterious Miss Jones. After two rings it picked up and a sophisticated woman's voice answered with a simple hello. That was all I needed to hear and I immediately felt excited. "Is this the adorable Deborah Rebecca Jones?" I asked.

"John, is this John?" she replied, almost jumping on my last word. She was pleased to hear from me, and we arranged to meet in the evening back in the funky bar on Sixth Avenue. I hadn't been there since our last meeting. How strange this all is, I thought to myself, that there is this woman who keeps re-appearing in my life and yet never totally disappears. I wonder sometimes if she is a figment of my imagination, as I thought about the Buddhist concept that 'Life is an Illusion.' I wondered if Miss Jones was my illusion. I felt like I had known her for centuries and yet I didn't really know her at all. We had slept together only once and yet I felt like she was my true love, but I knew deep down in my heart that she was no-one's true love.

I entered the smoke filled bar, and through the purple, blue haze recognized a silhouette at the bar. I took a deep breath, inhaling the second hand smoke and tried to contain my excitement on seeing Miss Jones. I weaved my way through the quagmire of humanity that were smoking and drinking and talking and shouting and laughing, until I made it to the bar where Deborah was sitting, talking to Patrick the Irish barman. It was déjà vu, but this time I got a hug from my friend as the schoolboy in me when we first met, had dissolved into my first margarita. I had shot a film in Mexico and was feeling more like a man of the world again, and besides I had spent the night beside this beautiful and fascinating woman that I still didn't really know. "Sir John," she said,

"Lady Jones," said I, as we hugged each other like long lost friends.

She introduced me to Patrick again, as he crushed my hand on shaking his and welcomed me back in his Irish brogue. It seemed like Deborah felt more at home here than at Odeon. It was definitely more of a mixed crowd that she seemed to like. It was a down to earth New York bar and I must admit I preferred it to the more pretentious establishments except when I felt like being pretentious. We talked excitedly about our experiences leaving out the love interests, at least the ones that I had. Whether she had any, was irrelevant and besides I didn't want to know, as I might have been jealous. Deborah was more accepting of this sort of thing than I, although I pretended to be quite nonchalant about all that messy stuff. It felt good being back in that bar again with Deborah and New York began to feel like home once more as I was pushed and shoved from all directions, as smoke was blown into my eyes and someone coughed in my ear, and the smell of cheap perfume wafted up under my nose. We had a few drinks together, Deborah sipped on her martinis and I, my margaritas, until the speech slowed down and the words became garbled, as it was hard enough to hear anyway. It was time to leave and we did.

We entered her loft space as she sent the elevator back down to street level. It looked pretty much the same as it was when I was last there, but with less swirly fabric hanging from the rafters. It felt more open than last time. I questioned her about the difference and she told me that she wanted to design a new theme. She liked the middle - eastern feel still, but wanted to combine it with some other culture. She broke open a bottle of French wine that she brought back from France and started to talk in French, then apologized to me as she realized that my French was limited. I wanted to speak French fluently, like Miss Jones and to have been so well educated although my education I had got from the street and from traveling and having a desire to learn about other places and cultures, so in that respect I did not feel inferior, in fact my experiences had been more down to earth having lived in an Indian fishing village, when Deborah would have been up to her ears in fluffy pillows looking out the window at the third world outside. We spoke about those differences and she told me that is why she liked me and the funky bar we were just at. She was capable at looking at the world from both sides, but she had a good security blanket, called money. Somehow we got onto the subject of India as I sipped on my second glass of the very fine French wine that slid down the throat so easily. "I am bloody starving darling," she announced," I haven't eaten anything all day - do you fancy a curry?" The talk of India had settled in her palette and as she mentioned it I could almost taste that first bite of Chicken Vindaloo.

The buzzer rang and the elevator doors opened and the smell of curry entered the loft along with an Indian boy, who carried two bags in his hands. I paid the lad and he descended from whence he came, and Miss Jones and I were alone again once more, except for two curries, six papadoms, two veggie samosas, two onion bhajis two banana pakoras, two garlic naans, two little white boxes of basmati rice and a mango lassie for Deborah. I helped Deborah get out all the plates and silverware and we laid the table together for our reunion feast. We toasted each other along with Gandhi, friendship and adventure, and good health and wealth. Clink! As the glasses hit each other, then clink again for the next toast, until they almost smashed in our hands. We laughed at our silliness, leaned across the table and kissed each other on the lips as Deborah Rebecca Jones said, "Now not another word," as we dove head first into our curries, savoring every bite as though it were our last. To me Indian food is the most exotic and sensual in the world. We barely looked at each other as our food consumed our very being as we washed it down with glass after glass of fine French wine.

It was an orgy of food and the two of us lay together on her oversized couch, looking like a couple of pregnant people as Ravi Shankar turned slowly at 33rpm on the turntable. Miss Jones was the magician of ambiance and with her I felt like we could be transported to anywhere in the world without leaving the comfort of her home. I loved this woman, but dare not tell her so, for fear that she would kick me out the door. It all felt so natural being with this woman and I not only had fallen in love this night, but I realized that I adored her and admired who she was even though she could at times act rather spoilt, but she carried it well, and no-one was going to get one over on Miss Jones.

The next thing I saw was the sun bleeding through the bamboo blinds. The two of us had eaten and drunk ourselves into oblivion. Deborah was purring like a kitten on the over-sized couch as I looked at her and then at the empty wine bottles that were strewn like dead soldiers on the floor. I rolled over to kiss her on the cheek as she was coming out of her dream state, her long black hair trailing across the Gujarati pillows. She mumbled to me that I should put the kettle on for a cup of tea as she stretched her arms above her head.

When I came back from the bathroom the kettle was whistling to me, and Deborah told me where the Darjeeling tea was. I made us a nice pot and placed it on a tray along with two large cups, a small jug of milk and two English Muffins and placed that on the little table next to the couch. Deborah sat up, looking like a beautiful twisted scarecrow as she squinted at the morning rays of light now creating godlike shafts that penetrated the dust that hung in the air. "How do you feel," I said. She answered in French then asked me where we were in English.

"New York," I answered. Miss Jones just sighed at my answer. It was a non - committal sigh, neither good nor bad. After our many conversations about travel and life and death that we had had in the past I began to realize that Deborah felt more affection for Paris than the Big Apple, because it was the city of romance and Deborah was a hopeless romantic like myself. Church bells rang off in the distance and Deborah mentioned that she loved the sound of church bells, especially the ones of 'The Notre Dame' in Paris. I jumped up and placed a small pillow under my shirt and did my Hunchback of Notre Dame impersonation for Lady Jones as I mumbled, "The bells, the bells," from my purposely deformed mouth and dragged one leg behind me as I made my way to the couch whereupon our lips met and she laughed then pushed me away after hitting me on the head with her Gujarati pillow. I stayed in character as I asked Deborah what her plans were.

"I want you to amuse me all day," she said, as though she were The Queen of Hearts. I bowed to her request, as she slightly moved an inch or two on the couch and realized that we were about to spend a very lazy day together. It was Sunday morning and Sundays were meant to be 'beautifully lethargic' as Deborah said. New York rattled and hummed outside of the window as the day slowly began, as the party animals of a Saturday night yawned and stretched and rubbed their eyes to face the most religious day of the week.

"Would you like to spend the day together?" Deborah asked.

I couldn't believe the question, as this was the woman who always seemed to be running off, going here there and everywhere. My heart suddenly beat faster and I played pantomime as I told her that I would have to look at my appointment book to see if I could possibly fit her in. My God, I would have cancelled my knighthood from the Queen

154

herself to have this most privileged opportunity to spend a whole day with the one and only Deborah Rebecca Jones.

"I will have to cancel a few appointments, but I think it would be possible" I told her.

She then ordered me to take a shower, whilst she called her sister in Paris.

"I've told my sister about you, you know?" She exclaimed, as she literally rolled off the couch and onto the Persian rug.

"I didn't know," I replied as her school - mistress character revealed itself once more.

The shower felt good and hot, as I lathered myself from some smelly French soap and poured some apricot shampoo onto my head as I massaged it into my scalp with a skill like Vidal Sassoon. I began to sing a song from the musical South Pacific as I watched the creamy lather slide down my legs. I was happy. When I got out of the shower I smelt very fruity like an orchard and hoped there were no wasps around to mistake me for a large apple! I slipped on a brown Moroccan djellaba that Deborah told me to wear and was now ready to spend Sunday with Lady Jones. As I stepped back into the land of make believe I saw Deborah hang up the phone with her sister.

"That wasn't a very long phone call," I said.

"She was on her way out, and look at you my Moroccan poet."

She then lectured me on Moroccan culture and told me that the djellaba I was wearing signified that I was a bachelor because of the color brown. I wondered if she had a collection of others - one for married men or divorcees. From the bedroom she produced a pair of Moroccan slippers for me that she called babouche, which sounded French to me. So now the masquerade had begun as I walked over to the full - length mirror to look at my new image as Deborah twirled into the bathroom. I wondered if she was resurrecting an old

Moroccan boyfriend by dressing me up like this. I feared to ask as I knew my boundaries with Miss Jones.

After twenty minutes or so the bathroom door opened and steam poured into the loft as Deborah disappeared into the bedroom to play her role in our Sunday pantomime. She came out masquerading like a Hindu Princess wearing a lime green sari and gold slippers. I thought us now to be a strange couple - an English Moroccan and a New England Hindu woman. So who was I to question anything at this moment in time, as this mysterious woman shrouded me in her magical sensual world, she looked wonderful and could have passed for an Indian Princess.

"Today I am Parvati, the wife of Lord Shiva," she said, "and you will be Ali."

I thought she was taking all this a bit far, but I thought why not? After all don't actors take on different personalities, and that's what we were doing for the day. I remembered our first meeting on the commuter train when Miss Jones seemed so conservative all dressed in black, looking like an executive and now here she was dressed as an Indian princess. She walked over to the record player and placed an album onto the turntable. It crackled and hissed for the first thirty seconds until the familiar sound of a wailing sitar blotted out the sound of the New York traffic that was now beginning to build outside of Parvati's world. So let the games begin, I thought to myself. I walked over to the window and looked out onto New York, the sun had gone and a black cloud darkened the loft space.

"They said there was a storm coming in today" said the Indian princess, and as she spoke beads of rain began to hit the window pane as I watched as people began to run for shelter on the street, as umbrellas burst open hiding the heads below. I loved to watch the rain and found it mesmerizing as the princess placed a bong filled with hashish into my hand. "Good morning Ali" she said, as she ignited the hashish in the bowl. I took a deep breath out and then inhaled the blue smoke as it bubbled inside the glass pipe. I passed it back and Deborah

156

inhaled, then blew some back out, as we watched the rainfall from the heavens above, as a thunder - clap shook the building losing the sitar music in the distance. We looked at each other, Deborah in her sari and me in my djellaba and we laughed then kissed as we watched the storm outside. She told me that this was her favorite weather and I had to agree, as it reminded me of the old country, then she took my hand and lead me back to the couch where she handed me the poems of Kahlil Gibran to read to her, but only after I told her the origin of the word hashish.

I told Parvati to sit down on the couch as it was now thundering and lightning outside which created the perfect atmosphere as I told her about the Hashishins, which meant hashish eaters that were a secret order that dated back to the time of the Crusades. Legend had it that they came from Persia, and Hassan who was the leader would kidnap his victims feed them hashish until they fell asleep and were then taken to a beautiful garden, and when awoken would be offered sensual pleasures by beautiful hand maidens or girls from the Harem. The kidnapped would then believe they were in Paradise. So now they were under the control of the kidnappers and would be sent out to assassinate whoever needed assassinating. So the word assassin was derived from the word Hashishin. I then went on to tell Parvati about the Thuggees who were also assassins, but from India and they were around from about the 13th Century to the 19th, who carried out their assassinations in the name of the Goddess Kali. These chaps as I told her strangled their victims who were very often travelers, with silk handkerchiefs or nooses.

Over the years they were responsible for about two million deaths. So the term thug as I told Miss Jones came from the term Thuggee of which in dear old England we have many, along with many wonderful Indian restaurants. So we decided that the world had always been a violent place and that things today were not so bad. Our pantomime continued and Parvati got up to get a stack of art books and books of poetry. There was a book on The Pre Raphaelite painters that she grabbed first then hurriedly flipped through the pages until she came

157

to the painting of The Lady of Shalott, by John William Waterhouse. "That's me," she said, pointing to the painting. "That is my destiny, see she is in a canoe with a few of her belongings."

I never questioned her about the remark. She then picked up a book on English poets and asked me to read Tennyson's poem

'The Lady of Shalott,' as she stared into the painting in the book. She asked me to read a verse over that she liked.

No time hath she to sport and play:

A charmed web she weaves away.

A curse is on her, if she stay

Her weaving, either night or day,

To look down to Camelot.

She knows what the curse may be;

Therefore she weaveth steadily,

Therefore no other care hath she,

The Lady of Shalott.

 Tears sprang from Parvati's eyes, as I closed the book. I asked her what was the matter. She told me that she had been cursed like The Lady of Shalott, but that I should not worry. Although the poem was about a mythical person, she related so much to the story. Once again I was mesmerized by this mythical woman and actually wondered if indeed she was real.

She then asked me to read the middle-eastern works of Omar Khayyan and Kahlil Gibran and I felt privileged once again to be in this woman's company. Parvati lit the pipe once more as we both became Hashishins and indulged in sensual pleasures but without the assassinations afterwards. I was instructed to place an album by a musician I had never heard of on the turntable and it hissed and clicked until the needle found some mystical middle-eastern music as Parvati blew the swirling surplus hashish smoke into the air. By now the storm had eased off and I walked over to the window to watch, as another storm front was moving in. Perfect! The stage was set for the reading of more poetry, as Parvati snuggled up close to me, as I flipped through the pages of the Prophet, and reading a poem from one page to the next I realized how simple and contemporary they were, and just as relevant to the world today as then, and that thoughts and fears and love, have always been in the mind of men from the beginning of time.

She told me that she was very aware of her previous lives and re-incarnations which was why she felt the way that she did about life - that it wasn't to be taken too seriously and that we were here to enjoy it quite simply, and to have fun and laugh and to pass on good will. "I am just traveling through this one and now wonder where my next life will lead me," she would say as though she were in a hurry to experience the next life wherever that would be. I believed she was a re-incarnation of someone very special - but who?

I left Deborah's abode at about ten the next morning. The weekend was over and most people were going back to work. I stepped out onto the thunderous streets and was immediately bombarded by the banging and crashing and horns a honking, like some distorted Buddhist ceremony. It was a beautiful morning however and the air felt crisp after the heavy rains of yesterday as New York had had a good bath. Once again I had to shake my head back to reality. I had gone back into the womb for the past thirty-six hours where Deborah and I played a wonderful game of fantasy, but it wasn't fantasy at all. It was as real as anything else - we had merely put a different perspective on life. I hadn't taken a shower and I could still smell Deborah's scent on me and my clothes smelt of Indian incense. I wanted to turn around and go back to that world, but the door was closed and I had to deal with the black and white world that New York

159

dished out. I meandered up Sixth Avenue, still in a daze - I was no longer Ali, but just plain old John, although in Mexico they called me Juanito and thought that maybe I should change my name to something more exotic like that. I traveled with my unrealistic thoughts until I found myself at The Museum of Modern Art. Then once again began to enjoy the diversity of New York as the crowds outside spoke in different languages as Europeans lined up to enter.

Outside the museum people were selling art books - they were stacked randomly on tables. I bought one on Sisley who was an impressionist painter of the time and who lived in Paris of course and another on Matisse. Sisley was more of a Landscape painter and Matisse was considered a contemporary of Picasso and I believe one influenced the other. The museum seemed crowded, so I didn't enter but decided instead to walk up to the park with my glossy new art books, pretending to be all - intellectual and artsy fartsy. I sat on a bench in the shade as the sun was getting hotter by the minute and started to read about these artist's lives in Paris at the turn of the twentieth century and realized why Miss Jones loved the city of Paris so much.

I know that for many, life must have been hard, but surely it was a lot simpler than it is today, I thought to myself. I was inspired by these books and thought that maybe one day I would be a painter and I imagined myself in a Parisian garret overlooking the Seine, canvass in front of me on an easel, paintbrush in one hand and palette in the other. My subject would be Miss Jones dressed in her sari showing a naked shoulder with the soft diffused light gently caressing her face, as she looked down slightly embarrassed. As I flipped through the book on Matisse I loved his colorful depictions of women and thought that is how I would paint Deborah. It wasn't until almost twenty years later when I did actually pick up a paintbrush (and now have over 600 canvases to my name).

I was broken from my dream state by the smell of hot dogs. I had been sitting on the bench for nearly two hours reading and dreaming and realized that I hadn't eaten anything and it was now early afternoon. I was bloody starving and indulged, not in a hot dog but a nice spicy Italian sausage that another vendor was selling. I smothered it in onions and ketchup and bit into it like a man possessed. I then realized I was thirsty and washed it down with a small bottle of water. I wiped my mouth with a paper napkin and felt satiated. It did not take much to make me happy and I enjoyed these moments alone with my thoughts as I wondered what was next.

What was next was a journey around the world? I had always wanted to do it, and so I did. A friend of mine called Hedley Garnet owned what was called a 'bucket shop' in Earls Court (also known at the time as Kangaroo Valley, because of all the Aussies that had decided to live there). A bucket shop for the uninitiated is basically a cheap travel agency whereby the agent would buy up tickets on flights around the world and put them together for a cheaper flight than normal. Sometimes they were on lesser known airlines that I had never heard of and sometimes well-established companies. Deborah went off to Paris for Christmas and New Year and I left the Big Apple on New Year's Day. I arrived at Heathrow early in the morning after having breakfast whilst flying over Ireland and touched down into a cold dank foggy morn. It always amazed me when flying in to London how many green fields there still are, and that it was still Blake's green and pleasant land.

After going through the green light at customs, my old friend Maurice of almost twenty years picked me up and delivered me to my mother's house in Stoneleigh Surrey, about a forty-five minute drive from the airport (depending on traffic). My dear old Mum seemed to have shrunk in height since the last time I saw her and I joked to her about it, after which she punched me in the stomach! So the three of us sat down and had a nice cuppa with some chocolate digestives as my mother asked me how my flight was. I was home. I looked up to see that the porcelain ducks had not flown off the wall papered wall as my mother knelt down to turn on the electric fire with the rotating flames that flickered behind the electric bars. "We'll put all four on for now, till it warms up love," There was a bit of a chill in the room, my mother

161

was used to the damp and cold of England. These old birds had seen it all - the V-1's and V-2's dropping on dear olde London Town - The Blitz, and rationing, things that Americans didn't experience in the War.

I remember my mum sitting around with her other five sisters in the past talking about the war years and how everyone helped each other out and what a great sense of camaraderie there was. Now unfortunately the world has become a greedier place, where it's dog eat dog. But enough of that! I was home and home is where the heart is and mine is still in England's green and pleasant land. It was good to be home once more and no matter how old as a man you are, you will always be mum's little boy. I would leave the house and my mum would say "Do you have your handkerchief, son?" To which I would reply "I haven't blown my nose once in twelve years mum." So everyday I felt younger and younger until I almost was sucked back into the womb. How could I have possibly survived all these years I wondered without my dear old ma?

I went to see most of my old friends, which usually ended up sitting around a burning log fire in a country pub clutching a pint of best bitter and telling bawdy jokes as though I had never left England's shores. Back outside after to see your breath leave your mouth, under a broad bright moon, and to hear the crunching sound of dead leaves under foot as you hugged old friend's goodbye. "Where you going now Drakie?" they would say. "Around the world" said I, and Maurice would drive me back to my mum's to be molly cuddled and spoilt until I left. So after two or three weeks I left from Heathrow, to catch a plane to what was still called Bombay where I was to meet up with Carlisle the following day.

Dear old London town.
Thames Embankment with St. Paul's Cathedral

OFF TO INDIA

My flight left at 6pm on the 24th January 1986 from Heathrow, a non-stop flight to Bombay. The plane was full, not one empty seat - February was to be the Chinese New Year, so there were many Chinese on their way to Hong Kong, the next stop after Bombay. My seat was on the aisle, next to an old Indian couple, the man reminded me of a man I met in Sri Lanka who fleeced me out of a bit of money over the purchase of a star ruby. The man also had a slight lisp, like the man from Sri Lanka - maybe it was the same man. We were half an hour late taking-off as we were all crammed into British Airways sardine can flight 003 for eight and a half hours, until we eventually arrived at 8.30 in the morning. It had been twelve years since I was last in India and the heat and smells that I immediately recognized made me feel like I had never left from before. I was back in India - land of temples, forts and forests, beaches, mountains, rich and poor, beggars and thieves, spirituality and materialism - a contradiction of a country. I took a cab to the South End, a hotel that had been recommended by the travel bureau in London. It was a bit funky - this was no high-end hotel, but I didn't care, I just wanted to crash out on the bed. I slept longer than I thought I would, suffering from lack of sleep on the plane and jet lag. I got up rinsed off my face and walked out onto those old familiar streets of Bombay. It was already dark and my nap had taken me into a hot Bombay night, into bedlam and a sea of humanity. A number of women in saris came up to me and enquired in a most charming Peter Sellers like accent if "I would like a bit." I nearly burst out laughing at the delivery of such an eloquent line and replied, "thanks but no thanks" in so many words. The street life of India was once more upon me, there was no other place in the world like it, the hustle and bustle and noise and smells and chaos was overwhelming and I felt like I needed more air, but there was none to be had only the choking pollution flowed into my lungs. I walked up and down the street a couple of times to acclimatize to this strange world that Kipling wrote about a century before. I walked up to a magazine stand that sold the Times of India and some English rag papers and bought myself a pack of beedies. It had been about twelve years since I had smoked one. A beedie for those who have not been initiated is an Indian cigarette that is a leaf of tobacco wrapped up at one end by a red piece of thread like a Buddhist's thread of protection. That is it - one is smoking a pure piece of tobacco with no chemical additives. I was never a cigarette smoker before except for a half a dozen puffs as a kid, 'cause I thought it was cool. Somehow the beedie was my indoctrination back into India, so I had to inhale India back into my lungs along with everyone else. I was home again and ready to face the consequences of returning to a place that was so extreme. I walked back to my funky hotel as a thousand images flickered like an old movie across my mind. I wanted to climb to the highest mountain and say thanks for letting me into this crazy insane world. I wanted to tell everyone to stop fighting especially in the name of religion and for everyone to appreciate the gift of life.

I got back to my hotel room and collapsed on the bed once more and watched the fan spinning around above me. I watched as a thousand memories spun around in my head in time with the groaning fan. I was now neither tired nor energized, but just felt like I was floating somewhere between heaven and hell. I got off the bed and walked down the stairs to the reception area for no particular reason. An old man was talking on the phone. He had long grey hair and a long grey beard to match and looked like a sardhu. He began to yell down the phone, shouting to someone at the other end, "I want to tell you the man is dead" he kept repeating this phrase as if it were his mantra. "The man is dead I tell you" he said one more time. Life and death - I was back in India and it was a fine line between the two worlds. I walked over to the corner of the lobby and sat in a comfortable chair and continued reading 'The Razors Edge' and thought how wonderful it must have been to travel around the world in the 1920's. That was when someone who wanted to see the world was called a traveler and not a tourist. I hated being called a 'tourist' as that was the last thing I wanted. Unfortunately it was too easy to be classified as a tourist, despite your intentions. I closed my book shut and retired to bed - I had to meet my friend Carlisle at the airport the next day.

I got up early, as Carlisle was arriving in the early hours of the morning and I had to meet him at the airport. I took a taxi and waited outside the arrivals gate. It was still dark, as the hot Indian sun had not yet lifted her head to greet the day. Carlisle appeared amidst all the commotion and chaos of street vendors, taxi drivers, beggars and the like. I could see he looked a little shocked at the sight that greeted his eyes, as I remembered the shock I had, arriving here in the early hours of the morning twelve years before. There is nothing that can prepare

165

one for that first step onto the vast sub-continent of India. He was relieved to see me and we hopped in a cab to take us to Juhu Beach where we slept and rested then made plans for our journey through India.

Wednesday 5th February   Benaulim Beach. Goa

Carlisle was outside sitting on the stoop and I was inside lying on the bed listening to 'Wish You Were Here.' We had rented a room on the beach for just a few dollars a day - a basic room with a toilet and a shower and two single beds. The sun was setting over the Indian Ocean and the big black crows screamed and screeched at each other outside the window. My face was covered in Nivea cream as it was drying up like a prune from the hot Indian sun. I had forgotten how intense the heat can be in India.

*Fishing boats on Colva Beach - same as they were
when I was there 12years before*

166

The sun sets slowly behind the palm trees as I sit by the window of my room in the Grand Hotel, sipping on a good strong cup of Indian tea that the chi - wallah brought in. India lies outside the window as I breathe in its scent of Jasmine and incense, sewage and dung, whilst the fan spins slowly inside this old room. It's hot and humid and the monsoon season is on its way. I am almost at the very tip of India, in the very south not far from Cape Comorin. The other day I saw the Moon come up and the Sun go down at the same time, from the very bottom of India where East meets West, but East is here and the West a very long way from this place.

We arrived here after a nine hour barge trip through an intricate system of canals and backwaters, past beautiful little villages lining the banks of these waterways. Dark smiling, happy faces greeted us as we slowly moved past on our barge, which was being punted by our Tamil captain. Little children waved to us as we passed them playing and laughing on the riverbanks, with the dense jungle behind them. I felt like I had stepped back in time like Sir Richard Burton about to discover the source of the Nile, as we drifted along past the lily-ponds and dense undergrowth, with the hot Indian sun baking down on us as we moved slowly through these people's lives in this place that probably hadn't changed much in hundreds of years of India's vast history.

A village on the banks of the inland canals

A month ago I had gone back to Goa to see some of my old haunts from the time I was there, in 1974 - twelve years ago. Calangute had completely changed, being overrun with tourists and hotels, but other parts of Goa seemed to have remained quite untouched by the hoards of lemmings coming from the West and Russia. I remember sitting at a restaurant in Goa watching the Arabian Sea roll in and feeling very old and even ancient and yet not even born. I had taken quite a few photos back in '74 of the kids in the village, so those that were eight years of age then, were now twenty years old! How would I ever recognize just one of them?

India hasn't lost its magic, although I think traveling here in the twenties must have been the time. I feel like an old adventurer from the time of the Raj, sitting here listening to the wailing outside the window. In a couple of days Carlisle and I will take a train to Madras and from there another train to New Delhi and then to the garden of India to Kashmir. New York is a million miles from here as I begin to think about the huge contrasts between the USA and India. The thing with travel is, that it becomes a very personal experience - it is you and the Universe and when you sit back and relax and meditate, you feel like you are being taken care of, even though you are in a place so strange and yet so familiar. Have I been here before, you ask yourself?

The canals on the way to Ernakulam

The Bucket Of Water

He came from a place where people walked in the rain.
He remembered holding out his hands, when he was young.
He wanted to hold all the oceans in his hand.
But he didn't understand where the rain came from.
So he went to school and asked his teacher,
But he didn't really know.

So he left school, not seeing any reason to be there.
And traveled on the sea for many years
Trying to understand the mystery of water.
Every time he picked it up, it ran out of the side of his hand.

He decided to buy a bucket and start a collection.
He placed his bucket out in the rain
And watched the water collect
He was very happy sitting out in the rain
And began to feel like water himself.

A tear fell from his eye
He was beginning to understand the mystery of water.

He sat by the bucket for years, waiting for the rain.
He stopped eating

170

He was too absorbed in his bucket of rain
That became a bucket of water.
He got thinner and thinner
Until he finally disappeared,
He had mastered the art of water

He realized that capturing it in a bucket
Was not the answer,
By the time he knew the answer
It was already too late,
He had gone back to the sea.

Southern India, 1986

It's February 24th the day after my birthday and I had just turned thirty-five. Carlisle and I are heading to Madras on a first class sleeper from the small town of Ernakulam as India slides past the windows under a full moon. The moon is bright enough to light up a range of mountains as we light up inside filling the carriage with sweet smelling puffs of smoke as India turns into a dream once more. I drifted off into never-never land as the past and present turn into the future. I began to wonder if I had crossed over into the fourth dimension. I pull down my bunk bed and climb aboard as Carlisle sleeps below on his. I look out of the window now in a dreamlike opium state of mind and watch as India flutters like a camera shutter past my eyes as I see images of film sets and white sandy beaches, dark skinned women walking upright and proud, balancing pots on their heads filled with water. I see The Tower of London and The Empire State building, the Greek islands with gleaming white houses contrasted against a deep blue Aegean Sea as I lay my head down to join the rest of my body as I seem to be floating off into space. I feel a smile crack on my face as I fall asleep contented like a young baby after a mouthful of mother's milk.

February 25th

I woke up to a clattering and banging as the train was just pulling in to Madras station. It was now seven in the morning and it had taken fourteen hours to get here from Kerala on the west coast. At the station we tried to book a ticket to New Delhi. We bought the ticket, but the office wallah couldn't confirm it, so we had to come back later, only to be sent on a wild goose chase, going from office to office. Bureaucracy established by the British Raj over two hundred years ago kept many Indians employed, but they took it to another level of rules and regulations and laws all wrapped up in miles of red tape. Finally our tickets for the Tamil Nadu express to New Delhi in a couple of weeks were confirmed and Carlisle and I celebrated our minor victory with a breakfast at an Americanized hotel where we washed and did our ablutions in style. After breakfast we caught a rickshaw to the bus station to take us to Mahabalipuram. We get on the bus and after a while, we hear a sound like a gunshot, then the bus swerves to the left and then to the right, then pulls over to the side of the road. There is a blowout in the front nearside tyre. All the passengers get out and Carlisle and I jump into a passing sand truck that is heading our way. The Tamils tell us to throw our gear in the back and they drop us off about 5km before our destination. We thank them for the ride and walk for the next couple of miles under a baking hot Indian sun with a back pack that is way too heavy. We finally make it to the town of Mahabalipuram where we check into a mosquito haven, but it felt good to collapse onto a bed. The moon rose full over the Bay of Bengal as we now faced the east. We found a decent restaurant where we ate a masala dal and a chapatti and retired to bed under a mosquito net.

February 26th

Woke up with a bit of a hangover having not had a good night sleep, thanks to the mosquitos sucking out my precious English blood. There must have been holes in the net, or else there were hiding inside waiting for a nice meal from the westerner with all that sweet tasting blood. Had breakfast of eggs toast and jam and a good pot of Darjeeling tea as I sat on the terrace that looked out across the Bay of Bengal knowing that beyond the horizon lies Thailand where I should be heading in about another two months, but first a train through the middle of India to Delhi, Rajasthan and then Kashmir.

Carlisle and I visited the temples of Mahabalipuram, the Pancha Rathas and the five chariots named after the Pandavas. The temples portray events that are written in the Mahabharata and the city dates back to the seventh century AD. Early stages of Dravidian architecture are seen here and in the streets there are shops selling stone sculptures depicting the head of the Buddha, Shiva and Krishna and many other gods, as the whole area seems to act as a school for young masons and stone carvers.

Temple in Mahabalipuram

We were thinking of visiting Madurai, but decided against it for some reason and within the next few days found ourselves on the Tamil Nadu express bound for New Delhi.

We boarded the train and found our first class compartment, which would be considered third class on any European train. Nevertheless it was private and clean and basic with two bunk beds. Bedlam was all around us, with vendors selling everything from chapatis and papadums and rotis, to chai tea and sweet pastries to wooden and stone carvings of all the Hindu gods. There were knick - knacks and scarves and cheap jewelry and this and that. Finally the train pulled out of the station leaving all the human commotion behind and we were off on a journey through the middle of India as I remembered a scene from

174

'The Man Who Would Be King' that wonderful story by Kipling that was made into a film by John Huston, starring Sean Connery and Michael Caine.

Eventually, the train pulled in to the station in New Delhi the capital of India, and we alighted amidst the usual pushing and shoving and begging and shouting. Outside of the station we hailed a taxi to take us to a small hotel near Connaught Circus, then hit the streets to get a bite to eat. The next few days were spent doing the usual touristy things like visiting the Red Fort named that because the walls are made of red sandstone. It was constructed in 1639 by the Mughal Emperor the Shah Jahan, who was also responsible for the building of the Taj Mahal which was built to house the tomb of his wife Mumtaz Mahal. The bazaars were all pretty interesting to meander around, the ones being Chawari Bazar in front of the Red Fort and the Chhatta Chowk. The India Gate was built in 1931 and was inspired by the Arc de Triomphe in Paris, so to the arch at Washington Square Park in New York. The Rashtrapati Bhavan is the official residence of the President of India and apparently is the largest residence of any Head of State anywhere else in the world and was formerly the home of the Viceroy of India. Other beautiful places to visit were the gardens at Buddha Jayanti Park. So after a few days in the capital we headed west on yet another train to the Thar Desert and Rajasthan. We stayed in Jaipur that is the capital of Rajasthan with a population of over 3 million. It is known as the 'Pink City' as many of the buildings are constructed with red and pink sandstone. The Maharaja Pratap Singh had the Hawa Mahal (Palace of Winds) built so that many of his wives and women of the royal household could observe the activities on the street below without being seen. A couple of the locals told me that the Maharaja had two hundred wives. From Jaipur we visited Ajmer and from there took a train to Pushkar.

Pushkar.   March 11th

175

Pushkar is one of the oldest existing cities in India. It sits on the edge of Pushkar Lake and legend associates Brahma with its creation. I awoke at sunrise after having slept on the roof of the Pushkar Hotel. Later we saw the masses go down to the ghats to do their ablutions with the banging of drums and ringing of bells. Pushkar is a vegan town where one cannot even get an egg to eat, nor any alcohol to drink. It is considered a holy city. I drank gallons of mineral water as I realized that I hadn't been drinking enough and was feeling a little dehydrated here in the middle of the great Thar Desert.

March 12th

I walked to the top of a hill where sat a temple that housed the goddess Savitri. While I was there I met this Australian woman who had made the temple her home. We sat down and spoke for a while about traveling and India, and then she proceeded to tell me her story. She told me that while she was living in Sydney she had dreams of this place, Pushkar, the holy city. She did not know where it was, but had an idea that it was in India somewhere. The dreams kept recurring and one day she took off to India with her boyfriend. They traveled around India and eventually separated and went their own ways. The woman ended up here. She was staying in the town on the lake, and looked up to see this temple on the top. It looked like the temple from her dreams. Something was calling her to the temple and she walked up the hill. The Brahmin who looked after the temple, started walking down towards her. As they met half way, the Brahmin told her that he had been expecting her. He knew he was to become her teacher. She was learning to speak Hindi. So that was this woman's story and she had been living in the temple studying the Vedas for the past four years. She got up with the sun and went to bed when the sun went down, she told me. In the morning she practiced yoga and then offered food to the goddess. In the evening she would meditate. She then explained how in the west people put too much energy into exterior things, which I understood only too well, having been a seeker of a simpler life myself. It was important to have a better understanding of oneself and to store energy instead of wasting it. She told me that she hadn't spoken to too many westerners, as she didn't need the interruption from her life. Her life was complete in that temple, with her teacher, as she was learning the meaning of existence. For four years, she sat and listened and greeted the dawn, staring into that fiery ball as it lifted its head into the hazy desert sky. Her eyes were clear and she had a most peaceful essence about her, as she was indeed at peace with herself and the universe. She had made a choice, she had gone from the west to the east, from the physical to the spiritual, from anxiety to peace, although it seemed from her story that she was summoned and sent for, so in that respect she accepted her destiny at least for the moment and moments are all we have. Strange things happen in India. It is a land of mystery, mysticism and magic and one does not question, but accepts what is. It is an ancient land full of extremes and different philosophies and once in it's womb, it is all encompassing and one becomes a part of India, whether you want to or not.

There is another temple that Carlisle and I considered visiting near the city of Bikaner. It is called the Karni Mata temple and is known for the worship of the rat. The temple is home to over 20,000 rats. They are pampered and fed by the caretakers and are left to run around freely. Only within the Hindu tradition could something so bizarre as this exist, because of its acceptance and reverence for all living things. Not being great fans of 'the rat' and knowing of the 'Great Plague of London' that was brought about by our rodent friends, we decided to opt out of this cultural experience and head out towards Udaipur in the south.

Udaipur

Time ticks by as I sit on the roof of the Hotel Lalghat, looking out onto Pichola Lake. The sound of the dobi wallahs can be heard banging their clothes as they wash them on the steps of the ghats. The dull thuds of wet clothes echoes back off the mountains as the hot sun bakes down on the little white washed stone houses that remind me of Greece. Carlisle and I have the honeymoon suite, but there is no honeymoon. The double iron studded door, leads into a cool white stone room that leads into a circular bedroom situated in the turret of the hotel. A lace curtain separates the two rooms. I imagine myself as a Maharaja dressed in fine silks colored orange and wearing the Rajasthani turban as I await my princess. My dream is quickly broken by the Austrian guy downstairs, playing Mexican mariachi music. A small motorboat leaves the Lake Palace Hotel laden with tourists. A small boy flies a red kite from a rooftop, it whips and jerks from the hands of its master and then slowly and sadly it falls against a wall. There is no wind to keep it airborne. I look across the rooftops and see the heat haze creating a mirage. I decide to write in my diary - it is far from complete. February contains just a few days and now it is already

March as you wonder where the days went. Many years later I will look at the diaries and see how much the world has changed. I look down at the purple, pink, orange and red saris that lay like a crossword puzzle on the ghats below. Bare chested women throw buckets of lake water over each other as they laugh and sing. The women are beautiful and their smiles glow under the hot Indian sun. Meanwhile vultures hover over a temple, they know that someone is dead or dying.

Pichola Lake Udaipur with the Kings Palace in the background

Rajasthan is filled with forts and palaces and pretty much every town seems to be fortified. Many battles took place over the years between invaders from the north and west. There were many wars throughout the centuries, between the Mongols and the Rajputs and one of the earliest battles, the Battle of Rajasthan dates back to 712 AD against the rising Arab powers. The Rajput army had over 3,000 elephants and cavalry and infantry of up to 300,000 men. The battles went on into the 12th century and again in the 16th century when more battles were fought.

Carlisle and I in Udaipur Rajasthan

Jaisalmer Rajasthan, India. 1986.   The North West Frontier.

I took a look in the mirror at my face, opened my eyes wide, then pulled down the bottom eyelid using both hands - it was as I had expected. Both eyes were dark yellow and my face was tinged yellow, it was jaundice all right–hepatitis. I looked beyond the jaundiced eyes in the mirror and like an old faded photograph turned sepia through age began to think about the last 10 years of my life. I had spent most of them in New York City, that part of my life that was the most recent seems very hazy to me, it was as if I had been asleep for a long time and that the last years were just a dream. The face in the mirror however was very real and so to this dusty place on the edge of the Thor Desert. Pakistan was only a few miles to the west and Delhi to the northeast. This was my time, the time to get hepatitis, there must be a reason why I got it, but now it was too early to say. I liked to think that everything happens for a reason, I know that sounds a bit ridiculous, but it helped me at times like this to get through it, or just get through whatever you had to get through. Everything must have a beginning and an end. I began to think, that at this time of my life I had had many beginnings and many endings. Life to me consisted of many little lives in one. Unfortunately to become a master of anything took a proper lifetime, that is to say 50 or 60 years. Because of this I wasn't a master of anything except maybe the master of dreams and illusions. The chief procrastinator! Unfortunately there were no jobs at the labor exchange with any of these job descriptions or titles. 'Chief Procrastinator needed at local Dream Factory.' So here I was in this hot dusty place sweating, looking in the mirror wondering what I was doing in this hot dusty desolate place. It was as if I wasn't in control of my actions and that somewhere in my subconscious this voice would tell me what to do and where to go. Half the time I didn't know where I was, or what I was doing. All I ever wanted was to live a simple life in the country with a beautiful wife, and perhaps a couple of kids running about. I had seen couples like this. It did exist and yet even though I wanted it, it was the hardest thing for me to achieve. For one thing I hadn't met the right woman, and the other was that this path that my subconscious took me on led nowhere to the country, but on the contrary to New York City.

So now here I was – me in the mirror and the yellow image and at the same time none of that mattered. At this point in time I was free as one could be. It felt good to walk away or maybe I should say walk to another spot, much like going on a picnic, if one place didn't suit you then you pack up and go to another. Maybe I had done it in a previous life–travel to faraway places when it wasn't such a common thing to do, perhaps that's why I had this little emptiness inside me that longed for another time. I poked out my tongue at myself, pulled down my eyelids once again just to check, perhaps it had gone away, but everything was still the same. There wasn't much else to do but look in the mirror, it's a bit like when you get a haircut or shave off a beard or moustache, it's hard to pass a mirror without checking up on this new person, after all you might not like what you see - it takes a while to adjust. I wonder if many people stood in front of the mirror and examined themselves and talked to their own reflection. I like to think so. Mirrors, however always fascinated me, it was a bit like looking at the past, I always wanted to walk through one to the other side, to my past just to be able to see objectively what you did. I didn't particularly regret anything I had done, except a couple of things that could create a little bad karma for myself, but I won't go into that, it's just that I think a lot of people if they were able to see their past would perhaps have done things a little differently. There were always thousands of questions, but never any answers - there was just nothing in the end, just one big unresolved question. Why? - As they crowded around you dressed in black. I often wondered if you'd hear them all. I think many people have the fantasy of being dead and hearing them mourn over your dead body, or maybe you'd hear things like, "He was a real bastard, you know." Perhaps it's better if we don't hear. Then I wondered if maybe it was the hepatitis making me think this way, perhaps I were a little delirious, I had a fever. I began to feel tired and thought I should perhaps go into the bedroom that was the only room. The room was the usual Indian low rent room. Ugly green walls broken up by fallen plaster revealing white walls and brick beneath, and lit by a dreadful fluorescent light, which just made my illness look even more hideous. The place was pretty dirty like most of India, the bed was incredibly uncomfortable and the mattress had seen better days and as you got onto the bed it would tip over to one side, which made you feel a bit like being at sea. Ants crawled in formation at one corner of the room, made their way across the ceiling to the other corner where they would meet another platoon coming the other way,

182

and for a split second they would stop as if saluting each other and carry on. Occasionally a couple would drop on my head and face. There was nothing else to describe about the room except there was a ceiling fan that actually worked quite well, lowering the temperature to a balmy 100 degrees. The room was drab as I glided into my temporary home and collapsed on the bed, hot and sweaty and watched the fan as it revolved around and around - and then a voice said, "You are sleepy very sleepy"– my eyelids blinked a couple of times until they became too heavy to keep open and I was gone, gone to the land of Nod.

I slept and slept and slept. Then I woke up, I was in the same room that I went to sleep in, even though I was expecting to awaken back in New York or in Deborah's arms. I looked across at where Carlisle had been sleeping, his bed was empty and he had probably gone out for a walk, as I was not too much fun just sleeping all the time. I decided I should see a doctor, and one from the town came by and examined me in the room. I sat on the edge of the bed. He looked at my eyes, I poked out my tongue and he decided that I had the flu, and gave me a prescription that I had filled at the local chemist. I took the pills that where probably highly toxic, as India would get the drugs that were not proven and didn't meet the required standards in America and Europe. These pills probably made my condition even worse. So Carlisle and I decided to get out of town and go back to New Delhi. We took the train for a few hours and found a hotel near Connaught Circus, where I crashed out on yet another bed. I found another doctor in New Delhi, who told me immediately on seeing me that I had hepatitis, which I knew anyway. So my trip to see the Taj Mahal was cancelled it seemed for good, and Carlisle went to see it in Agra on his own, leaving me with more hallucinogenic fever dreams as my temperature rose into the hundreds.

I lay in bed all day as I had no energy, but managed to read 'The Snow Leopard' by Peter Matheson, which inspired dreams of the Himalayas and the illusive snow leopard that not many people have ever seen. Through my hazy eyes I could see a camel chewing on a palm leaf outside the window - yes I was still in India. The woman in the hotel was very kind and every day she would bring me a bowl of yogurt with honey and that was my diet for the next week or so. I had no appetite anyway and the yogurt seemed enough to sustain me. After a week I managed to get out of bed and walk around and I met someone who told me about the Tibetan Medical Institute here in New Delhi. I decided to go and check it out, after all what did I have to lose? So I jumped in one of the three-wheeler black and yellow taxi cabs that screeched around in every city, town and village of India and arrived at the Institute. I was introduced to the Tibetan doctor there, who could not speak a word of English, so had an interpreter with him. We walked into his surgery and the doctor looked at my eyes and felt the various pulses in my wrists. The interpreter told me that the doctor told him that indeed it was hepatitis, which I already knew from my own self-examination from day one. When the liver is not functioning properly it distributes what should normally be excreted out, around the body there by poisoning the system, so one's excrement turns white or grey in color, the urine turns a dark yellow, almost brown and the whites of the eyes are jaundiced which as we know turns them yellow. So what should be brown is white, and what should be white is yellow, and what should be yellow is brown, so basically putting it into layman's terms, I was fucked! So now it was time for me to take a pee into a bottle in the bathroom whilst the Tibetan doctor and interpreter waited outside. I was told to leave the bottle there, which I did and the doctor walked in, after I came out. I wondered what he was doing in there, when I heard a strange gargling sound and then the sound of someone spitting. I was told that is how doctors in the middle ages diagnosed people by gargling their urine thereby tasting how much salt or sugar is in their system, apparently this was what this doctor was doing and by doing that gave his diagnosis. The doctor came out and he said a few words in Tibetan to the translator and he told me that things were not so bad in so many words, and that it could have been a lot worse, but nevertheless I had all the symptoms of hepatitis and that I was going to live to see another day, especially after I take the prescription down to the in-house pharmacy. I thanked the doctor by means of the interpreter and the Tibetan gave me a lovely toothy smile and I was on my way.

I took the prescription to the pharmacy and in return they gave me a bag of what looked like rabbit-turds with pieces of hay or straw sticking out of the sides. I was to take two of these turds every morning with a nice cup of Darjeeling tea, just like having breakfast back in jolly olde England! And so I did, and not only did they look like rabbit turds - well you guessed it, not that I had eaten a rabbit's turd before. So I took this strange Tibetan medicine and Carlisle and I booked a flight to Srinigar in Kashmir. We wanted to go by train through the Punjab but there were skirmishes going on between the Hindus and Muslims or Sikhs, and fifteen people had recently been killed by indiscriminate firing by state police, and civilians had been shot by terrorists, so it was deemed unsafe to go by land, and so we flew there to the garden of India, where a few years later war was to break out between India and Pakistan over who owned the land. The Muslims wanted ethnic cleansing and targeted Kashmiri Pandits and a few years later an Urdu newspaper asked all Kashmiri Pandits to immediately leave the beautiful valley of Kashmir, and there was over time, an exodus of over half a million people.

So Carlisle and I flew to Kashmir. After we landed we caught a taxi into town and Carlisle jumped out at the Indian Airlines office to book his ongoing flight to Ladakh. The doctor advised me not to go there because of the altitude, as I was still under the weather being jaundiced, and not having too much energy. Srinigar was already at about 6,000 ft and Ladakh a few thousand feet more. So I sat in the taxi and as I did so, I noticed two Australian girls who we had spoken to earlier that flew up on the same plane. They were being hassled by about fifty men all wearing long pherans, who were surrounding them, offering them places to stay. There was a lack of tourism here because of the skirmishes in the Punjab, so the locals were desperate for money.

As I looked on I could see the girls were afraid, and so I opened the door of my cab and yelled and beckoned to them to get in, which they did and shut the door. Because I did this, all hell broke loose. The driver told me in English that the men were very upset, that I intervened in their affairs, and that I probably should have done nothing, but I felt I had to do something and couldn't let these women lose at the hands of these crazed men. By now the taxi was surrounded by about fifty men yelling at me, and shaking their fists and beckoning me to get out of the taxi. The driver told me not to move, that if I got out they might kill me. (Later I heard about an Australian man that was indeed killed by a similar incident a few weeks earlier). We locked the doors and suddenly the taxi was being rocked back and forth, and a couple of men had jumped onto the hood, others were banging on the windows screaming like madmen, and for the first time in my life I thought I might die - here in the foothills of the Himalayas. As I looked out the back window I could see two or three policemen with batons fighting their way through the crowd, but were able to do very little. The adrenaline was pumping through my veins and I felt like jumping out and telling them I was British, but would not have been for long as I would have been a deceased member of the Empire! What were we to do? The taxi was surrounded and couldn't move and the rocking of the cab continued till at one point I thought we would turn over. I looked to see if the girls were OK, but they were gone and only I remained and the crowds dispersed and the rocking stopped. Carlisle came out of the Indian Airlines Office and asked me what all the commotion was about that he had heard.

Me in Srinigar on a bridge over the river Jhelum

Kashmiri men wearing the Pheran

So that was my welcome to Kashmir, I don't know what happened to the girls, but there was no report in the paper, so I presumed they were eventually OK. Carlisle and I booked into a small hotel and I proceeded to tell him about what happened. The next day we got up early to catch the floating vegetable market on Lake Dal and I took a lot of photos with the misty Himalayas as a backdrop. It was peaceful on the lake and after we walked around the town over an old bridge that crossed the river Jhelum. It was quite cold there as it was still only April and the men sat around fires called kangris, which is an earthen pot filled with flaming coals, and some of the men had these under their pherans that were loose woolen coats that went down way below the knees to keep warm. There were only men everywhere and I don't think I saw a woman all day. Such is the way in this part of the world, where the majority are Muslim.

Kashmir is called the garden of India because it is very fertile and lush and green, not dry and dusty like Rajasthan. Srinigar is called 'The Jewel in the Crown of Kashmir.' It is very beautiful and picturesque, but I felt unsettled there and after a couple of days my traveling companion left for his adventure in Ladakh, and I stayed on for a day or two, but then caught the plane back to Delhi to continue my around the world Journey. I was now alone and of course for the next day or two I missed my traveling companion.

Lake Dal   Boats called Shikaras
with the Victorian houseboats in the background

Srinigar is situated at the foothills of the Himalayas and on Lake Dal that at one time was the summer capital of Jammu and Kashmir. The British built beautiful houseboats, which they called "a little piece of England afloat on Dal." I went into a tourist trinket shop there that looked over the River Jhelum and the man in the store told me that it was from the window where one of the last scenes from 'Passage to India' was filmed that was David Lean's last epic film. Lean was the master of film making, responsible for 'Lawrence of Arabia,' 'Doctor Zhivago' and 'Ryan's Daughter'.

New Delhi

I was beginning to feel a lot better although I still got quite tired especially in the heat of an up and coming summer, as by now it was April. I went out to buy a newspaper at the local newspaper stand and on the front page I read that a nuclear power plant had blown up in a place called Chernobyl in Russia, which caused the release of radioactive material that was blowing over a lot of Europe especially Scandinavia, and was the worst nuclear disaster to date. Hundreds of thousands of people were displaced from the area for hundreds of miles around. It was beginning to feel like the year of disasters as back in January the space shuttle Challenger exploded shortly after takeoff turning it into a ball of fire. The event was televised live around the world. NASA had apparently been warned about a design fault, but chose to ignore the warnings. An O - ring caused the fuel tank to become damaged that caused Challenger to explode and disintegrate in the air. I remember there was a woman teacher on board, but can't remember how many astronauts died with her. I was glad I was in India after hearing about the Chernobyl disaster and hoped that the fall out would not reach England. Off course this event reminded me of the Bhopal disaster in India back in 1984 where a gas leak from the Union Carbide factory, which was a pesticide plant exposed over half a million people to methyl isocyanate gas which was highly toxic. It was considered the world's worst industrial disaster. The government of Madhya Pradesh confirmed a total of 3,787 deaths, but others estimated that over eight thousand died within the next two weeks and since then another eight thousand died bringing the total number of deaths to almost twenty thousand, and yet very few people heard about it. Carlisle and I passed through the town on a train earlier on our trip from Madras.

In the town of Bhopal

I flew off to Bangkok on the next leg of my trip with my fingers crossed.

So I landed at Suvarnabhumi Airport in Bangkok and took a tuk-tuk, the three wheeled taxi cabs similar to what they have in India, except they seemed more souped - up than the Indian counterpart and screeched a lot louder. I found a room in a hostel type place on Khaosan Road where all the back-packers stayed for about $3 dollars a night. It was just a small room with a bed and the bathroom was down the hallway, which was shared with my fellow travelers. I did the usual tourist type things, like visiting the temples and the area of Pat Pong road that was a very sad state of affairs where pimps sold off young girls for sex. It became more famous by visiting US Marines on leave from Vietnam during the war.

Siam. *The Wat Phra Kaew Temple that houses the Emerald Buddha and is regarded as the most sacred temple in Thailand.*

The Golden Buddha at the Wat Traimat Temple.

It weighs 5.5 tons and is made of solid gold. It was lost for about 200 years as it was covered in a thick layer of stucco and plaster to hide it from the Burmese invaders in 1767. It remained amongst the ruins, until it was moved in the mid - fifties when a chunk of plaster fell off thus revealing the Golden Buddha beneath.

I had a few rabbit turds left that the doctor had given me from New Delhi and took them with me to the hospital in Bangkok where I was getting glucose shots to give me energy as I was still suffering from hepatitis. I showed them to the doctor there who was this lovely woman and she in turn showed them to another woman doctor, when on seeing this medicine broke into a good laugh. The two doctors examined the turds and shook their heads. They told me in broken English that they had no idea what this strange Tibetan medicine was. I finished up the rabbit turd medicine the next day with a nice cup of tea whilst sitting in a cafe on Khaosan Road. Whether the Tibetan medicine helped me or not, I have no idea, but I continued with the glucose shots for the next couple of days until I left Bangkok on an overnight bus to Phuket. There were armed guards that got on the bus as we neared Malaysia as there had been skirmishes down there between the Thai army and some separatist groups, that had been crossing the border into Thailand. Once on the island of Phuket I was beginning to feel more relaxed and had to find another place to stay for a week or two so as to convalesce from my illness. I was still jaundiced, the whites of my eyes were now a light shade of yellow, instead of a dark yellow that they were, but I felt like I was getting my energy back. I started to walk off towards the ocean when I got approached by a young Thai girl who asked me if I was looking for a place to stay and led me down this path into the jungle where there were little huts on either side. She showed me into one, which was basic with a bed and toilet outside and a shower. It was all I needed and agreed to take it. By now my Thai friend was beginning to flirt with me and asked if I wanted her to stay. I had a suspicion whilst walking down the path to the hut that something was amiss or should I say this was not a miss! Her hands were bigger than normal on a member of the opposite sex and the Adams Apple bounced up and down as my she-male friend spoke. This person was certainly attractive and I am sure that on many a night had fooled many a tourist that had had one too many into an awkward situation for some, or a fun evening for others. Needless to say I declined my newly found friend's offer and she left a little disappointed I think. I looked around my new residence and thought that I could find something a little better and closer to the beach.

It was now later in the afternoon, but the day still had a few more hours left. I decided to leave my backpack there by the side of the bed and take a walk down the path hoping it would lead me to the beach, which after about a ten-minute walk did. There in front of me was another exotic looking beach with waving palms and turquoise seas. I took a left turn and walked down the beach for a hundred yards or so when I saw a sign that said 'Happy Hut' on it with an arrow pointing back into the jungle. I followed the arrow for just a few yards and came upon these lovely little huts set back into the edge of the jungle surrounded by tall coconut palms and banyan trees. The place seemed quite deserted as it was nearing the end of the season, except for one fellow who was sitting on his porch smoking a pipe. He yelled and beckoned me over to his hut. His English was tainted with a heavy German accent. Gunter introduced himself and told me that the proprietor of the establishment would be back in half an hour. He was a very talkative chap, slim, about six feet tall and seemed quite well versed with English literature that he said he studied in Berlin. We seemed to hit it off immediately and while we were getting to be better acquainted the manager of Happy Hut came by after the German beckoned to her. I was introduced and decided that I would stay in one of these sweet little huts. It had a connecting bathroom and toilet that had no roof but was open to the stars. I paid her up front for the next week. This was the perfect place for me to recuperate. The woman left and the German produced a bong from behind his chair, loaded up with a good bud of Thai stick. He asked if I would like a puff or two to which I indulged in the sticky sweet plant, and blew the smoke into the sky that was now beginning to change color as the sun was slowly sinking. I thanked Gunter for his hospitality and help and thought it

196

best to return to my other hut back along the path into the jungle, before the sun set. I had secured my new place with a good payment and decided to spend the night back in my original place that I had already paid for. I waved goodbye to Gunter and walked along the beach feeling high as a kite.

The Thai stick was beginning to take effect as the sky was growing darker and it seemed like the topography of the place had changed and I couldn't for the life of me decide what path I had ventured to the beach on. I took one and it didn't seem right, so back tracked to a fork on the path, then tried another, but nothing seemed familiar to me or perhaps it was that everything looked the same, and I couldn't tell one path from the other and I was beginning to regret smoking that stuff! Now it was quite dark - the sun seemed to just drop out of the sky suddenly and it was gone for the day. I started to get a little worried that I may never see my backpack again and was beginning to get a little paranoid because of the smoke that I had inhaled earlier. I took a deep breath and counted to ten when my she-male friend appeared from behind another hut, where maybe she was living. She knew I was lost and gave me a big smile and at that moment she was the best thing I could have seen. She grabbed my hand for a little while and pointed to my hut that was only a few yards away. I thanked my she-male friend and she walked off into the direction of the beach.

The next morning I grabbed my backpack and walked down the path that I had walked down the day before, arrived at the beach then took a left turn and saw the sign for 'Happy Hut.' Happy was a term used quite a bit in Thailand - there was 'Happy Endings' that you could get at 'Happy Hut' if one so desired. I picked out the hut that I wanted, as there were quite a few that were empty, as it was the end of the season and the rains would be coming soon. I threw my pack into the corner and laid down on the bed as I watched a gecko scamper into the palm leaf roof. Maybe he was going to be my roommate for the next couple of weeks?

The next day I decided to go into town to get some provisions for my new place to make it homey. I was feeling a lot stronger now and my jaundiced eyes were almost white again, as I thought about the rabbit turd medicine that I was given as I walked into the market place. I bought some pillows and soap and shampoo and a mug or two for a nice cuppa and some fabric that I would drape from the beams in the ceiling, to add to that eastern feel. I loaded them all into a bag and began my journey back to Happy Hut, feeling rather pleased with my purchases, when all of a sudden I felt this pain on my right buttock and turned around to find a dog standing there, panting with its tongue hanging out the side of its mouth. It was a straggly looking canine with brown fur and a wild mad look in its eyes. I kicked out my leg to send him on his way but he just stood there challenging me. I did it again, my leg making contact under his jaw this time. The mangy looking dog yelped and cowered back, then turned as he had met his match with the Englishman. This was certainly a case of 'Mad dogs and Englishmen go out in the midday sun.' I was praying that this dog was not mad and that he didn't have rabies, as I knew what the series of shots consisted of.

I continued my journey back to my new residence, walked up the stairs to my hut and threw my purchases on the bed. I was anxious to look at my arse, to see what damage the mangy dog had done. I went into the bathroom, took off my shorts, then took the mirror off the wall, and took on a yoga pose as I turned to look at the bite, like a contortionist, trying to turn my head around like the girl in the exorcist. I just managed to see the damage that man's best friend had done. The dog had certainly pierced the skin and I wondered what kind of bacteria and crap was on its teeth. I decided to deal with the problem first thing in the morning and went over to see Gunter who already had the bong up to his lips. He asked me where I had been all day and I told him of my adventure. "You better have some of this," he said as he handed me the bong loaded with Thai stick. I took a good dose as I wanted to forget about the mad dog, and then Gunter asked to see the wound on my arse. He took a look and put some antiseptic on it. I was hoping that no one was passing by, as it must have looked a little strange from a distance, one man putting his arse in the face of another like this on a sunny afternoon. This was Thailand however, and I am sure the locals had seen a lot stranger things than this. Gunter told me that my bum had been punctured and that I should get it checked out at the hospital first thing tomorrow, which is what I had already decided to do.

Gunter had been living in Thailand for the past five months and he returned every year. He was quite the authority on Thailand and it's culture and seemed to think that the dog didn't have rabies. I must admit he made me feel a little better about that as I took another hit of the bong along with a shot of the local brandy. By the time I returned to my happy hut I was in another state of being and slept through the night with dreams of packs of mad dogs chasing me. I woke up feeling exhausted from running all night and got myself ready for my trip to the local hospital.

I went to the emergency part and walked right in. I told two lovely Thai nurses what had happened and they started to laugh, then laughed even more once I pulled my pants down. I was just another crazy Farang (a term used for Europeans and maybe whites in general). One of them cleaned it up and it stung like hell and the other gave me a tetanus shot, although I think I may have had one about a year ago, but another couldn't hurt. I paid them in Baht, thanked them after they thought that it would be unlikely that I had rabies, but to keep my eye on it which was difficult, as I would have to do the exorcist thing again, and didn't want to ask Gunter either, as he may think I was beginning to like more than just his company.

After a while I started to bark like a dog and ate my meals on all fours out of a dog's bowl. OK - so that's a joke! But apparently when people have full - blown rabies they do bark like a dog. (Hence the term - barking mad!) The remedy for rabies is a series of thirteen shots to the stomach, or so I was told - not a pleasant experience. After a week I had forgotten about mad dogs, but every time I walked to the village from that point on I would be looking all around me, and carried rocks in my pocket like I did in India to throw at the beasts if they came anywhere near me.

After being at Happy Hut about three weeks I went out to one of the local bars. I still wasn't drinking, so I ordered a Coke, not a drink I would normally have. There were a few girls at the bar and one came over to talk to me in her broken English. I bought her a drink and she seemed quite sophisticated, not like a lot of the girls that hung out in the bars down Pat Pong road in Bangkok. At the end of the evening she came back to Happy Hut with me where she spent the night. She was quite beautiful and probably in her mid-thirties. In the morning she asked me for money, to which I refused, as she never mentioned it the night before, and I really didn't think she was a prostitute. I thought she genuinely liked me for my English wit and charm and so felt slighted that I was just another monetary transaction thereby hurting my British pride. She asked me again for money, with a big smile on her face, and with a big smile on mine I said "no". At this point she went into a rage and tore up my 'Guinness is Good for You' t-shirt and left down the steps to the beach. I sat on the bed looking at my torn t-shirt. I loved that shirt that had traveled to many different countries with me, now here it was in shreds.

A couple of nights later I went back to the bar where I had met my true love and was in a conversation with a chap from Newcastle, who had a strong Geordie accent. We were swopping traveling stories about India. He was a bit of a rough lad, but a good sort, a working class hero with a sense of adventure. He didn't realize it at the time but he was soon to get a bit of adventure here in this bar. It came to be joke-telling time and I had him laughing over one that I kept in my repertoire. Out of the corner of my eye on the other side of the bar I spied my true love from the other night. I pretended not to see her, but for some reason I glanced back at her and about six feet from me I saw a beer bottle flying through the air aimed at my head - I ducked instinctively and it hit my Geordie friend on the noggin and knocked him off his seat. I turned to look back at the woman but she was gone. My newly found friend was OK, as he had a head as hard as a breezeblock, but was definitely dazed and kept repeating, "What the fuck, what the fu, fuck, what was that, fuck!" as he was rubbing his head. I tried to explain the circumstances of the incident, but he decided that I was not a safe person to be with and I never saw him again. I began to wonder why I was having such a hard time making friends. A local Thai boy told me that if you insult or hurt a Thai person they will hold a grudge and get vengeance on you. The next day I left Phuket fearing for my life at the hands of a mad woman, and took a boat to Ko Phi Phi Island, which was about twenty-five miles South-East of Phuket and boasts one of the oldest communities in Thailand. It is a beautiful island with Limestone Mountains and cliffs and caves and long white sandy beaches. There was a beach called Monkey Beach, where you had to keep an eye on your belongings as the monkeys would run off with whatever you had around. I met a couple of people who had their cameras stolen by the little thieves. I cooled off on this island and stayed away from the Thai girls, where I began to center myself once again before the next part of my journey.

Bali Indonesia

I finally made it to Bali with dreams of meeting a native girl and falling in love with her, having children, and living in paradise for the rest of my days. I made my way from Denpasar to Legian, next to Kuta beach that was where all the Aussies hung out, and found a place to stay as soon as I got to town, dumped off my bag, then went out for a bite to eat. I found a place called Goa, which sounded good to me, and was ready to meet the girl of my dreams. I sat down at a table and ordered a curry - I was starving, as I hadn't eaten all day. It seemed like I grabbed the last empty table as the place was filling up. I ordered a beer, probably something like a Tiger beer - took a swig, and was now feeling relaxed after a day of traveling. A blonde Australian girl walked in, whom was a little over weight with a pretty face. There were no seats left and she asked if she could sit at my table. "Of course," I said, and added that I would be pleased of the company. She ordered a beer and drank it fast, and then another as I was still on my first. "I'm so bloody thirsty, mate," she said, and I just nodded. We chatted for a while, in between mouthfuls of rice and after her fourth beer started to get quite flirtatious with me, which I was not expecting, as all I could think about was my Balinese princess. I didn't need to get involved with a westerner at this point so was trying to just smile and be courteous, when suddenly in the middle of a fairly normal conversation she blurted out, "I'm on the blob right now, but you can shove it up me shitter if yer like?" I put my fork down as I almost choked on a piece of chicken, then thanked her most heartily for her very generous offer that I had to decline. I began to wonder what kind of upbringing this Sheila had? She seemed like a nice girl at the start of the evening, until she made that remark, and it seemed like the

202

demon alcohol was beginning to get rid of all her inhibitions. She was obviously very generous in offering up her collection of orifices to someone she had just met, but I told her that I was going to go back to my place, to lay on my bed and just look at the stars as I was feeling a little tired. She seemed a little upset that I never took her up on her offer. We said goodnight and I went home to my new abode, and did lie on my bed and look at the stars and wondered what happened to my new romantic life here with my Balinese princess.

The next day I awoke after a good night sleep under the mosquito net and thought about the Australian girl that I had met last night and wondered if I actually attracted a certain type of female, that were either sex mad or just mad. My journey so far had not been boring and even when I was trying to mind my own business trouble seemed to find me. Dada Viswani once said "Don't trouble trouble, unless trouble troubles you" well trouble did seem to be troubling me and wondered if I could have a chat with him about this predicament that I seemed to be finding myself. For instance I didn't ask for that dog in Thailand to come and bite me on the bum, so then I had to put it down to karma. I was a nice person and hoped that I still was and didn't remember anything particularly bad that I had done to anyone. I thought that maybe I should just stay off the streets and out of bars for a while, or perhaps I needed the refuge of an ashram.

After an uneventful couple of weeks I was sitting in a bar somewhere in Bali when an Australian guy approached me as if he knew me and gave me a wide opened look like I was a long lost friend. I must admit he did look a little familiar to me - that is what happens on the road- it is an appreciation of a kindred spirit that is recognizable almost immediately. He walked over to the table and said, 'I know you don't I?' I replied that I didn't think so, and yet he did look familiar. He asked if he could join me at my table, to which I replied a quick, "Of course." He introduced himself as Tommy White and I told him my name. He grabbed the waiter's attention and immediately ordered two beers, one for me, and one for himself. I thanked him for the beer, we clinked our glasses together and right on cue said, "cheers."

We started to swop traveling stories and Tommy told me in his broad Aussie accent that he was born in England, in the West Country and when he was twelve years old his parents took a ship to Australia, with young Tommy of course. They emigrated there as part of a government scheme to get people to move and work there. The Commonwealth countries were still being developed and needed a huge work force of artisans, of plumbers and brickies, builders, carpenters, roofers etc. basically a labour force that could build houses and factories. During the sixties, families left England for a new life in New Zealand, Canada and Rhodesia and of course Australia and all it cost was ten pounds to be paid to the government. For that price you would be found accommodation and a job, but you would have to stay a minimum of two years. If one left before that time, you would forfeit the deal and would have to pay the price of the passage back to the government. In a way this was one of the best all - inclusive life changing deals of the time.

Families left the working class areas of terraced houses, with grey slate roofs under grey cloudy skies for the sun and heat and space that Australia had to offer. Some families returned back to England, as they missed those grey skies and green fields of the English countryside, but on the whole I think most stayed. Of course there were those who chose to go to Canada and didn't consider the harsh cold Canadian winters. New Zealand of course had a fairly mild climate probably the closest to England out of all the commonwealth countries. My sister had two friends that migrated to Rhodesia, and had a farm there and had the most luxurious life. So this was Tommy's story, a twentieth century version of being shipped off to Australia, unlike the convicts that were shipped off to Botany Bay a hundred years and more before.

After babbling on for an hour or so and a table laden with empty beer bottles we were both in hysterics laughing at I can't remember what, but it did seem like he was an old mate, and he was after all from the old country. So after a series of questions like did you know such and such, or what's her name from you know where, we decided that we had never met before, which was sort of obvious as he had been in Australia most of his life and I had been in England and America. Then he tells me of his travels in the north of Thailand up near Chang Mai and Chang Rai and produces a photo of a women from his inside pocket whilst explaining to me how he met her. As soon as the photo hit the table I recognized the women immediately. "That's Noga!" I said, in a high pitched voice, as I even surprised myself. "You know her?" said the Aussie. So then I went on to explain that she had worked on a film with me in Mexico the year before. So there you have it, the serendipity of travel. Although we had never met, the theory of six degrees of separation came in to play, and we both thought how extraordinary this meeting had become and we became good pals after this. So Tommy and I hung out together for the next few days, drinking and guffawing like good old colonial boys should, until he thought the time was right to tell me of another of his amazing stories, the one of which he was still living.

In the seventies Tommy tells me, he was working for the Australian government as a cartographer, plotting maps and that sort of thing when he got an assignment to fly into New Guinea into a village in the middle of the jungle, in the middle of nowhere. So he and three or four other guys landed by helicopter out of the sky, out of the heavens, like gods, into a clearing in this village to map out the surrounding area. The tribesmen and women were in awe of these gods who came from the heavens and were scared and inquisitive at the same time. These gods were wearing strange costumes, with floppy hats covering their heads and big leather wrappings around their feet that ended almost at the knee. After the initial shock and the giving of gifts were over Tommy and Bruce and Lindsey or whatever their names were, were accepted and revered by the tribe. These people had never seen white men before and certainly not arriving from the sky. After the work had been done and they were due to go back to Sydney, Ted told me that he decided to stay there as he had found himself a nice Sheila there in the tribe, and in the meantime they had made him a King. The others flew back into the heavens, as Tommy told me and he stayed as their King. While he is telling me this amazing story he produces some black and white photos of a couple of his wives, with himself sitting between them. "Come on mate, why don't you come back with me - we could make you a prince and you could have yerself a couple of good looking Sheilas on yer arm."

Well once again the table at whatever bar we were at was strewn with empties and the demon alcohol had once again changed my perspective of things, the Dutch courage had taken over, and I was considering his proposition. I had been on the road for at least seven months at this point, had contracted hepatitis, was bitten by a dog, and had a beer bottle thrown at me by a crazed angry Thai woman, so I thought why not. I was not the same person that I was when I had started this journey, and shouldn't life be an adventure, as I was beginning to convince myself more and more of my new calling in life. I imagined myself sitting on a throne with a crown on my head, with a bunch of wives around me pandering to my every need and whim, I could be a new page in a Rudyard Kipling book, a story to tell the folks back home, an adventure way out of the norm. Drake, prince of Ugga Ugga Land or whatever the village was called.

The imagination was running wild as I heard the sound of drums being beaten by calloused black hands and men and women worshipping at my feet, as I sat with a gold staff in my hand, and that crown on my head and women singing my praises as they danced in full regalia with plumed headgear, the men doing the same as they banged their feet on the ground and chanted my name as they worshipped this white god from the heavens. And then I had another beer and suddenly the dream changed as I saw myself being boiled in a big pot, soon that white meat to be a feast for the tribe. I was glassy eyed and Tommy asked me if I was feeling OK.

"So what do yer think cobber, can yer see yerself there?"

My dream had turned to horror, as I thought of Colonel Kurtz who had lost his mind up the river of no return.

"Oh we'd have a ball mate, the Sheilas would love yer" I heard Tommy say somewhere off in the distance, as he shook my arm to bring me back to reality wherever that was.

"I'll have to think about it," I said.

On top of the volcanic Mount Agung

The next week I rented a beautiful little cottage with a veranda that overlooked a river with the rice terraces in the background. The cottage was traditional Balinese style made from big bamboo poles with a thatched roof and interior trimmings made from coconut wood and teak. This was to be my home for the next week or so where I would scribble down notes about my existence on this Earth. I bought provisions for my temporary home from the town of Ubud and made it back without being bitten by any mad dogs or wild women. I had decided to be a recluse for the next week and only go out to see other humans when necessary. At night I would light the candles and sit on the veranda in my bamboo rocking chair and look up at the star studded sky that was not polluted by the lights of Ubud as I was sufficiently far enough away from the town.

I began to examine my life once more and realized that a man's relationship with supreme isolation springs forth from the emptiness of being, and from that isolation emerges inspiration and imagination resulting in creativity. I was happy with my thoughts, as they were mine, and nobody else's. There were times when I felt like a cursed King, exiled from his kingdom to spend the rest of his days in this supreme monk like existence. The only person to talk to was myself, or I would talk to the rocks and the trees, which never argued with me. I was content at this moment in time and felt pleased with my journey so far, despite being infected by hepatitis. My health was getting better each day as I was not drinking again except on two occasions with Tommy! My existence was dreamlike and inexplicable. I was on an existential journey through time and space.

I needed this time alone here as I felt that there was not much mystery left in travel as so many places had been turned into tourist destinations. I smiled to myself as I listened to the squawks and trills and primeval sounds from the jungle - like forest and imagined myself a traveler from centuries past. I used to carry The I Ching (the Chinese book of Changes) when I traveled in my twenties. Now I was more certain of my decisions and felt like I had no need to consult anything or anyone. A little advice was always accepted of course, but there was no ideology or religion that I would adhere to, except some teachings from the Buddha that was all basically common sense.

I remembered a line from one of Kahlil Gibran's poems from the wonderful day and night that I had spent with the mystical and magical Deborah Rebecca Jones. The line was: 'You talk when you cease to be at peace with your thoughts.' Well I seemed at peace and the talking I did was only to myself. There were times when I felt sad and forlorn, but realized it was just a part of the human condition, so I would immerse myself into that sadness and realize I was feeling the sadness of the world, and that I was a part of this world, even though I wanted to escape from it at times. I thought about Deborah and our strange but lovely relationship and wondered what she was doing at this time. I sent her a postcard from Kerala in India and hoped that she received it. I thought about all the islands in the world that I had visited and began to make a list as I listened to the singing from the jungle.

I was attracted to islands because I was born on one. It was an island probably about the same size as New York State that floated out there alone just twenty miles from the coast of France. I wondered if my enjoyment from being alone had anything to do with the fact that I was born on this island called England, which was broken off from Europe and isolated in its own stubborn way. I finished my list of islands from Crete in Greece to the Cyclades Islands, the Ionian Islands and many more that were scattered like jewels in the Mediterranean. I continued with the islands of the Caribbean from Tortola down to Barbados and Hawaii and Tahiti and even the Isle of Wight in the English Channel and the Isle of Man where they held the motorcycle TT racing. I wondered if I had become an Isle of Man myself, as I seemed to be cutting myself of from so - called civilization day by day. I then laughed at Tommy's offer of him making me a Prince in New Guinea and on that thought I went to bed under the mosquito net and traveled as the earth slept.

June 5th Thursday

I have rented a 125cc Yamaha motorbike from Kuta Beach. Since the 29th May I have been touring Bali. I reached Ubud last Friday after an hour and a half ride and checked into a beautiful room about 1Km out of town, overlooking the rice fields. They wanted 9,000 rupiah, for the room but I managed to knock the price down to 6,000 rupiah - just under $6.00. For the next four days I explored the hills in and around Ubud visiting beautiful waterfalls, rice fields and incredible vistas. I visited a beautiful little town where there was a public bathing pool, where the locals took their baths. There I met two brothers who were

209

selling some land for $10 a square meter, that overlooked a river. I stayed in Ubud two more days than planned as I heard about a cremation down the road from Ubud that I wanted to see, as it was a public event. The body was placed inside of a wooden horse, like the wooden horse of Troy and underneath they lit a fire.

I saw a Legong dance performed by young Balinese girls in beautiful Balinese costumes. Bali is steeped in magic and the locals can be quite superstitious and many important decisions are not made without consulting the priests. The Balinese do not go into the rice fields after midnight as they believe the spirits live there and I was told that some locals had seen fire balls rolling through the fields, which they believe are indeed spirits. I left Ubud on Tuesday morning and headed for Candidasa on the South East coast where I rented a room for 3,000 rupiah a night in a place called Kelapa Mas that was practically on the beach.

I am staying in a losman in Besakih in the hills and listen as two young sisters sing sweetly in the courtyard, as a boy and a girl sit quietly in the shade playing chess, as two other kids play badminton out in the street. The Balinese are a lovely people, they always seem happy and content with life and the children amuse themselves as they play with each other, laughing and smiling till the end of day.

In Kintamani I listened to the prayers to Allah as it is now the beginning of Ramadan. I left Kintamani early the next morning on my rented Yamaha and journeyed through the mountains, past little villages and peasants attending to their daily chores as kids balanced colorful buckets of water on their heads going who knows where? Women old and young work in the rice fields as men talk to each other by the roadside.

I decided to climb to the top of Mount Agung the sacred mountain in the centre of Bali that the Balinese believe is the navel of the Universe. So with the help of a couple of young guides we left at about two in the morning from Pura Pasar to make the climb so as to reach the top by dawn. I didn't take the right clothing with me and by the time we had reached the top at almost 10,000ft I was almost freezing to death. The volcano is still active and in 1963- 64 it erupted killing about 1500 people in the lava flow. We made it back down and I was exhausted and slept for about a day as I realized that I still hadn't fully recovered from hepatitis.

Mount Agung lay behind me now as I climb into another range of mountains. The daylight is blue because of the low clouds as rain hangs high in the air, as a black cloud blows across my path ahead of me, as I was expecting to get soaked. It was cold in the mountains and I was wearing practically all my t-shirts one on top of the other and then a long sleeved shirt over those. The ride through the mountains was exciting. The mountain people were different to the ones at the coast. They seemed less friendly and weary and suspicious of strangers and at times almost hostile. Travelers merely pass through their villages, so there is little or no communication with foreigners. The mountain people are descendants of the original Bali Agee people who were the original Balinese. After coming over the mountains I arrived in Singaraja the biggest town on the north coast, then following the road along the coast I found myself in Kalibukbuk, where I found accommodation for 3,000 rupiah a night at the Kalibukbuk Beach Inn, which seemed to be the going rate for a basic room. The beach here is narrower than at Candidasa and is made up of black volcanic ash. I had a meal of sweet and sour fish which was quite tasty, then took a shower and threw all my dirty clothes into a pile on the floor, and as I did so a terrible sense of loneliness overtook me as I stood and looked at the crumpled pile as I realized that my life lay in there somewhere. I had no one to talk to, as I seemed to be the only western traveler here. Most westerners didn't leave Kuta Beach or Ubud and it was also the off - season. I thought about my ex-girlfriends and my trip with Abby to Sri Lanka and knew that had I been here with Abby I would not be feeling so lonely. Then once again I wondered what I was doing here on this black beach alone on the north shore of Bali.

I was to be thirty-six next birthday and here in Bali as in many other places I could have had children of eighteen or sixteen years of age, but I didn't. I began to wonder about destiny again and took a walk along the black volcanic beach and sat down under a palm tree. After a few minutes I heard a thud and a large coconut hit the sand a foot from my head. If it had hit me on the head I could have been knocked out or even killed. I thought about the headlines in the paper - 'ENGLISHMAN KILLED BY COCONUT IN BALI'. I thought about destiny again and knew that my time was not yet up, as a foot of space separated me from life and death. I remember reading in the paper a while ago, of a man who had been struck by lightning seven times and lived to tell the tale! Something in the cosmos was trying to tell me something as I moved away from under the tree. The sun was hot and the black beach showed no mercy. Two straggly looking canines, sniffed at each other as they dragged their carcasses along the beach as I remembered the dog that bit me in Thailand. A pregnant lady undressed not too far from me, as soon a Balinese baby would be dropped into the world to laugh and cry to live and die.

The locals stare at the foreigner, as they wonder why he comes here alone, to sit on this black beach. The pregnant lady ties up her hair, her teeth brilliant white against her dark smiling face. Four children gather around her, as I wonder if they all belong to her. As I look up again, the children are naked and walk into the sea. The woman is naked except for her sarong. Her breasts are big and swelling as she sits in the sea and pours sea - water over her head, smiling and laughing all the time as the children play about her. How can life be so bloody simple and why are they all so happy? I ask myself. I look at the mother again - she is no older than twenty-five. She sits with her children as I sit alone. I think too much and she doesn't have to. Her life is much simpler than mine. I began to feel better as I looked around me. Two more volcanoes like brother and sister appeared through the clouds. They were not there a few minutes ago. Miracles can happen. The coconut that just missed my head was a miracle. Two fat Americans break the silence, their voices crack the harmony of the moment - my moment, I don't know where they came from, but they are not miracles! I got up from where I was sitting and walked further down the beach, as my legs were beginning to come back to life after the climb to the top of Mount Agung.

Last night I heard the prayers to Allah from the local mosque. As I sat down a young handsome boy sat next to me and offered me some fruit to buy. I bought a couple of bananas and then he started to sing 'Three Blind Mice' to me. I realized then that my mood had changed 180 degrees as the sun began it's descent into the Java Sea.

Tuesday June 10th

I sent off a birthday card to my sister today, tomorrow she will be forty years old. Somehow I don't think that she will get it on time.

The view from my cottage overlooking the rice terraces

Time For Battle

Drake sat upon the top of Mount Agung

Way above the clouds

Looking at the coastline of Bali

Floating like a gem in the Java Sea.

He knew what it was like to stand on the bow of a boat

Hand upon the hilt of his sword

With the wind blowing in his hair

Arriving in new lands

On distant shores.

What a feeling!

The feeling of discovery

He wanted to discover his soul again

And wanted his pound of flesh

He was ready to do battle again

He was ready to die with a sword in his hand

And go to Valhalla

Heads were going to roll.

Bali summer, 1986

Lala Land. The Fall of 1986

This is a letter that I wrote to my dear old Ma, that I never mailed!

My dear Mrs. Drake,

Finally I have reached the shores of America, after crossing the great Pacific Ocean as Magellan and Drake had done four hundred years before. Unfortunately I flew instead of sailing. I left Sydney about three weeks ago, after short stays in Tahiti, which I found to be very expensive and a week or so in Hawaii. I sit now in a friend's house overlooking Mandeville Canyon and the coast of Santa Monica and Catalina Island way in the distance. My friend points out Frankie Avalon's house to me across the ridge, as I remember 'Beach Blanket Bingo' and films like it from the sixties.

This then is Lala Land, the land of make believe, Mickey Mouse, celebrities - a dime a dozen, fast expensive cars and women with abnormal sized breasts, that are creations by plastic surgeons. The car is worshipped here, so too money.

Meanwhile here I sit outside a million dollar home in one of the more exclusive parts of LA, writing to me old mum, whilst listening to Indian music on my headphones and remembering the look of a smiling, starving Indian girl with the most beautiful big brown eyes. My friend sits inside the house typing a script for United Artists. A part of India swims in my blood after contracting hepatitis in Rajasthan as I look back on my around the world journey. As I look in another direction I see a house built in the style of a castle. My friend tells me that it has tennis courts and a swimming pool and even an indoor bowling alley. The homes all around here are large - large enough to house a dozen Indian families each.

I lie back in my reclining chair and feel the hot sun on my face, the same sun that I worshipped in India. I drift off into a dream state as memories of a fan revolved above my head as I squint to look at it through jaundiced eyes - the whites of my eyes the color of a lemon.

215

I remember the beggars, some with no legs, propelling themselves along on a handmade skateboard. Where an eye should be there is only an empty space. I saw lepers where the nose had been rotted away and a mouth with no lips. I saw men with no arms, people with no legs. I saw blind beggars weaving their way in between the stalled traffic, being led by small children. I saw so many people close to death and yet there was still a strong feeling of spirituality. These poor people needed all the gods they could get as they worshipped in the temples to Ganesh and Krishna and Shiva and a host of others, hoping and praying that their next life will be a better one.

A Spitfire from WWII buzzes the canyon, as I am broken from my dream state. My friend tells me that the Spitfire belongs to Cliff Robertson, the actor. It only takes money to be who you want to be here in Lala land. The price of fame however was sometimes too high and many wanabees ended up dead from drug over-doses or alcohol and sometimes just good old - fashioned murder. I decided I didn't need fame at that price. The smell of eucalyptus entered my nose as I was reminded of when I was a baby and almost dying of whooping cough. I remembered having to breath in those fumes in a dark bedroom in the North of London. Now the smell was pleasant and didn't need it to save my life. I thought of the burning bodies on the banks of the Ganges as the Spitfire came by for another pass of the canyon. I wondered if he might spray the houses with machine gun fire next! I stretched myself out on the lawn chair and felt like I had escaped death once again and realized how fortunate I was. I had no money except a thousand dollars in the bank in New York, no work, and no real home to speak of and yet I felt complete. The trip to India had broadened my mind and perspective on life, and I was ready to go on living.

Only two months before I was in Bali and had a servant and a Javanese actress for a girlfriend. I never wanted much from life. Simple living and high thinking said the Buddha. I felt contented and pleased with my adventure and thought about the days when men were press ganged into the Royal Navy and went to sea for the rest of their lives.

I had been to the East and now once again I was back in the West, in fact the very epitome of the Western world with its material wealth and power and everything seemed to be here except a soul! I missed the little kids of India that had been replaced by snot nosed spoilt little buggers of LA. There was probably not a greater contrast in culture and life than LA and any Indian City, such as Bombay or Delhi. It takes extremes to realize what we have or what we want or don't want in life. Travel can create knowledge and experience and also confusion. It was easy for me now to look back on India as I basked away the afternoon laying on a lawn chair, with a beer in my hand. Paradise was a place invented by Catholics as an alternative to hell. By being a good person, one place would save you from the other.

To be continued… Your son John xx

I found this letter a few years later that was scribbled in an Indian notebook. I can't remember much more about Los Angeles, but within the week I found myself back in New York where my journey around the world had begun.

After finally getting back to New York I had to readjust to the western world again and the hustle and bustle of the big city. An old girlfriend was having a Halloween fancy dress party, so I went as a mad cow. (The mad cow disease had been identified in the UK and thousands of bovines were being put down). So I managed to find a rubberized cow's head and a straight-jacket which wasn't too hard to find as most of my friends were nuts! So that is how I went to the party, but the only trouble was that my hands were tied behind my back, so to be able to take a drink someone would have to place the drink in my hand and I had a long straw from the glass to my mouth. After a while I got someone to untie my arms, as beer from a straw didn't taste too good. It was a fun party and I was applauded for my ingenuity!

So that ended the year of 1986, as Mike Tyson became the youngest heavyweight champion in history, Oprah Winfrey show debuted and smoking was banned from public transportation on planes, buses and trains thank god! The Bangles 'Walk Like an Egyptian' came out and Aliens scared the living daylights out of everyone when the 'Alien' came bursting out of John Hurt's stomach!

Back in the Apple '86

After flying back to the Big Apple from the plastic land of Los Angeles I settled back into life in the big city once again. I didn't know it at the time but by this time next year I would be living in LA. If only there was such a thing as a crystal ball that could really see one's future? I had met a couple of sardhus in India this past year that told me a thing or two about my past, just from the lines on my face, but what did the future hold in store for me? I began to wonder if people knew what day or in what year they would die if they would suddenly change what they were doing. I don't think that I would change anything, perhaps give up work altogether if I had the money and just keep traveling. I realized that it was not the things that I did that I regretted, but it was the things that I didn't do that haunted me more.

I had written a couple of letters and three or four postcards to Deborah on my travels from Bombay and Rajasthan, Thailand and Bali and she had written back to 'Poste Restante', to a couple of post offices one being in Bangkok. Obviously it was easier for me to contact her, as I was a man with no fixed abode. She had told me in her letters that she was once again living back in Paris, but was beginning to spend more time in the south of France. I wondered where she was now and I gave myself a couple of days to re-adjust to the hustle and bustle of New York. I couldn't wait to see Deborah and to tell her of my experiences of the past few months. It felt good to be back and I felt secure in my old tenement apartment on dear old Sullivan Street. I called Deborah a couple of times the following day but there was no answer - maybe she was still somewhere in France. I felt anxious that she was not around and a little concerned about her. I knew she was a strong-minded woman, but I also knew of her sensitive side and weaknesses.

218

I telephoned her the following day again, but there was still no answer and no answering machine. A couple of more days went by and I tried to contact her again, but with no response.

By now a week or so had gone by, so I decided to go around to her loft. I looked up and I thought I saw a light on. I buzzed the buzzer and waited, but still there was no response. I had a feeling though that someone was there, so I walked down the street and called again from a call box. The phone rang five, six, seven times and then a women's voice said hello. I was relieved- I loved the sound of her voice, it was a voice from another world.

"Lady Deborah, is that really you?'' The voice answered,

"It's her sister, is this John?" she asked.

"Come back to the door and ring the doorbell and I will buzz you in."

She sounded just like her sister and I wondered if she was playing a joke on me. The lift shuddered to a halt and a woman's hand slide open the metal gate and for an instant I thought I was looking at the woman I loved. She looked almost exactly like Deborah, a little taller and a little older, although she was ten years her senior. There was a strange sadness about her as she introduced herself to me. "I'm Marie, Deborah's sister," she said as we shook hands. She pointed to the oversized couch for me to sit down, the couch where Miss Jones and I made love on about eight months ago. Marie took a deep breath, then sighed, she need not have said anything, as I knew what she was going to tell me. "My sister is no longer with us, she passed away six weeks ago."

I couldn't talk and my eyes teared up and then I just bawled my eyes out as I cradled my head in my hands. Marie sat on the couch next to me and held me in her arms and we cried together. It was as if Deborah was now Marie as I felt her spirit enter through her sister. Marie then proceeded to tell me what happened, that Deborah had contracted this strange illness when she was a child and was told that she didn't have

219

long to live. She did live however and lived on and with grace for many years beyond all the doctors and experts predictions. I was not completely surprised, as I always knew from our conversations that Deborah was quite aware that one day she would not be with us. I also at the same time could not believe that I would never see this interesting beautiful woman again, that had a life force so strong, that it had now been taken from her in her prime. Marie told me that they had a funeral for Deborah in Paris, which was her favorite city in the world. Then she gave me a box and told me that Deborah wanted me to have it. I opened the box and it was the Eye of Horus that she always wore around her neck. Then she handed me the Ravi Shankar album that we listened to when she became Parvati on that wonderful rainy stormy day in the loft where I was now sitting.

"She wanted you to have these," she said, and kissed me on both cheeks.

"I didn't know - I should have been there with her," I said.

Marie told me that it was a shock to everyone and that it all happened so fast. I thanked her, and then Marie told me that Deborah used to mention me to her from time to time. We hugged and said it was good to meet each other but would have been better under different circumstances. She opened the gate for me, and as I looked at her I saw Deborah standing there, and then she was gone as I descended into what seemed a living hell.

I walked down Sixth Avenue in a daze as I remembered the time when I became Ali and Deborah, Parvati. I remembered how wonderful I felt when I left her loft on that beautiful Monday morning after the stormy Sunday. I remembered how I walked north to the Museum of Modern Art and now I was walking south for no particular reason. The difference from how I felt from that time to this time was literally like night and day. It was daytime, but it was dark, darker than the darkest night. My heart and soul had been ripped out of me and I felt empty. Deborah knew that her life expectancy would be shortened which is why she didn't want to get too close to me, but we did get close to

220

each other - very close and now she was gone. I didn't know if she had another lover in Paris and it didn't matter. The last couple of times we were together felt complete as though there had never been anyone before. Our relationship had been a mythical experience and when we were together the real world seemed remote and ridiculous. I felt like an ancient mythical being when I was with Deborah as though she had captured me like a Siren from ancient Greece. I believe if she was still alive and we kept on seeing each other that I would have asked her to marry me. I had felt close to other women before, but not like the connection that I had with Deborah the mysterious and mythical, the conjurer of spells and make believe. Now however the mystery had been revealed in a cruel twist of fate. I began to wonder if I could live without her as I dragged myself down Sixth Avenue.

I found myself on the pier at the end of Bethune Street as I looked out across the Hudson River. I kept seeing her in her green sari and wondered if she might appear from the mists of despair on the river in her canoe like The Lady of Shalott. 'A pale, pale corpse, she floated by, my Lady of Shalott.' Then I remembered what she had told me on that Sunday about her being cursed and about being in her canoe with a few of her belongings. Deborah Rebecca Jones knew of her destiny much like The Lady of Shalott. I remembered that stormy magical Sunday when she got me to read Tennyson's poem to her after looking at her art book of the Pre - Raphaelite painters. I had seen John William Waterhouse's painting of The Lady of Shalott at the Tate Gallery in London when I was a lad and I remembered the haunting mythical quality of it. Now here I was in utter despair caught between myth and reality, that to Deborah and I were the same thing.

As I continued to sit on the old wooden pier that smelt of creosote, I felt Deborah's spirit enter my body and I felt myself smiling as a tear rolled down my cheek. I knew that this woman would live deep in my heart forever in this life and that we may meet again in the next.

Life is an illusion say the Buddhists and it certainly felt like that, at this particular moment as on this sunny day a huge dark cloud sat above my head as I sank into a world of darkness. I wandered around the streets, not knowing where I was going, as nothing seemed familiar anymore. I had just returned from traveling the world but the experience meant nothing to me now. I walked up the crooked stairs to my apartment as the sun was going down. The day had left without me, as I entered my empty apartment. I walked over to the turntable and placed the haunting music of Ravi Shankar on the turntable, then took the Eye of Horus from the box and placed it around my neck. I walked up to the mirror and stared at myself as the sad wailing strings of the sitar echoed in my mind. I continued staring into the mirror with the Eye of Horus around my neck and watched as my face turned into Deborah's face for a second or two and then she was gone as she said goodbye to me for the last time. "Goodbye my darling," I said as her face morphed back into mine. I never took the necklace off, but I lost it many years later while I was swimming off the south coast of Crete. Maybe it wanted to go back to Egypt that wasn't so far away.

The next morning I woke up to face the world without my dear friend and soul mate and I sank into a deep depression for the next two weeks. I didn't see anyone, nor did I want to. I didn't answer my phone messages. I didn't care about anything or anyone anymore, but just felt like dying.

After about a month or so I received a call for work. My spirit had lifted a little during this time and I realized that I had to get on with my life.

The Address Book

She bought him an address book,
So that he could write down numbers.
He filled his book in a matter of months,
He was very pleased.
He knew everyone from A – Z.

But no one ever came to call,
He wondered why?
He threw away the address book,
He didn't need it anymore.
He started to collect names on pieces of paper.
People came and went from the paper in his pockets.
There were names from everywhere.
Some were long names and difficult to pronounce
Like Fyodor Dostoyevsky
And other names were short,
Like Billy Hayes.
They were both names from the past,
He thought that maybe it was the end of an era.

The names came and went
Until they didn't matter.
Names had no place in his life anymore.

He didn't know anyone well enough to call them by name,

So he decided not to speak,
Because nobody listened to him anyway.

He bought himself a camera
From the money he'd saved from not talking,
And started to look at his life through the camera
And found the world to be a better place.
Someone told him that the camera never lies.

He was happy with his camera,
And collected hundreds of photographs
Of people and places,
Until the photos began to drown him.
He needed to talk to someone,
Then realized he never had an address book,
He knew no names.
Words had become redundant,
He had forgotten how to speak.

He didn't know what to do
With his hundreds of photographs.
He had no – one to talk to,
So he took a photo of himself

Then went out to buy an address book.
He wrote his name in the book
And placed the photo in the back.

He donated the address book
To the Museum Of Modern Art.
People from all over the world
Came to see the address book,
But nobody ever saw him again.

New York City   January 1987

The Bag Lady

It was a hot steamy day in the Big Apple and a friend and I were down in the Wall Street area after walking down through Soho and Tribeca. We had a pint in one of the pubs down there and then decided to take the subway back to the Village. It was now rush hour and the Wall Street types, investment bankers and those wearing suits and ties were cramming themselves into the subway cars to take them back uptown to the upper west side and upper east side.

My friend and I joined them feeling rather out of place as we were wearing shorts and t-shirts. Some men took off their ties to save themselves from being strangled and to let whatever bad air there was in the subway help cool them down. After a stop or two a bag lady pushed herself into our subway car. She was big and fat and dirty looking and looked like she hadn't seen a bath in years. She was wearing a baggy looking dress and had two big bags with her full of god knows what? She snuggled her way in between the suits, and started muttering something to herself. The suits were trying to ease away from her as she probably smelt bad, but there was nowhere for them to go. Some turned their heads away as others lifted their heads, their noses searching for fresh air, but there was none.

My friend and I sat and watched from comfortable seats. The train slowed down in the tunnel and came to a stop. A terrible smell of dung wafted under our noses as we realized the bag lady had taken a dump right there and then as she was standing up. There were screams of disgust from the men and women that surrounded her, but there was nowhere to escape to. After a minute or two the train continued its journey to the next stop where almost everyone in the carriage fled through the doors onto the platform gasping for air. The bag lady had emptied the carriage as she stood there laughing, her mouth wide open showing gaps where her teeth used to be, and on the floor of the subway car sat a big steaming turd. My friend and I decided to alight the train also and decided to walk the rest of the way home. It was at this point that I took this as a sign to leave the Big Apple for California and did so within the next couple of months. The old bag lady had made a statement and couldn't have picked a better time and place to have made it. It was real performance art and obviously made quite an impact on the fleeing audience. I almost felt like applauding this one-woman show. She seemed pleased with her performance as the train pulled away leaving just her in an empty carriage during a New York rush hour.

The Old Man On His Knees
On Bleecker Street

Age looked at age as it crossed the street
Horror in its eye,
Youth sits and laughs in sidewalk cafes.
They don't see the old man on his knees
Praying on the corner,
People pass him by.
Some look down, as others look away.
The old man makes them feel awkward,
He causes an embarrassment.

Desperation is pathetic
The old man on his knees
Clasped his hands together
And looked up to Manhattan's choking sky.
Is this where God lives?
The old man had nothing but a tear in his eye
And a prayer in his heart.
He was so alone amidst thousands.
How could this happen?
There were no real answers anymore
It just is that's all.

*I saw this in an antique shop on Bleecker Street
and decided it was time to go sailing*

The Job in the Caribbean

I got a job through a friend of mine called Rusty Ford, who by the way was no relation to Broken Chevrolet, shooting a video for a kind of travel show to promote holidays for those with lots of money, so that they can stay at very luxurious locations throughout the Caribbean. So we got a hold of a Betacam camera (state of the art, back then) and off we all went - myself, my friend Carl (who worked as a grip/PA) a technician from New York, where we got the gear, a friend of Rusty's and of course the guy whose company it was who was promoting these vacations.

First stop was Bermuda where we filmed in a couple of hotels. I found Bermuda to be rather stuck up with the quintessential English snob bobbing around all over the place in their Bermuda shorts, (of course) wearing black shoes with black socks pulled two inches up to beneath the knee. To me these people looked like over grown English schoolboys and I was immediately taken back to my schooldays in England when I used to get a good canning for doing very little, which was probably the problem. Stiff upper lip an' all that - these people were effigies of England's once glorious past resting on their laurels from centuries past, bored and boring people who hob-nobbed from one dull function to the next pretending that England still ruled the waves, somnambulists from privileged backgrounds who may have been posted there and forgotten in old yellowed manuscripts. Snoozing in rocking chairs on porches that looked out to sea and shaken (not stirred) once in a while by black servants to see if they were still alive or not. Of course there were some good sorts there, some who were the real thing, old battle scarred veterans from the days of the Empire who really did serve their King and country and had interesting tales to tell. Nevertheless our rowdy crew enjoyed ourselves sipping on Bermuda rum in the evenings as the sun dipped its head into the Atlantic Ocean.

After a few days filming in Bermuda our jolly crew flew back to New York to get ready for the big adventure which was to be photographing these exclusive resorts from the British Virgin Islands, the American Virgin Islands down to the British Grenadines not far off the coast of South America. The production company commandeered a nine - seater plane out of Beef Island, Tortola and we took the door off so as I could shoot the beautiful turquoise seas and coastlines from about a thousand feet above. This was not the worst job of my life, and I couldn't believe my luck as I looked through the eyepiece at the astounding beauty that greeted my eyes.

So we flew from island to island, and where we couldn't fly in because there were no landing strips, we would jump on board a beautiful schooner to take us into the next exotic bay more beautiful than the last. We shot on Cooper Island, Norman Island that was close to where Sir Richard Branson bought his own island that was Necker Island, but at that time was just another large rock in the sea. We landed at

Union Island that had a very short landing strip and the plane had to fly over quite a large mountain then drop down hundreds of feet fast to land before hurtling off into the sea at the end. I remember there was a great bar that was on a small ship that looked like a pirate ship and flew the Jolly Roger and you had to get to it by dinghy as it was anchored somewhere off the shore. We had a few Rums on board with a lot of talk about scurvy and how us Brits got the name of Limey. There was a lot of "arrghs" and "aye ayes" and "shiver me timbers" in conversation as Carl and 'meself' took on the identities of Black Beard and Captain Morgan and not forgetting Drake himself. It was the perfect environment for a bit of skull duggery and drunken debauchery as none of us wanted to leave this scene from Treasure Island, but continue to pretend we were back in those days when men were flogged at the mast and made to walk the plank into a sea of sharks. Of course the imagination was better than the real thing as life in those days was 'ard mates! So back to reality - we all left the pirate ship with the skull and bones flying in the wind and we all flew off to another exotic location to film the life styles of the rich and wealthy. The next location may have been Antigua then onto somewhere else, till after a while one beautiful hotel or complex of south sea like cabins with thatched roofs that were for rent all began to look similar, not that I was getting bored, this was a job that to me could have lasted a lifetime and I even got paid for it!

Eventually we landed on the island of Mustique (which in French means mosquito) not an inviting name for a holiday destination and at some point in time the mosquito there ruled the roost, so to speak, and somehow or other they managed to curb this nasty pest, but of course mosquitos are everywhere in the Caribbean and most hotels would have mosquito nets over the beds. However this pesky insect did not stop the jet set and English Royalty from getting a foothold on the island, and we stayed at Lord Lichfield's rather luxurious home there. It consisted of one good - sized house and two lovely little cottages further down the hill that overlooked the glistening blue waters of the Caribbean. I had one of the cottages and everyone else had their own fabulous room. Lord Lichfield was a cousin to the Queen and was quite a renowned photographer who photographed his family that happened to be the Royal family of England, his real name was Patrick Anson and he inherited the earldom of Lichfield in 1960 from his paternal grandfather. In his professional world he was known as Patrick Lichfield. He was the official photographer for the Prince and Princess of Wales in 1981 and subsequently became known as one of England's best known photographers. He died at sixty - six years of age of a major stroke. Next door, well not exactly the next door as if I were talking about a terraced house in Streatham, but quite a few yards away was the home of Princess Margaret who had quite the reputation on the island. From my little cottage I could see the building of Mick Jagger's house that was in a state of construction - 'It's only rock 'n roll but he likes it!' So Royalty and rock stars was the order of the day on the island of mosquitos!

Rusty, Myself and Carl on the island of Bequia

Colin Tennant, who was a close friend of Princess Margaret, bought the island in 1958 for 45,000 English Pounds. He built a new village for its inhabitants and planted coconut palms, vegetables and fruit. We visited and filmed him in front of The Great House that was inspired by a Mogul Palace and looked a bit like a miniature Taj Mahal. Inside was a silver four-poster bed and a harpsichord made from mother of pearl.

Basil's bar was the notoriously famous bar there and Basil the owner had many a tale up his sleeve, and many that I am sure where he is sworn to secrecy concerning certain members of the Royal family.

Rusty's family had a house on the island of Bequia, which was also part of the British Grenadines. 'Bequia' means island of the clouds in ancient Arawak, but when we were there, there wasn't a cloud in the sky. The island was also known for whaling and the locals were allowed to catch up to four humpback whales per year using old methods of hand thrown harpoons in open boats. I saw a postcard of the bay there and instead of being that beautiful turquoise blue, it was completely red from whale's blood. The island had also been a hideout and staging point for Sir Francis Drake's raids on the Spanish. It also was home for a while for Blackbeard (Edward Teach) and Henry Morgan who also anchored there in Admiralty Bay and a good drop of Morgan's rum always went down the hatch very easily during sunset, or any time for that matter. I was in good company then and home away from home feeling some kind of distant connection to these old sea dogs of long ago. I loved the Caribbean and the history attached to it.

Behind the house and up the hill a little was the house of Sandy Meisner who was an acting coach and had formed his own technique called The Meisner Technique. Meisner trained as an actor under Lee Strasberg who was considered the father of 'Method' acting which was an acting technique derived from the system of Konstantin Stanislavski and apparently all three were good friends.

233

In 1983 Meisner founded the acting school on Bequia and had an acting course there on the island for a few weeks a year and his students would come from all over the world but mainly the USA. He had developed throat cancer and spoke through a voice box and microphone through his throat, which was quite eerie sounding as I sat in on one if his sessions one day. One evening his students, aspiring actors and already working actors were at a 'jump up' which is basically the name given to a Caribbean party. It was held at a local bar near the beach and our scraggly crew decided to join in. I had ordered another rum and was ready to set sail when I saw a rather beautiful woman with amazing bone structure and long black wavy hair sitting at the bar a few bar stalls along from me. I got off of my stall and with a little Dutch courage aided by another rum approached her and in my best Scots accent, which I put on for certain auspicious occasions said,

"You're a beautiful looking woman, could I get you a drink?" or something to that effect. She turned to look at me and said that she hated my accent. So of course I continued with my fake brogue, when she interrupted me and asked if I were really a Scotsman, so of course I had to come clean and tell her that I was really English, which she seemed rather relieved about. Her revulsion towards the accent was not revealed till after about our second date together when she proceeded to tell me her story. I had met Theresa Saldana, who was an actress and had played Joe Pesci's wife in Scorcese's 'Raging Bull' starring Robert De Niro. She gave me a copy of her book, 'The Theresa Saldana' story after telling me in person what happened to her in Hollywood six years before.

So that was how I met this wonderful, beautiful and funny woman. She had a zany sense of humor and a great disposition and positive outlook on the world. We had a fun time together on Bequia and took a scuba diving course together. I remember her calling her doctor to ask if it was OK to dive, and it was, and so we both got our certification together. The whole course was conducted in the sea, which is probably better than learning in a pool.

234

I had to leave Bequia as I was still with the video crew when we heard that the Queen was visiting the volcanic island of Saint Vincent for an Independence ceremony - another island where the Union Jack was lowered and folded away nice and neatly, never to be seen again and replaced by an independent flag. We got to the dock where film crews were there already as the Queen's ship Britannia had just arrived and the red carpet was rolled out ready to be stepped upon by the Queen and Prince Philip. I placed a tape in the camera and started rolling and there was my Queen of England just a few feet away and despite what a lot of people say about Royalty, I honestly felt quite honored to be there. The actual Flag lowering/raising ceremony was to take place at the football stadium more inland, so we packed up our gear and hurried to the stadium where all the locals had gathered and the local gentry and Governor General of the island. The Queen gave a speech, the Governor General gave his, the band played and the bugles shrieked and the Union Jack fluttered gently in the warm Caribbean breeze as if waving to her subjects to say goodbye and another bloody colony hit the dust!

A tea party was arranged on Bequia and we made it there by boat. Carl and I stood together wearing the smartest un - ironed white shirts we could find like a couple of bedraggled rascals as we lined up to meet the Queen and the Prince. I was wearing a tie with the Beatles faces on it and as her majesty came by, I bowed and said,

"Your Majesty."

"I like your tie," she replied.

"Thank you your majesty," said I, as she moved on to greet Carl.

The next second I was facing Prince Philip and I can't remember if we shook hands or not, but he was very funny when he said to me, "I'm with her you know." Then moved on. The Tea party was all very grand and I tried not to make a fool of myself. There were the usual watercress and egg sandwiches with the corners turned up enough to ensure that they were the real thing and plenty of pastries. I popped a couple in my pocket to save for later, being a working class lad from North London, but nevertheless a subject of the crown. And so a rather splendid afternoon was had by all, with Lords and Ladies and local dignitaries from the Grenadines and in the evening I am sure that we all imbibed in a few glasses of rum.

Carl and I getting dressed up to meet the Queen

The Queen and Prince Philip on the island of St. Vincent

Sir Colin Tennant's mini Taj Mahal on the island of Mustique

Theresa's Story

Theresa had worked on 'Raging Bull' and was at the time living in Hollywood with her husband, when one day her manager or agent called on the phone telling her that something suspicious had happened, that Theresa's mother in Brooklyn got a strange phone call from a man claiming to be Scorcese's agent, and that he had misplaced Theresa's phone number and address, and would her mother give her the details. Overjoyed by this of course, thinking that another project was in the works she gave this man Theresa's address in Hollywood. Theresa's agent or manager became suspicious and told Theresa to be careful as they thought she may have a deranged fan on the loose, which does happen a lot apparently. So Theresa took note of this and when she left the house was accompanied by her husband who was a martial arts expert. A couple of weeks went by and there was no more word from this particular person. Theresa began to relax, thinking it to be yet another hoax from a fan. One Saturday morning at about ten or eleven she was getting ready for a piano lesson and walked outside to her car, about to open the door. (Her husband this time was not with her) when a man approached her and asked in a Scots accent if she was Theresa, he barely got her name out when she realized that something was not right and tried to run, when he grabbed her arm and with his other arm produced a kitchen knife from his bag and proceeded to stab her not once or twice, but a dozen times right there in the street on a sunny day in Hollywood. There was a seltzer delivery - man on the corner who saw this and ran over and disarmed the man Arthur Jackson, the Scotsman. Jackson was arrested by the police, and Theresa was rushed to hospital in an ambulance.

Arthur Jackson had been living in Scotland and one evening was watching TV, a show that Theresa was in, I don't believe he had seen her before but apparently he fell in love with her and Saint Michael told him to find her and kill her, then kill himself so as they could be in heaven together. He had flown from Scotland to New York where he hired a private detective to find out Theresa's address in Brooklyn, where her parents lived. So it was then that he contacted the mother on the phone. While Jackson was being taken away in the police vehicle he kept asking a number of times if she were dead, because if she was he would kill himself to be with her in heaven.

Theresa told me that she died and came back and saw the white light at the end of the tunnel with Jesus there. She was a Catholic, being half Italian and Puerto Rican, an orphan whom her parents, adopted when she was five days old, and who were the sweetest couple in the world. Apparently when her father heard the news he turned grey overnight. Theresa wrote a book about the whole experience and starred as herself in the TV movie of the same name. She also played Maria Scicolone in the story of Sophia Loren.

After a week or two the crew and I flew back to New York. I spoke to Theresa a number of times when she was back in Los Angeles and she told me she was coming to New York for Christmas. I spent Christmas day with Theresa and her parents in Brooklyn somewhere. Her parents were very sweet and gentle people and we spent a good Catholic holiday together. When Theresa and I walked out onto the streets of Brooklyn it seemed like everybody knew her and would yell out. "We love you Theresa!" People knew of her terrible ordeal and they all had a lot of respect for her. She was a very special person and cared for people with her big heart. She stayed with me on Sullivan Street a few nights in between staying with her dear old mum and dad and we decided that I should move to Los Angeles so as we would live together. Theresa left for LA the following week and we spoke on the phone everyday as I began to pack up and box up my apartment.

Sooner or later I flew to LA where I moved in with Theresa on the corner of Hollywood and La Brea into her penthouse apartment. The view from the balcony was looking directly down Hollywood Boulevard as I remembered the Kinks song about all the stars on the sidewalk on this famous street. I had arrived in Hollywood! The year we spent together was difficult as Arthur Jackson, the man who stabbed her six years previous, was up for parole and possible release on August 6th 1988 and could possibly be free to roam the streets again. This would mean that he would have only served six years of a twelve-year sentence. The man was as good as a murderer and it was only by a miracle that Theresa's life was saved. The man should have been executed - he stabbed this beautiful woman ten or twelve times in front of witnesses in broad daylight. It was a case of pre-meditated murder, and like I said it was a miracle that saved her. People serve more time for offences like fraud. There is something seriously wrong with the whole system that this evil, sick demented person could have been out walking the streets. Theresa was stressed out because of this, and we had a bodyguard living with us in the other bedroom. I was about to get trained by an ex FBI agent on how to use a gun, so as I would be able to protect her.

Theresa was in and out of hospital the following year as the scar tissue from the original stabbing was breaking up and causing her pain, along with the terrible thought that this sick individual could be out of prison and stalking her again, causing her a lot of stress. As it turned out, he did not get released and while he was in prison admitted to a bank robbery that he had committed in England, and I think a murder also. He was therefore extradited back to England to serve time, where he eventually died of heart failure in prison in 2004, at the age of sixty-eight. Unfortunately our relationship didn't work out, as it was a bit too stressful all round. I had to go away on jobs which made it difficult when she was on her own and perhaps I was not the right person for her to be at her side more. One time when I was back in New York she called and told me that it was probably best for both of us if we went our own ways. I was heartbroken but realized that she was right.

Theresa formed a movement called 'Victims for Victims' that was to help victims of attacks so as they could get some kind of help from the government. She went to the White House where she met President Reagan concerning this and kept a photo of herself with him in a frame in the living room of our apartment. She would fly from place to place giving talks about this issue whereby trying to get more help for these victims of serious crime.

One time she had a party in the apartment for her movement where I met Sharon Tate's mother, who would attend every parole meeting for Manson to make sure he never got out. I also met an ex British fighter pilot from WWII who was blind and was attacked on the streets of Hollywood, and a girl in a wheelchair who was beaten in a bar because she refused a dance with a certain individual and was reduced to a life in a wheelchair because of it.

The stories were horrendous and heartbreaking how one individual can ruin another's life in an instant. Theresa was the strongest and bravest and most spiritual person I had ever met and once she told me that she thought I was going to be her Guru, but she ended up being mine. (I saw from the newspapers earlier this year that she had died at the age of 61). My heart goes out to all her family and friends, and I know that she will be missed by many, including myself by just knowing that such a wonderful woman as this had so much to give in this cruel and ruthless world in which we all now live. She was that breath of fresh air, and I will always remember her great smile and whacky sense of humor, and I know her spirit lives on.

The Bathroom Mirror

He felt the time go through him,

Like a razor.

He glanced at his life, that hung off his wrist

And it said, TOO LATE NEXT TIME.

He glanced around and caught a reflection of himself

Gazing at her, gazing at him.

The razor slipped, he cut his chin, just by looking.

He bent his head down to the bowl

His blood dripped and turned the water red.

He looked back into the mirror

And thought about the scar

And she was gone.

There was only a faint smell

That lingered and clung like a cloud to a mountain.

He asked her about the road to freedom

But she just laughed,

And the mirror steamed up from her smile

As water ran off her back.

He scratched his nose, then rubbed his chin

He looked into his eyes

And saw her breasts behind frosted glass.

He wondered if he was home
But home was light years away.
Would she do, he wondered,
The toothpaste fell from his smile
As she sang like a siren from the bath
He blinked, then flushed away his dreams.
She told him that showering washed away her nightmares.
He feared that he might have been one of them.
He wondered if he might be her and she him.
There were too many mirrors in the bathroom.

He span himself around until the tears began to flow
And faster and faster he spun
Until he became as one,
And a bright light shone from her reflection.
He opened the frosted door
And joined her in the shower
Until the water washed away their souls
"See these hands," she said,
I HAVE THE TOUCH

Los Angeles, 1986

After Theresa and I broke up I went back to Sullivan Street for a short while. I met a woman through a friend who lived on Cochran Street in LA. She was looking to move to New York and I thought that I should probably stay in LA. The weather was better than in New York and the film business in the city had hit a bit of a slump. It seemed like people in the business were migrating to the west coast, so I decided to do an apartment swop. I moved to Cochran Street and Diane took my place in Soho. As far as apartments went I got the better deal as her apartment on Cochran St. was twice the size of Sullivan Street, but Soho was a far more interesting area to be in. After a year or two Diane moved to Amsterdam to become a singer. I had established myself as a DP in LA (somewhat) working for a Tabletop Director out of GMS Productions. I didn't particularly like the area where I was living and actually never really liked LA. Thinking about it all now in hindsight I probably should have just moved back to Manhattan after Diane left for Europe. I found LA to be plastic and to this day I still do. While I was living on Cochran Street, I wrote another script called 'Sugar Reef' a drama/love story set in the Caribbean, a good spicy tale, I thought, but once again I never knew who to get these scripts to, even though I had been in the film business for years.

There was one redeeming factor about the area where I lived and that was the Farmers Market at Third St. and Fairfax, that had many little restaurants and stalls serving everything from Cajun food to French and Italian, Japanese - you name it they had it there. There are also a couple of bars where the regulars hang out and a couple of bookshops. If ever I was going to meet someone it would usually be at the Farmers Market. It is considered an historic landmark and dates back to the early 1930's. I continued to live in that neighborhood for about five years, until I met Sandra, when I escaped to Laguna Beach. Apart from work and a couple of trips here and there, this was probably one of the most boring periods of my life.

A Fool and His Money

In 1989 or 88 I shot a film called 'A Fool and His Money' starring a guy called Jonathan Penner with his love interest being Sandra Bullock. I believe it was Sandra's first film. It was a story about an advertising executive called Morris Codman who receives a message from God off the TV. God tells him to start up his own religion based on greed and selfishness, which is actually quite relevant to today's world. Perhaps Dan Adams the director and writer was ahead of his time. It was a good premise, but was not well received. I however got a good review as cinematographer from Variety magazine. It was quite a star-studded cast with George Plimpton as God, Gerald Orange as head of this new religion and a cameo performance by Jerzy Kosinski (writer of Being There and Painted Bird), Tama Janowitz, Chuck Pfeiffer and the boxer Jose Torres playing himself. We shot in and around New York over the course of about five weeks. Sandra Bullock was very professional even back then, and always hit her marks, which is all a cinematographer and focus puller care about, as an out of focus actor is of no use to anyone! I remember thinking that this actress may do well - the rest of course is history! We had a lot of fun on the film as it was a very zany story, but unfortunately it didn't quite hit the mark!

...pearance a final viewing of the director's cut.

Script's problems are worsened by actors apparently unfamiliar with film acting and sound recording that highlights their playing to back rows. Writer Jerzy Kosinski, who has acted before (in Warren Beatty's ''Reds'') fares best in a cameo as a panhandler.

Strongest plus in the film is its look, with credit going to director of photography John Drake and production designer Paola Ridolfi, whose contributions suggest film might play better with the sound off.

Most likely prospects for film are quick theatrical playoff followed by sale to cable. Pic will probably work a lot better on the small screen. —*Kimm.*

I got a good review from a film magazine

246

Fort Liquerdale Florida

I got a call from Andre of Bond films, telling me about a job he was bidding on for Tavist D allergy pills with me as the director/cameraman to be shot in Fort Lauderdale, some of it at the bottom of Andre's garden which backed onto one of the inland canals. The nickname for Fort Lauderdale was indeed Fort Liquerdale because of the amount of drinking that went on their during Spring Break, when all the hooligans from colleges would meet up, get obnoxiously drunk and shag their fellow students, as the testosterone in the male would be at it's height. There was also a fair amount of drinking there anyway, as it was known as a holiday resort and a place where the cruise liners would dock.

So I had the obligatory conference call with the agency and client, then off I flew to Miami from LA, where I was driven up to Fort Lauderdale. The first thing to be done was the casting as well as scouting locations that were quite contained being around the grounds of Mr. Bonds' house. The casting was quite hilarious, and as in a lot of commercial actors their performances were over the top, as they were so desperate to please the director and get the job and if the commercials went national, the pay packets were huge, as residual checks would keep coming in every time a commercial was played. I had a friend in New York that got a national spot and he moved to Mexico where he survived solely off his checks. This however was not a national spot.

The first thing that would happen would be to review the preliminary performances that were put on tape by the casting director. I would decide along with a couple of other people from the agency who were the most suitable to look at after screening a lot of hopefuls. So, myself as the director, Andre the production producer, his assistant, the client consisting of four or five people and the agency with about the same amount of people went to the casting agent's studio where the actors would perform in front of us. All that was really required was a sneeze, as the commercial was to be about allergies and Tavist D would cure them! This was not a job for a Shakespearian actor. So men and women came in and sneezed then left, although quite a few dragged out the sneeze for seconds that would have taken up the whole spot being about twenty-five seconds plus the tag at the end. I would say to them, no I just want a quick sneeze, without all the motivation behind it. Of course there was more to the spot than just a sneeze. There was one gentleman who came in who had stopped off at McDonalds and had stuffed one of those little pepper sachets up his nose after opening it first. His eyes were streaming and his nose was all snotty. It was a very convincing performance for someone dying of a terrible case of influencer or the plague, but a little over the top for just a sneeze in a commercial. Anyway he had to be taken to the hospital afterwards, as he couldn't get the pepper sachet from down his nose. God knows where it went - maybe to his brain? The job went off very well and we all went off to a good restaurant afterwards with the client and agency. The commercial world of advertising was fun when one got the job, but there was a lot of under hand things that went on and could be quite an incestuous business at times, but one got to travel, and most of the time work with decent people and the pay was good. I directed a number of commercials for Bond films and loved coming down to Florida usually once a year around my birthday. I had friends, a married couple that worked for a scuba diving company in Tortola, which was part of the British Virgin Islands. I flew from Miami to Tortola, via Puerto Rico, where my friends met me at Beef Island airport, then stopped off on the way at my friends favorite bar for a welcoming drink of rum (of course) and coke, known to professional drinkers as a Cuba Libre! It was always good to be back in the Caribbean, land of pirates and adventurers. There was a strip of water off Tortola called Drake's Channel, so I felt very much at home here.

I had known Barry for years and we went back to my early days in New York, as he was the cameraman on the kid's films we did in Connecticut in the late seventies. Now here he was after giving up the film business, captain of a dive boat and instructor for scuba. Nicki his wife was also an instructor. After a couple of days I went out on the boat with them as I had my license after being certified in Bequia. It was beautiful in the crystal clear depths of the Caribbean and I saw many different types of fish and coral. In the evening we all went back to the house where a lot of rum was drunk and stories of the old days in New York were bounced around amidst uproarious laughter.

The following year I went back to Fort Liquerdale to direct a Nationwide Insurance commercial and afterwards flew from Miami to Puerto Rico where my friend Barry met me and flew me down to Tortola in his twin engine Aztec. He had since changed occupations from being a dive master (the last time I was there) with help from some very rich people to start his own company called Fly BVI out of Tortola. We landed on the runway on Beef Island that was part of Tortola after a beautiful flight about a thousand feet above the turquoise blue Caribbean as the sun was setting.

Nicki, Barry's wife was there to greet us as she was running the administrative side of the business from a small office just a short walk from the runway. It was good to be back in the hot steamy Caribbean. There were not many small airlines in the islands to fly people around, so there was plenty of room for another company. The smaller airlines were called puddle jumpers as they transported passengers and small cargo from one island to the next. Barry and his wife had about eight of these small planes from single engine Pipers to twin engine Aztecs and could hold from four to six or eight passengers. The boy looked great in his white pilot uniform and was no longer the bedraggled unshaven captain of a dive boat. I had to hand it to Barry that he did what he wanted to do. After meeting Nicki, Barry and I went off to a local bar for a couple of drinks and some coconut shrimp. He introduced me to some of the locals there who were all pretty much alcoholics.

Back in the day - the day being the days of the Vietnam War, Barry was a news cameraman. He once told me that a bullet hit the side of the camera, instead of his head that actually saved his life. We had met as I had mentioned before on a film in Connecticut when he was

249

a Director of Photography. We became closer friends later on as we both had a lot in common regarding the Caribbean and travel stories. Every year I managed to direct a commercial for Bond Films out of Fort Lauderdale that got me so close to the islands that it would have been a sin not to visit! (I was living in LA at this time, and never really wanted to go back, so I would do everything in my power to delay my return to the land of la la). I think I visited Barry and Nicki about half a dozen times, the first time being on my fortieth birthday. A few years later I brought Sandra down with me when we were living in Laguna Beach and we would drive down to a beautiful bay called Little Beach or Little Bay that could only be reached by a four wheeled drive vehicle. There was never anybody there and so would have the beach to ourselves, sunbathing and swimming naked in the crystal clear sea.

A few years later Nicky who was only in her mid-fifties if that, died from cancer, which left Barry alone. Broken hearted he dissolved the business in Tortola or sold it and went to live in Paris, which was a dream he had. He was studying French and enjoying the life that Paris had to offer. I had an old girlfriend, who I hadn't seen in years and she came to visit me in Santa Monica after I had broken up with Sandra. She then came to visit me in Vancouver after I had moved there. She told me that she wanted to settle down and get married. I liked her a lot but for some reason I wasn't ready or perhaps I might never be. She told me she was going to Paris and then to Toulouse to see her family and asked if I knew of anyone in Paris. I gave her Barry's phone number and they met and before I knew it they were married. After a few years I believe they got divorced and Barry got Leukemia and eventually collapsed and died so I heard in a bar in Paris. He was in his early sixties.

Nicky Me and Barry on the dive boat.   Tortola

Van Gogh And Friends

He was a regular guy, like Van Gogh.

He felt it was time for a change.

A new image – he called his agent,

His agent was a modern man,

But he was too old fashioned

An out-of-date boy.

He wondered if Van Gogh had an agent.

Time for a change he said,

He wanted to dye his hair

He never wore hats.

There were days when he never had a head.

He looked in the mirror at his head that wasn't there.

It's a suitable image, someone said.

You've lost the essence, said a little voice.

He looked around wondering where the voice came from.

He thought it might be the bogey man

So he kept the lights on all night.

The lights blinked at him and grew hotter.

He studied the night-life of the big apple,

But opted for the mushrooms that grew wild.

He became an animal once more.

Poisoned by the apple, like Snow White,

It burned a hole in his skull

They found it at the Natural History Museum.

He didn't know whether he'd been on the road too long,

Or not long enough.

He wanted to give them all a bit of stick,

He wanted to perform, but couldn't find the audience,

So he covered his room in mirrors

And saw a thousand images of himself.

He began to perform, but couldn't trust his image.

He began to scream louder and louder,

Until the mirrors cracked and fell.

His image lay on the floor looking back at him.

He'd been waiting a long time for this.

New York City   January, 1987

Madrid. Winter

Café Central.

On the road again – back in Spain, shooting a "Frudesa" commercial - 6000 miles to film vegetables. Across the continent of America to Atlanta, across the Atlantic Sea to Spain. Flying high, higher and higher. Europe seems to be calling me back. I'm the man from the future from the land of America, California, Los Angeles. I visit my past my history – Europa! Europa! I scream. I see her face looking up at me, she looks confused, the wall is down but the barriers remain. I still don't know you she blinks, I'm gone – that was New York, gray, cold, warm and wet, sweat and dust–deserts to jungles, dark to light, the Sun and Moon.

My life seems to encompass everything and everything encompasses my life and a Mexican song plays in this bar in Madrid. Every glance or look or smile or tear reminds me of a time. It never ends. One experience affects the next - I don't feel lonely any more even when I am alone. I feel the circle the wheel of life, as cerveza wets my lips and the music is happy. I must publish a book. He told her the truth she didn't like it. Sometimes a little deception is better. Life really is a game I don't intend to lose, but you never know. The Mexican music reminded the traveler of Guaymas in Sonora, Mexico. I remembered the beautiful Mexican model–she was young, the dust from the desert blew away my thoughts. Not everything I had was recorded on Kodachrome. Thank God I still have my memory I thought to myself, as I had just visited the Thyssen-Bornemisza Museum in Madrid, and was inspired once again. Paintings by Van Gogh, Dali and Picasso, the list goes on. I saw glimpses of so many lives, the desire to record, the need to put down on paper, canvass or film. I'm glad I have the need, I thought to myself, although I hadn't written too much in quite a while. A couple of scripts–one about life as a schoolboy in London in the 60's, and the other about a writer's strange experience in the Caribbean. I scratched my head with the pen and looked around the café. I heard German accents next to me, two girls were sipping on their cappuccinos - they seemed very young, perhaps teenagers. I looked across into the other direction - two more beautiful girls laughed and smiled, they were young too. My God I thought to myself, I wanted to be with them all. I was feeling a lot more eccentric, the girl opposite me had pock marks in her face, it wasn't unattractive in fact it added to her beauty. I wondered how she felt about it. The woman next to me was writing furiously, was it a race?

I remembered having to write essays at school in a short period of time. I preferred this. Sitting in a bar on my own time–no judges. I ordered another beer and when I looked up I noticed more people writing. I wondered what they were writing about - there must be a universal translation somewhere. I blew the dust from my mind for a split second and was lost. The girl next to me caressed her hair out of her face, while her friend shook a packet of sugar in time to the music. The coffee machine was working again and people were happy. A French song played. I caught the waitress' eyes - I liked this café life. Perhaps I should start wearing a beret and smoking Gitanes cigarettes. Somehow this café bar seemed a little more real than the ones in Los Angeles. I liked Europe because it was old.

The girl opposite had piercing blue eyes and of course she was German. I thought perhaps she was a product of the Lebensborn programs, but after reconsidering knew she was far too young. Another young German joined the group she looked like the sister of the one with the very blue eyes, she had blue eyes too. I took another swig of beer and drops fell onto my writing, the ink ran and cried off the page. I looked up again and the music changed, I heard the sound of hands clapping "Camarones de Isla" wailed from the speakers. I felt fire burning in my loins, and wanted to dance - I loved the music. A grey-haired man behind the column stuck his tongue down a woman's throat. She was blonde. I couldn't tell what she was like, but her profile was interesting. She was more the age of the writer. I wanted to play guitar like a flamenco guitarist, Camarones de Isla was a junkie and died of a heroin overdose. I wondered if the woman next to me was writing about me. Probably not–why should she. I

255

wondered how people perceive me. The two Germans seemed to grow younger, they laughed and smiled their blue eyes caught the reflected sunlight from my beer glass it was quick–the grey-haired man kissed the blonde profile again. Could they be in love I wondered? "Where is my canvas?" I cried. Was there time for love in his life? A man in a maroon coat walked into view he wore a white silk scarf and trilby hat with a black band around it - he proceeded to read a book, he might be gay. He reached into his inside pockets and produced a map of Madrid - he was a tourist like myself. A chill ran up my spine, it was getting cold, but it was great to be here in the winter. Winter blubber hung over my jeans, I wondered if that mattered. It wasn't a big concern at the moment although I never wanted to be fat. The girl next to me reached down into her shirt and pulled out her talisman, not unlike the one I wore around my neck. The Eye of Horus that Deborah left me to protect me from evil. I closed my book and decided to buy a tape of 'Camarones de Isla,' then glanced across at the couple now staring into each other's eyes. I thought the image ridiculous. I then asked for "La cuenta por favor," paid and then left.

Isabel

I went back to Madrid the following year, but this time as a director of photography for a Spanish detergent commercial. I had just returned to New York after finishing up 'Primary Motive' in Boston. The rest of the film had been shot in Luxembourg and now it was the beginning of summer and I had to get back to Europe. I didn't want to spend the summer in America. I called Amelia in Madrid to see if she had any directing jobs for me. She told me that she hadn't but did have a detergent commercial for me to shoot if I wanted to. The director was from England and his usual cameraman wasn't available so Amelia who owned the company asked me if I wanted to work as his director of photography. Off course I jumped at the opportunity, anything to get me back to Europe. She was the producer of her own production company and was also a lover of mine. The first night I

256

was there we went out to dinner and Amelia came back to my hotel room that night and we made love. The next day I went to a meeting with the production company and the agency. I was introduced to the director and assistant director, a girl called Isabel. Isabel and I shook hands, looked into each other's eyes and I knew immediately that I was in trouble. The meeting ended and the next day we were filming in a studio just outside of Madrid. Isabel kept looking over to me - I kept seeing her out of the corner of my eye staring at me. Amelia was there sitting by the monitor with the clients and agency people. Isabel yelled Silencio! And then performed her duties as an assistant director. The director called ACTION! And the film rolled through the camera, my eye pressed against the eyepiece as I watched as detergent flakes fell through the air, which we filmed in slow motion.

"CUT!" Said the English director, and Isabel walked over to the camera.

We had to reload as we were shooting 120 frames a second, which meant that a 400 ft. magazine ran out very fast. While the assistant cameraman was reaching for a new film magazine, Isabel told me in broken English that she loved it when I put the long lens on, she smiled and turned, then walked away. We shot for about twelve hours which is a normal film day and in the evening after work, myself and some of the crew and Isabel all went out to a sherry bar, deep underground, close to the King's Palace. Amelia wasn't there as she had other commitments. We all sat at a long table and the atmosphere was electric. A guitarist sat in the corner and played Flamenco music. Isabel got up to go to the bathroom and I followed after her about a minute later. When she came out of the bathroom down the corridor I was there. We looked into each other's eyes and kissed heavily on the lips, it wasn't a long kiss, but long enough to know that an affair had started there and then. She came back to my hotel room that night and we made love all night long. We became obsessed with each other and the next day on the set we couldn't stop looking at each other. I think Amelia must've picked up on the vibes between us and I had already told Isabel the situation between Amelia and myself that we were old lovers. Isabel said that it was okay, and that she understood the situation. The next night I was with Amelia she seemed a little distant and a little annoyed with me and with good reason, but nothing was said. I did feel bad about the whole situation, as Amelia was a good woman and she was the one paying me. I normally wouldn't have done such a thing, but the connection and chemistry between Isabel and myself was too strong to ignore. The commercial was over - it only took two days to film and the day after I was paid in cash in Spanish pesetas. Two days after, Isabel and I took a train to Toledo where we found a great little hotel overlooking the square. Toledo is where they made some of the finest swords in Europe and Toledo steel was known throughout the world. I suppose to have been run through with a blade made from Toledo would have been a good way to die!

We visited the Cathedral, which was very dark inside, as we had just come from the blinding sun outside. I remember the atmosphere in there was intense and a feeling of sadness came over me. The Cathedral had probably sheltered many poor depressed people over the centuries. It was built in the 13th Century and was inspired by the great Gothic Cathedrals like Chartres in France. Many historic events had been hosted in the Cathedral over the years including the proclamation of Joanna the Mad and her husband Philip the Handsome as heirs to the throne of Spain.

We went back to the hotel room where we made love again, it seemed that's all we ever did, we couldn't keep our hands off each other, there was a remarkable obsession and we fell in love. Isabel had wild curly hair and dark brown eyes and was originally from Lima, Peru. I believe her father was a famous photographer there and she had moved to Madrid years ago. It was by now the middle of the summer and I suggested to Isabel that we should go to the island of Hydra in Greece as I'd heard so much about it, so we both flew to London where we stayed at my mother's house for a couple of days, then booked a flight to Athens from Gatwick airport. A couple of days later we were in Athens and we did the usual site seeing of the Acropolis and the Plaka and the wonderful museum of Archeology, where I looked at all the Mycean art. The next day we took a hydrofoil from Pireaus and an hour or so later were on the island of Hydra. We got off the boat and there I was back again on the Greek islands, a new set of Islands (Saronic Islands) and with a new woman. We were right there at the port, it was very hot and we immediately found a Taverna. We sat outside and I drank a Myrtos beer. I think Isabel had a glass of wine. We walked through the village up the hill until we found a nice little hotel. There were no roads on the island, no cars, only donkeys that were laden to carry things around. The next day we found a beautiful little cove in amongst the rocks. I don't think there were too many beaches on Hydra and although it was the middle of the summer there wasn't too many people there, so every day we would go to our own private little rock where we would make love naked in the sun every day all day for the next week. We took the ferry over to Spetses, which was not as nice as Hydra as it was more commercialized and attracted more tourist types. It was also very flat - we just went for the day and took the ferry back in the evening. Hydra has an art school on it and is a bit more elite than Spetses, and also more expensive. We stayed there for almost two weeks then flew back to Gatwick where we stayed at my mother's house again back in Stoneleigh. Every time my mother went out shopping we would be making love again wherever and whenever we could, usually in my old bedroom so I could look out the window to see when my mother was returning home in the car. I had become a naughty eighteen-year old boy again and was enjoying every minute of my newly found youth. I rented a car in Epsom, a little car, and we drove down to Brighton where I had my business on the pier many years before. We found a hotel on the front in Hove an old hotel with high ceilings and big bay windows that overlooked the English Channel. It wasn't exactly the Greek islands, but Isabel really enjoyed England with all its eccentricities.

We would have an English breakfast of toast and fried eggs, sausages or bacon, or both, and baked beans with a nice pot of tea. We drove the car along the coast to Hastings, where the famous Battle took place and where King Harold got an arrow in his eye that killed him. Isabel gave me a Nikon camera that was her brother's that he had given to

259

her. She felt she had to pay me for something as I had paid for the trip to Greece. She insisted that I take it. I drove her back to Gatwick airport a few days later and I never saw her again. I can't remember what happened but somehow we lost touch with each other - it was a long-distance relationship and I was the gypsy cameramen. I always felt bad that I had lost touch with her, as she was a great woman.

I called my agent in Los Angeles and he had got me a job booked as a director cameramen shooting in São Paulo Brazil, it was for Banespa Bank, so the next thing I knew I was on a plane to São Paulo. I flew business class. It was a horrendously long flight of about 16 hours and flying over the Amazon jungle we hit an incredible electric storm and the plane seemed to fall for hundreds of feet, some people were screaming and my stomach entered my mouth. By this time I was already pretty plastered on champagne and I thought wow, if I had to go, it would be down into the Amazon jungle drunk on champagne - a first class death! I must admit I was frightened and for a few minutes I really believed we were going to crash. We didn't - and a few more hours later landed in São Paulo Brazil. I was met at the airport by Max, who later I called Mad Max, as he was a wild character. He drove me to my apartment that had a small kitchen and then they left me alone to sleep after my nightmare flight.

The next day I went to their production office that was called 'Blow Up' funnily enough, which was the name I used for my shop on Brighton Pier. It seemed like life kept going around in circles in a good way - that somehow on this journey there was some kind of connection as though my destiny had already been laid out in front of me. The next day I was introduced to the owner of the company and we all went off to a meeting at the production office to meet the clients of Banespa, the bank of Brazil. The job was basically a Tabletop job as that's what I was known for and that's what I had become - the new tabletop director. We shot for two days and they paid me in cash! They paid me in cash. I had a pair of cowboy boots at the time and I remember I stuffed a couple of thousand into each boot when I left to fly home. I can't remember what I did with the rest. After the second day of shooting Mad Max and Enrique the editor took me to a samba place as I told them I wanted to experience some Brazilian nightlife. We went to this dance hall but Enrique suggested after about an hour that this really wasn't the real thing - it was for tourists, although Brazilian tourists. It seemed like the real deal to me, but he insisted that we should go to this other place he knew which was in the real black section of town - the real Brazil as he told me. We drove down these very dark streets they were very poorly lit and the air was heavy - it had been raining quite a bit in the area and it seemed very seedy and dangerous. I didn't care - I enjoyed experiences like this. We climbed up a wooden staircase and entered into a room that was about 50 feet square. There was a Brazilian band playing - conga drums were beating and the air was filled with smoke from marijuana, and cocaine was laid out in long lines across the table where we sat. I had entered a wild world and I indulged in everything. Within minutes I was flying as high as a kite on good South American cocaine. A black girl with wild and crazy hair like Isabel's, came over and asked me to dance and before I knew it I was on the dance floor dancing the Samba and minutes later I was playing congas with the band. According to Max the girl I had been dancing with was a hooker and he told me I should take her back to my apartment. She was absolutely gorgeous - from the jungle, she was from Salvador in the north of Brazil. I didn't partake in the offer fearing that I may get some strange disease and I was immediately reminded of my days in the Dominican Republic when I did indulge myself in a sexual act and remembered the stories of the light bulb clap where one's penis glowed in the dark!

I got back to my apartment as the sun was coming up and of course I couldn't sleep because of the high-grade cocaine I had snorted. I stared out of my window and watched as the rain poured down once again and laughed out loud at the night I had just had. The day after this, the production company treated me to a stay in Rio de Janeiro as a little gift to me as they were pleased with the work I had done. I flew in a small plane from São Paulo to Rio de Janeiro which means in Portuguese - River of January, as that was when the Portuguese sailed there in 1565. I was met at the airport by one of their reps and was driven to a hotel that overlooked Ipanema beach. I was in Rio and I wanted to see the girl from Ipanema, but unfortunately it was raining and there was no one on the beach. When we flew into Rio I saw the statue of Christ the Redeemer high on the hill near Sugarloaf Mountain.

The next day my driver took me there and I climbed the steps to the see the statue of Christ that was one of the world's famous landmarks. This is a wild part of the world – a city of 10 million people. I love the Brazilian people they seemed to be happy back in those days - always smiling and dancing and singing. Of course not everyone was like that, for there was incredible poverty much like I had seen before in India, and the favelas house thousands of people that live in extreme poverty. The only way for lots of them to make money is to sell drugs. The Brazilians with money, the middle classes usually had barbed wire around their property to prevent burglars and many had bodyguards, as kidnapping was quite a common trade there. The favelas, the shanty - towns, had their own system of survival and codes, for instance, they would fly flags of different colors. When the police decided to raid they would lower one flag and raise another one, a code that everyone knew thereby allowing the drug dealers to escape out of the top of the town. (These days of course there are numerous raids by the police and shootouts occur quite often and lots of people are shot. Now drug dealing is an everyday occurrence and is the only way a lot of people can make any money there).

When I was in São Paulo a cab driver who drove me back to the airport told me that when it rains heavily the kids from the favelas run down to the freeway which was the size of the 405 in Los Angeles and block up the drains, thereby flooding this particular section of road that was in a dip, so the cars had to stop. The road cut through the middle of a favela which probably housed a quarter of a million people in total, so the kids would come down as the cars had to stop, and would hold up everyone at gunpoint and get whatever they could. It was the Wild West out there and one always felt a sense of potential danger. When I was in São Paulo Mad Max would drive through the

262

red lights slowly at night making sure nothing was coming of course. When I asked him why he did that, he told me that if you stop at red lights you can get robbed by bandits. "They come out of the shadows with guns." Said Max. In fact the next time I returned to Brazil, Max had been kidnapped at gunpoint at the beach and held for ransom. His family had to pay a large sum of money to his kidnappers to get him back. He had bodyguards with him the next time I saw him. I must admit it was an exciting few days there, so anyway here I was now in Ipanema and the famous Copacabana beach. I went to a club where Ronald Biggs' was supposed to hang out. I don't think he owned it, but I was told he frequented a club there in Copacabana.

Ronald Biggs was known for his part in the Great Train Robbery in England. It wasn't carnival time here and I went out at night a couple of times, being warned not to take any cameras with me and not to wear any gold chains or jewelry which of course I didn't own anyway. I went to a Disco called 'Help,' because once you got inside the door that's the word that automatically came out of your mouth. The bar was lined with prostitutes and American tourists spending all their money on them, it was jam - packed and I didn't stay too long. There were a lot of seedy types in there, Brazilian and American alike. I wasn't so impressed with Rio, the streets were dark and there was so much poverty it just didn't feel right to me. I know they had a convention there on the environment or something for World Peace - something like that and I was told that the police took the kids that had no ID, (the street kids) and loaded them up into vans. They drove them out of town and then shot them, so I was told, so as to clean up the streets to show the world that Rio was a safe place to be. It is a police state and although I loved the Brazilian people and the music and their love of life it all seemed way out of whack to me. I went back again the following year as I had another job there and once again this time flying back to the States over the Amazon again another death-defying ride - another electric storm. I saw bolts of lightning either side of the plane shooting down into the Amazon jungle below me, and once again I thought I might be meeting my maker. But this time I arrived back at Kennedy airport safe and sound.

Statue of Christ the Redeemer   Rio de Janiero

So that was Brazil and that was the summer of '91 and I was on the road - it was sex drugs and rock 'n' roll. I had shot a film in Luxembourg, a commercial in Madrid, and one in São Paulo, Brazil and was now back in New York City and life was grand. I kept my apartment on Sullivan Street for a few years after I left and had a number of sub renters through there. They basically destroyed my apartment. I suppose soon after this I left my apartment in New York for good as this time I was living in Los Angeles near Hollywood on Cochran Street. I had done an apartment swap with a singer. She ended up in Amsterdam and I took her apartment for about five or six years until I met Sandra who persuaded me to live with her in Laguna Beach and that is another chapter of my life.

1992 The LA Riots

The riots began on April 29th after the trial of four police officers who were acquitted for the excessive use of force and beating of a black man called Rodney King. After the verdict was announced all Hell broke loose in the City of Los Angeles (and there were no Angels to be found at this time). The beating of Rodney King was videotaped by a passer-by and was used as evidence, although some pieces of the tape had been edited out. Widespread looting and assault took place that started in an area called South- Central. Fires raged and spread throughout the city as I watched the news on the TV from my apartment on Cochran Street. Sammy's Camera was set on fire that was on La Brea and Third Street that was only a couple of blocks from where I was living and rioting even spread as far as Hollywood Boulevard. So I decided to jump in the car and spend the night with friends in the Hollywood Hills. My friend had a view of the city and from there we watched as the city burned below, like some kind of perverted July 4th.

After two days of rioting a total of about sixty people had been killed and two thousand had been injured. Damages amounted to almost a billion dollars. Korean store- owners were targeted by gangs of looters and so the Koreans armed themselves with guns and semi- automatic weapons and shoot-outs took place like it was in the days of The Wild West, which it had once again become. One gun-store was looted and over one thousand weapons were stolen. Neighborhoods such as Beverly Hills and West Hollywood were barricaded off and were protected as the rest of the city saw a free for all. Eventually the National Guard and the Seventh Infantry and even the Marines were called in to stop the looting and destruction of the city. On the second day a curfew was called for the city from dusk to dawn. The rioting went on for a further four days until it died out and over 11,000 people were arrested.

Rodney King was awarded $3.8 million and founded a hip-hop record label with some of the money. King died many years later from accidental drowning. Alcohol, cocaine, marijuana and PCP were all found in his body.

In the same year Hurricane Andrew hit Florida, TWA the airline, went bankrupt and Bill Clinton became president. While in England Prince Charles and Lady Diana separated.

Laguna Beach

I flew off to Columbus Ohio to direct and shoot a spot for Pizza Hut. The day after I finished the job the rep for the company that hired me, suggested that we should get a bite to eat at a restaurant called Hyde Park (named after the Hyde Park in London I presume). She had arranged for another woman to meet us there who was also in the advertising business, whose name was Sandra. We were both introduced to each other and had a good meal with some stimulating conversation. Sandra told me that she was moving to California to work on the client side of the business for Taco Bell in Irvine. I at the time was living on Cochran Street, in the area known as Miracle Mile (where it got the name from I don't know, as I found the area to be anything but miraculous!) I went out with Sandra the following night and the next morning I flew out of Columbus to Aspen Colorado, to film a 'hair product' commercial with Chris Evert who won the Wimbledon Championship in 1974 and was the number one tennis player in the U.S. and the World's number one player for five years.

CUT TO:

California. A few weeks later

Sandra called me on the phone telling me she was about to have a meeting at a hotel on Sunset Blvd. but after would I like to join her for drinks at The Mondrian afterwards. So I drove up to Sunset Blvd and stayed the night with Sandra - and that is how it all began. A few weeks later Sandra moved to Laguna Niguel and started her job at Taco Bell. At the weekends I would drive my beaten up old Ford Mustang down to Laguna Niguel early on a Saturday morning where I would spend the weekend, then drive back to my place, which I was really beginning to hate. I was never a big fan of Los Angeles, and only came here originally to be with Theresa. Of course the weather had a little to do with it, being out of New York where the summers were too hot and the winters too cold. I enjoyed getting out of the urban mess of LA at the weekends and found the Laguna area to be more open and felt a greater sense of freedom there. After a while Sandra and I decided to move in together and we or should I say she, found us a beautiful three bedroom house to rent high in the hills of South Laguna, in an area called Arch Beach Heights which was all the way up the beautiful Bluebird Canyon Road. It was three floors, and one entered at street level into a large living room with an open kitchen and a wood burning stove and a balcony at the other end that looked out over the Pacific Ocean. The next floor down consisted of two bedrooms with en suite bathrooms also with a deck and a view of the ocean even whilst lying in bed. The third floor down was a big open space that I used as my office and meditation area. I had not started to paint at this time but it would have made the perfect art studio. This area also had a deck where I hung a hammock to look out over a Japanese style garden from next door with a huge bougainvillea plant in our garden bursting with bright purple petals. We also had a lemon tree in the back garden and would pick lemons right off the tree for our special foo - foo drinks. Life was grand here and every night we would sit on the deck with a banana daiquiri or a gin and tonic or a margarita that had been whipped up in our blender and watch as the sun would sink into the ocean, only to leave the most beautiful sunsets behind.

Laguna had been a haven for writers and artists since the early 1900's. It attracted plein-air painters and does to this day, and very often one would see a painter near Las Brisas with his easel set up and brush in hand ready for the next brushstroke, as they looked out across the beautiful bay. The Laguna Art Museum opened in 1918. In the 60's and 70's it was the epicenter for the hippie culture and people with alternative lifestyles and even Timothy Leary lived here for a while.

During this period I was working as a director/cameraman and very often I was able to fly out from John Wayne airport, which was a fifteen minute drive from our house, to cities such as Dallas, where I would direct commercials for Ci Ci's Pizza and the like. There was no reason to go to Los Angeles. Sandra didn't particularly like the world of advertising, even though she had a degree in marketing, and after a while left Taco Bell and got a job downtown in LA. It was too far to travel in from Laguna, so we rented a tiny studio apartment back in the Miracle Mile area that added to our expenses. Now the situation was reversed - she would come to see me at the weekends to our lovely house overlooking the ocean. Sandra was studying acting in Fullerton and kept trying to get me interested in being a thespian. It was hard to avoid actors being in the film business and I must admit that I did have a small desire to be an actor, as I was always fooling around and people would always remark, "You should be an actor!" I did understand what it takes to be a successful actor and many had spent their whole lives as barkeeps or waiters and waitresses hoping for the big break. I was not that driven and without that focus and determination, it would have been a hopeless cause. I was quite happy being on the other side of the camera and directing actors in the commercials that I directed. One didn't have to be a Stanley Kubrick or Spielberg to direct commercials! So life went on and I believe I had some of the happiest times of my life there in Laguna at the house that overlooked the ocean.

It was time to get rid of my old Mustang as it was beginning to make some very strange noises, like a bad orchestra trying to warm up. I sold it to someone, and then went off to a car dealer in Anaheim where I had my eye on a Jaguar XJS that Sandra knew about, and liked the design of the car. Sandra was at work this day so was not with me. I got in the car to give it a test drive, but it didn't start, so the sales rep replaced the battery. It roared into life with all twelve cylinders singing in English to me. I hit the button for the electric window to open but it didn't open, then I looked around at the beautiful leather interior and the classy design that the English are so good at with the walnut wood finish. The trouble is that it wasn't a convertible and now that I was in Laguna I wanted a convertible because it was sunny almost all of the time.

The car was for sale for $11,000 and was only a few years old with about 30,000 miles on the clock, but it had a few electrical issues already. As I sat there in the driver's seat the salesman poked his head in the window as I was telling him about a few of the defects that the car seemed to have. As I was telling him he was nodding his head in agreement, then told me if the water pump broke it would cost so many hundreds of dollars, and if this went wrong or that went wrong that would be another five hundred or so. I sensed he was trying to talk me out of it when he motioned with his arm and pointed to a blue Chevy Camaro. "It's a t-top, which is really better than a convertible," he said, as I was already half out of the door. He ran me through the reasons why I should buy the Camaro over the Jag and I was convinced after I took the muscle car for a spin around the block. It was an 89 RS Camaro six cylinder, and it was now 1992 and it had 25,000 miles on the clock.

I gave the man $8,000 in cash and drove out of the dealership, not in my classy XJS Jaguar but in an American - built muscle car. Back in Laguna I drove it back and straight into the garage hiding it from the outside world. Later I was out on the deck and saw Sandra driving up the road in her white Nissan, I then ran out to the front of the house to meet her. She stopped the car on the street and asked if I had got the Jag, then I opened up the garage door and surprise! - There was the '89 t- top Chevy Camaro staring right at Sandra. She gave out a scream of surprise and shock as she said it reminded her of her hometown of Hicksville, Ohio, that she has spent her whole life escaping from, and now here before her very eyes I reminded her of that little town in the Midwest and the rednecks that would be driving these muscle cars along with the Trans-Am's yelling at the girls with their tattooed arms hanging over the door. I explained to her the trouble with the Jag and the fact it wasn't a convertible and she immediately understood. I reversed the muscle car out the garage, and took off the t-tops while Sandra was getting into her civilian clothes. Five minutes later we were flying down the Pacific Coast Highway with the wind in our hair and smiles on our faces!

Our House was one of those that overlooked the Ocean

So life went on as life does, and Sandra and I were having fun sitting on the deck of our house sipping on Pina Coladas and other foo - foo drinks we made in our blender, whilst looking out over the blue Pacific Ocean. Of course I never realized what I had at the time - a millionaire's life style as far as the house and view were concerned. I was working enough, directing commercials here and there and making some money - not huge amounts, but a day rate for a commercial director was nothing to be sneezed at. In January '94 I got another job with Bond films, directing and shooting a spot for a supermarket chain in Columbus Ohio. A blizzard had just blown into town, but we were shooting inside as the snow was piling up outside. Meanwhile back in LA the rumblings started near Northridge which created a 6.7 earthquake and caused considerable damage, casing a ramp off one of the freeways to collapse. The total damage from the quake was estimated at over $15 billion dollars and caused 57 deaths, while over 8,000 people were injured.

I called Sandra in Laguna, and she told me that everything was OK there, and that she felt a little rumbling but there was no damage done. I got back to Laguna the following week. Sitting on the deck I read in the Times that a woman called Lorena Bobbitt had cut off her husband's penis with a knife while he was asleep in bed. She took it and threw it into a field, then later realized what she had done and called 911. John Bobbitt's penis was found after an extensive search and then surgically attached, hopefully the right way round! Lorena Bobbitt (who was born in Ecuador) declared that her husband abused her and she was found to be not guilty due to insanity. But the craziest part of this story was that John Bobbitt appeared in an 'adult' film called 'Frankenpenis'! I was reluctant to show the article to Sandra as we had had a little tiff the day before. Fact is stranger than fiction as the saying goes!

Bill Clinton called for health care reform and a ban on assault weapons, but to little or no avail on both issues. Someone stole 'The Scream' (one of the most recognizable paintings in the world) by Eduard Munch from the Munch museum in Oslo. The Winter Olympics were held in Lillehammer, not so far from Oslo and Norway voted a big NO to joining The European Union. That may have been the smartest thing they could have done.

Nelson Mandela was sworn in as first democratic president of South Africa after spending twenty- seven years in prison, which put the end to apartheid.

Meanwhile back in dear old England the IRA announced 'complete cessation of military operations,' as I remembered my days traveling on the tube trains in London, with bomb warnings everywhere telling people to be on the lookout for unaccompanied bags and packages. Many years later terrorists hit London again, but not by the Irish.

On a positive note The Eurostar between London and Paris was launched through 'The Chunnel,' that was a major engineering feat, especially as the French started from their side and the English from theirs. I was expecting there to be a huge loop in the middle where the two tunnels wouldn't connect, but they did and it seemed that together French and English technology and engineering seemed to work hand in hand quite well as did the development of Concord - that magnificent flying machine. So now one could travel from Waterloo Station in London to gay Paris in about three hours. The town of Waterloo that is now in present day Belgium was where Wellington defeated Napoleon that ended his rule. So relations between the English and the French were a lot better than they were back in 1815!

The Eurostar terminal was later transferred from Waterloo Station to St Pancras where the journey now takes under three hours.

Sitting watching TV one night Sandra and I saw police cars chasing a white Ford Bronco that was being driven by the ex-football player OJ Simpson, nicknamed 'The Juice.' This then was to be the start of a long drawn out reality TV show concerning the absurd trial of OJ Simpson and all the nonsense concerning the very tragic murder of his wife Nicole Simpson and the very unfortunate murder of Ron Goldman who happened to be in the wrong place at the wrong time. People were glued to the TV mesmerized as we all watched American justice at work, with infantile buzz phrases like 'If the glove don't fit then we must acquit' as one realized that if one had enough money in America one could literally get away with murder. OJ was found not guilty after over one hundred pieces of evidence that pointed to his guilt. He was found liable, (for what?) in Civil Court. So one court finds him not guilty, while the other finds him liable. I wondered in what kind of strange judicial system we were living?

The World Cup for football was being hosted by the USA and so because of the lack of enthusiasm for the game here Sandra and I were able to scalp two tickets to see the USA v Colombia at the Rose Bowl in Pasadena. The USA won after an own goal from the Colombian defender Andres Escobar (any relation?). Unfortunately for Escobar the fans were not happy about this and he was shot dead on his return to Medellin. We later managed to see Brazil v Sweden in the Semi-Final that was a great spectacle as the Brazilians had brought their conga drums with them and danced and sang in the stands, whilst the Swedes blew horns and banged drums whilst wearing their horned helmets. It was a spectacle not to be missed, and the chance of getting to see a semi-finale game in the World Cup would have been impossible anywhere else in the world. Brazil beat Sweden and went on to win the World Cup by beating Italy in the final by 3-2 in a penalty shootout after a goal less game.

On a love note Lisa Marie Presley married Michael Jackson, while Curt Cobain of Nirvana committed suicide.

Woodstock '94 happened which ended in violence. So much for the 'Love and Peace' of the original festival of '69! Meanwhile back in Deutschland the last of the Russian troops left ending the Cold War.

Senna da Silva was killed in the San Marino Grand Prix. He had won three Formula One World Championships and was regarded as one of the greatest Formula One drivers of all time.

Jacqueline Kennedy died and so did film director Lindsay Anderson who was responsible for such films as 'If,' 'O Lucky Man' and 'This Sporting Life'. Telly Savalas of Kojak fame also passed away. Meanwhile Schindler's List picked up seven Oscars at The Academy Awards, and to top off the year Yassar Arafat won the Nobel Peace Prize. So that was the year of 1994 as I once again realized what an insane world I was living in, as the battle cry of 'Freedom' was soon to scream out from the mouth of Mel Gibson!

Sandra's female clock was ticking and the conversation of children arose its head from the abyss of love. Children - those miniature adults, which are full of joy and laughter and look at you with those big blue or brown or green eyes asking for an ice cream and then an i-pad and then an i-phone and - then a small car and then college and then...

I love children in third world countries that play in the streets kicking a ball around or just playing with a couple of sticks. Little boys who carry their little sisters on their backs and watching the little children amuse themselves running into the ocean and laughing when they fall down. If I lived on an island and lived simply, I would have half a dozen of the little buggers running around - but here in the western world? The question became a bone of contention. It wasn't that Sandra was desperate to have kids, but the subject would crop up once in a while and if I jumped out of my chair and said let's have kids, well then we would have had kids. However I didn't jump out of my chair and so needless to say we didn't have kids! To this day I often wonder how my life would have been had I wanted kids. I know people who deep down wished they had not had them, sometimes they would say things like, "One is enough, don't think we'd have another" and then of course most love and adore their children. With us, it was a question of economics, I could not afford to keep a struggling actress with little or no money coming in, not knowing where my next job was coming from. I know there are many who succeed at this but I suppose I wasn't willing to make the sacrifice or maybe it was because I was too selfish, or just the fact that I didn't want kids to grow up in this crazy world or just the fact I just didn't want them - although I must admit that now I look around and say where is my family?

It was time to look into that mirror again. After the question of children came up, it was once again the turn of the acting career.

274

Sandra was not sure what she wanted to do. She liked the idea of being a playwright and also an actress at the same time. In a casual conversation one time I mentioned the New School in New York that took in students and had that show which was connected to the Actors Studio that was hosted by James Lipton. Sandra applied for that and a couple of weeks later got a letter saying that she had been accepted and jumped for joy around the living room holding the letter of acceptance high above her head, as my heart sank into my feet. I didn't want her to go anywhere, as we were both quite happy living together. Looking back on it I should have told her that I didn't want her to go, but she was so excited about the idea that I said nothing. Of course I should never have mentioned it in the first place. We didn't really know it at the time but this was the beginning of the end.

A few months later we loaded up Sandra's Nissan, till one could hardly see out of the back window and headed Eastbound. I drove with her to Denver and from there I caught a flight to Amsterdam as I had the possibility of some work there. Her father met us in Denver and he became co-pilot for the rest of their journey to New York. I had found Sandra an apartment through a mutual friend on 17th St between 7th and 8th Ave in New York.

When we arrived in Denver we checked in to the usual middle of the road motel that was privately owned and was clean, with a paisley cover on the bed and lace curtains on the windows and heavier curtains to match the paisley bedspread for complete privacy. There was a watercolor of the Rockies over the bed and another on the adjacent wall - this one had a river running through it with the mountains in the background. The next day Sandra's father arrived and he somehow had a connection to the baseball stadium there, so the next evening we saw a game with the Colorado Rockies v some other team. I am not an American football fan, neither a baseball fan and after almost twenty years in America I had never been to a game for either sport. The stadium however was fairly new or had been renovated and was the home field of The Colorado Rockies. After loading up with hot dogs, smothered in relish and onions and ketchup and a drink we sat down in the stadium surrounded by the Rocky Mountains. I must admit I found the game quite entertaining especially during the seventh innings when everyone stood up and sang 'Take me out to the Ball Game.' As an entertainment I found it amusing and a little boring at the same time, just as an American would find the game of Cricket incomprehensible and boring. Nevertheless there we were sitting outside in a beautiful location breathing in the sweet clean mountain air.

The next day Sandra and her father drove me to the airport and I caught a flight to Amsterdam. I felt bad leaving Sandra with her father to drive the rest of the way, but business was calling and I felt like I had an opportunity to work in Amsterdam. My ex. - Ingrid had given me a contact there and I had spoken to the woman at this particular production company and was set to see her in a couple of days. I landed at Schiphol Airport and I was back in Amsterdam.

I checked in at The Prince Hendrick Hotel near the train station. It was raining now as I looked out onto the square and decided to soak in the big deep bathtub for a while after my day of flying from Denver to New York and then across the Atlantic to Schipol Airport Amsterdam. The train from the airport to the train station was the easiest part of the trip and I was very relieved to throw my backpack on the bed in my new abode. I had been traveling for a good fifteen hours or so after waiting for the KLM flight from Kennedy to Holland. After the soak in the tub I felt somewhat rejuvenated, but still had the sensation of flying. I was also starving and so hit the streets of Amsterdam and walked into the nearest restaurant that was Indonesian. I ordered a Nasi Goreng and memories of Bali came flooding back to me. I don't think the cook was Indonesian as it was some of the worst food I had ever tasted. I washed it down with a beer and floated in a daze back to the hotel and hit the sack.

The next day I called the production company and the woman I had spoken to when I was in California was not around and wouldn't be for the next two weeks so I was told, which threw a spanner in the works. I had flown all the way to Amsterdam to hopefully connect with a production company and now nobody was there whom I could talk to. The flakiness of the advertising business was obviously worldwide and now I was stranded in Amsterdam, all dressed up with no place to go!

Amsterdam winter 1993

I sat on the bed and wrote my log. It was now dark, lights glistened on the canal outside the window and Prince sang on MTV - images flickered on the ceiling. I decided to go out for a walk and heard the happy music of the organ grinder. I was suddenly walking around in 'Wings of Desire,' where everything had turned into a monochromatic world. I meandered back to the hotel and the music got softer as it floated back into a time past. Along the canals it was damp and rain was hanging in the air - it was the beginning of a long grey northern European winter and I shuddered a little as I closed the collar around my neck. I called Cecilia a friend that I met in Luxembourg. She was visiting a friend here in Amsterdam. We got together for a quick drink, but then she had to leave on the train. I walked her to the train station, her eyes shining under the red beret, her black hair, long and tangled beneath. She was a bit like a gypsy and a lot like myself. She was very sensitive and very hard as well, a little bit hardened by life and wise and foolish at the same time. She said she felt old. I hadn't seen her for a year and a half, there were lines around her eyes that weren't there before, and she looked a little older but also more beautiful. She had since contracted malaria in Gambia and had a raving love affair with a guy with some Greek sounding name. She had been battered by this affair and another scar was added to her life and yet another chapter had been added to her book of wisdom at the same time. She told me she loved me in Luxembourg and gave me the key to her place, but that was two years ago.

277

That was then, and now I was in Amsterdam on a wild goose chase, with no prospects of work here it seemed. I stayed a couple more days to see the city again and visited the Van Gogh Museum after a puff or two at one of the Bulldog coffee bars. The last time I visited Vincent was on a previous visit to Amsterdam quite a few years ago and once again I was enamored by this artistic genius. I spent a few minutes in front of each and every canvass mesmerized by his wild yet carefully placed brush strokes as each one was laid down thick and with purpose. My next visit was to the Rijksmuseum, which is close to the Van Gogh Museum that housed the works of Rembrandt, Frans Hals and Vermeer. Although I appreciated the amazing techniques of these three painters I preferred the works of Van Gogh as his colors were more vibrant and the subject matter more interesting to me. The Rijksmuseum was dark and dreary in keeping with the dark northern European winter outside. I visited The Ann Frank house again as I imagined what it must have been like in those years when Amsterdam was occupied by the Nazis. In the evening I walked over to the Rembrandtplein where I drank a beer or two.

I booked a flight to London to see my dear old Mum again and once again my good friend Maurice picked me up from the airport and delivered me safe and sound to dear Mama. I didn't tell her about my visit and when I knocked on the front door she almost had a heart attack. Her response was "You should have told me you were coming as I would have gone out shopping."

Ah Mums! Where would we be without them? So as usual I did the rounds visiting old friends and sitting in on old wooden chairs in pubs in front of roaring fires with a pint in my hand as I entertained all with my stories of agony and ecstasy!

One of the canals in Amsterdam

Amsterdam

Back in Laguna Beach and the retreat at Joshua Tree

While I was living in Laguna Beach an English friend of mine who was living in New York told me about these meditation workshops that took place all over the country. There was one coming up in Joshua Tree that he told me, which was only about a two hour drive from Laguna Beach. So I signed up and left Sandra at home to watch the sunsets. It was a four-day workshop on meditation and holotropic breathing where one would get into a trance -like state from just breathing, but in a certain way.   The classes were conducted by Jack Cornfield, who had been a Buddhist monk in Thailand, Ram Dass and Stanislav Grof, a Czech psychiatrist. It was Grof who discovered the holotropic breath work and researched the non-ordinary states of consciousness for purposes of exploring the human psyche. He was known also for his early studies of LSD and its effects on the psyche in the field of psychedelic therapy. He connects the holotropic to the Hindu concept of Atman Brahma the divine, which is the true nature of the self. There were teachings given by Jack Cornfield, and we were taught different types of meditation practices, such as a heart meditation and walking meditation. There was a large hall where the lessons and meditations took place, and in the evenings I shared a cabin with three other men. Early pujas started at about six am and lectures and talks were given throughout the day. There was no talking until dinner in the evening. We each assigned ourselves a partner for the breath work that involved one person lying down on a mat in the large hall, amongst another hundred people. The other person - your partner would be the facilitator and would give you a drink of water when necessary. Tribal and new age music was played and the person on the mat would work through a hyperventilation state into a trance. People would be crying all around, men and women together, some would be screaming as the demons that each of us carry around were released. Apparently in my trance state I was on all fours breathing fast, my stomach contracting and releasing as though I was running. In my trance I was a cheetah and I was tracking down a gazelle on the

280

plains of Africa, until I dragged it down from behind by its neck. I remembered the dream state or trance, but I didn't recall being on all fours. After these sessions we would congregate into groups of five and discuss our experiences, and it was at the group session where I was told of my behaving like an animal! We each had two breathing sessions each, which could last up to two hours or so. It was like a re-birthing kind of experience where one went back into a previous life or form.

My second experience of the breath work I saw myself walking ahead of a horse and caravan. I was leading the horse by the reins and sitting on the seat of the caravan was a beautiful young woman with wild red hair, nursing a baby that she had in her lap. It was the same woman that appeared in all my dreams. This was my wife and child. As I walked ahead very slowly the leaves on the trees that were golden brown fell to the ground, and as they did so skulls grew from them, and on either sides of the road the fields were covered in crosses for the graves that were there. I had no doubt in my mind that I was traveling on a road through Germany during the time of the Black Plague and I was trying to get my wife and baby girl to a safe haven.

There was an older black woman in our group and in one of the breath works I saw her as a kind of witch doctor standing in the middle of a circle of tribesmen. I was a voyeur watching, as I didn't see my physical body. In the group meeting after the breath work, she told me that she saw herself as a witch doctor or tribal elder in the middle of this circle and that she saw me there, just as I had seen her. It was a strange connection. She lived in San Francisco and after the breath work I saw her once for a coffee and we vowed to stay in touch, it was as if she where a long lost family member. We never saw each other again but spoke on the phone a couple of times. The whole experience in the desert was cathartic as demons were expelled and the true meaning of life was put back into place and that basically we are all one tribe, and what one person does, be it good or bad affects the next, therefore it is better to pass on the good thoughts with love than the hatred that is so prevalent in American society today. All the religions basically teach the same thing, the answers are simple and as John Lennon said,' All you need is Love, Love is all you need.' Unfortunately now being 2016 we have entered a dark time, but hopefully we will transcend it. I returned to Laguna Beach as though my heart had been cleansed and scrubbed and I felt almost religious and fragile. Sandra told me that my face was clear and that I looked ten years younger. In the evening we sat on the deck and watched the sun set over the Pacific Ocean once more, feeling very blessed.

The Trip To Europe

It was time to get Sandra out of America. She had never been to Europe, like a lot of Americans and I understood why. It was a long way to go across the Atlantic. For me of course growing up in England it was just a ferry ride across the English Channel, that little strip of water separating England from the rest of Europe that managed to keep Hitler at bay. It was a little over twenty miles to France and beyond was the rest of Europe with its vast collection of cultures and languages and food. Sandra was studying acting and play writing at 'The New School' and I was there visiting from our house in Laguna Beach. So we booked a flight from New York to London and my dear friend Maurice picked us up at the airport. It was the month of June and the blossom was on the trees and it was a sunny day. Maurice dropped us off at my mother's little house in Worcester Park. She had downsized from the house that I grew up in from the age of eleven, to a smaller place that she said was more manageable. I never liked the new house nor did I like Worcester Park and felt like she could have managed to stay in the other house that was in a nicer part of Surrey.

So I introduced Sandra to my mother and they seemed to hit it off. Sandra was easy to get along with and had a good disposition and a good sense of humor. She was a little uninformed about the rest of the world which is why I thought we should take this trip together. My mother gave up her bed for the two of us and took the single bed in the small bedroom. While we were there in England we managed to

282

see a match at Wimbledon, not centre court, but some other one, but I can't remember whom we saw play. I rented a car and we drove to Stratford upon Avon, home of the Bard and saw William Shakespeare's house and the church where he was laid to rest, which was by the side of The River Avon. We walked around the village (that had been a bit commercialized) since last I was there, after we checked in to a lovely bed and breakfast place with a thatched roof on the edge of town. Sandra loved looking at all the Tudor style buildings and the wiggly windy roads and the back streets. We visited the house where William was born in 1564 and also Anne Hathaway's cottage and had a drink at The Dirty Duck, where a lot of thespians go to imbibe whilst learning their lines for the next up and coming production. We went to see 'Much Ado About Nothing' at The Royal Shakespeare Theatre that Sandra appreciated more than I. Lots of expressions came from Shakespeare's plays such as 'dead as a doornail' 'full circle' 'laughing stock' 'something in the wind' 'in a pickle' 'forever and a day' 'good riddance' 'heart of gold' 'not slept one wink' 'break the ice' and so on. So much of the English language is owed to William Shakespeare.

We could have stayed in England the whole time and driven down to Devon and Cornwall, which is my favorite part of England, although I must confess that I had never visited the Lake District, but had been to Scotland. However what I needed was to touch the land of Homer again and dive into the turquoise blue Aegean Sea once more. Sandra was excited about going to Greece as well and so we booked a flight to Athens. We stayed somewhere in The Plaka beneath the Acropolis which I had visited so many times before, as it was always an interesting experience, although this time it had scaffolding around it as the stone work was being eaten away by acid rain and pollution from the modern world. My favorite ruins in Greece were those in Delphi that were set amongst the olive groves. Two days in Athens were enough after Sandra wanted to see The Theatre of Dionysus, which she had learned about at The New School. It was built at the foot of The Acropolis and was dedicated to Dionysus the god of plays and wine, which to me seemed like a good combination. It was the

283

birthplace of the Greek Tragedy since the sixth century BC. And plays were performed there written by Sophocles and Euripides and other playwrights of the time and seated approximately seventeen thousand Athenians.

We hopped on a ship to take us to Mykonos and we stayed in a place I had stayed in many years before, that was just back from the beach. Mykonos was always fun, although grossly commercialized and the best time to visit was at the beginning or the end of the season. The first time I visited the island was in 1969 the year of the Woodstock festival. How different and undiscovered it was then! From Mykonos we did the usual ferry hopping from island to island through the Cyclades, but the first little trip was to the island of Delos where I had visited many years before, which was just off the island of Mykonos. It was known as the birthplace of the twin gods Apollo and Artemis and the island was considered to be one of the most important mythological and historical sites in Greece. The ruins contain the sites of The House of Dionysus, The Temple of Isis and The House of Cleopatra. Nobody lives on the island except for a handful of caretakers.

Lost their heads on the island of Delos

From Mykonos we took the Ferry to Santorini, but stopped off in Naxos as Sandra was feeling a little sea- sick, so we jumped ship there and found a little place to stay for the week. According to Greek Mythology Zeus was raised in a cave on Mount Zas.

Ia on the island of Santorini

I had been to Zeus' cave on Crete also many years before, so whether he moved around from cave to cave - I don't know?

I did a little writing while on Naxos as Sandra wrote her morning pages and so I decided to become Yanni the Greek for the rest of our Greek journey.

YANNI   Naxos, Cyclades Islands. Greece.   Circa 1993

Yanni laid on a bed in a white room staring at the ceiling a long way from home. He wore a soft gentle smile on his face as if his newly born feeling of detachment had taken him back into the centre of the universe, "It just is that's all," he remembered that line from a Van Morrison song. He had known that line for a long time, back from the days when he lived in India in the early 70's. He remembered the beggars with palms outstretched with that look in their eyes - that well-rehearsed look of pity and humbleness. They understood those lines, "It just is that's all." Yanni was now on the island of Naxos south east of Mykonos in the Cyclades Islands. He was feeling a little under the weather, taste of a sore throat with a feeling of a hangover that was clouding his vision a little. He had had a few drinks the night before with his American girlfriend, but now was feeling just a little run down as one gets on the road. "It just is that's all." His American girlfriend was sitting on the balcony writing her morning pages like she did every morning. They had decided to take a break from the hustle and bustle of American life and piss off to the Greek islands. Yanni had been on the islands many times before and the Greek islands were one of his favorite places in the world. It was probably the light that fascinated him most of all about Greece, and the white washed houses that contrasted against the deep blue skies. It was a magical land to him and he felt very much at home there.

Yanni was here to forget. He heard the Sirens calling from the rocks. He was in the land of the Cyclops and the Titans, so names were not important here. The name is just a way of stopping everyone from just saying Yo or Buddy or Dude as people called each other in America. So Yanni (Greek for John) seemed to work well for him. He liked the name and felt himself more of a Yanni than a John. He had been Yanni for the last 20 years. He officially changed it after one night of indulging in a drinking contest in a bar called Homer's cave on the island of Ios. The next morning his eyes cloudy from the ouzo, was transformed like the Phoenix into Yanni and he stayed that way ever since. It had a better ring to it than just plain old John, besides in

America a John was a place where you took a shit and Yanni felt it was a desecration of his name. A word or two about his American partner - He had met her almost 4 years to the day on a pizza commercial in Columbus Ohio a small town compared to New York or London, somewhere in the wilds of Ohio. He was at that time working as a director/cameraman in the indulgent world of TV commercials. It was a living too dependent on whose arse you were willing to kiss or how many times you were willing to bend over to get the big banana shoved up between your buttocks. He didn't like too many people in the world of advertising and found a lot of them to be a bunch of cornflakes. Friends came and went like farts in the breeze, well that was then, and this was now. His girlfriend Sandra who had changed her name from Sabrina a long time ago had met Yanni in Columbus where she was living. After she moved to California, Laguna Beach where the two of them lived for two years. She got tired of the advertising world and moved to New York City to become an actress in the theatre. A noble thing to do thought Yanni. She gave up a so-called stable secure career in advertising as an account executive for the unknown world of the theatre. The change made her throw out all her business attire which brought a smile back to her Midwest pretty face that opened up a whole new world of possibilities. "Jump and the net will appear," she would say to him a line she got from the 'Artist's Way.' It's a good line thought Yanni. He felt as though he influenced her life quite a bit, she was sweet and a little innocent although she had spent a night in jail in a small town in Ohio for drinking and driving. She was a good mix of decency with high morals and yet entertained a wild adventurous side to her character. So now the two of them were together on the island of Naxos.

He had gone to New York to pick her up from California then to fly off to Athens. Two nights before they were due to go they were making love and Yanni's knee popped out - an old war wound from dancing up a storm whilst working as a gaffer on a horror film in Mobile Alabama. He was with a few film cronies in a redneck bar, when he decided to show everyone how to Cossack dance! He flung

288

his legs around as though they were not his and one of them landed on a table and the rest of him descended to the floor. There was a loud resounding crack and his leg popped out. He completely tore his arterial crucial ligament and had lost all support in his knee. He ignored the injury for eight years trying to strengthen it by cycling and swimming etc. but there was no support left. Once a year or so it would pop out and he would pop it back in again. This one night however it stayed out for about 30 hours and on the second night he went to bed he awoke in the morning his knee had popped back in the next day. The day after they jumped on a plane to Athens. It was about 4.15 in the morning when they arrived in Athens and a lot cooler than Yanni had expected. He had been to Athens many times before and had remembered the heat surrounding him and engulfing him as he stepped off the plane into what seemed like an oven. Those times had been later in the summer around July or sometimes August, he had remembered.

There was one year when he was about 19 or 20 when he and a friend drove to Athens from London that was about the end of May he reminded himself. In those days he was coming to Greece from chilly London so the difference in temperature was therefore much more noticeable. This time Yanni came from sunny California. The Greeks had had a cold winter and it will take a while for the Aegean Sea to warm up. In July it would be warm enough to play in the sea all day. Yanni remembered those long hot summers in Greece particularly the summer when he drove out with his friend Barry in his Triumph 2000. They took two weeks to make the journey starting at Harwich, they took the car ferry to the Hook of Holland and then traveled to Amsterdam, Rotterdam through Germany, where they camped deep into the thickly wooded Black Forest. Then on to Salzburg over the mountains, down through Yugoslavia to Split and a Dubrovnik a beautiful mediaeval city on the Adriatic coast. Around Albania they drove, through a small town called Pec where the gypsies threw stones at their car as they passed by. In those days 1971 there was barely a decent road around Albania. Yanni remembered having to push some large rocks out of the road to allow the car to pass. He remembered that they only traveled a very short distance one day as the road was so bad. Yanni and his friend finally got to Athens after visiting Thessaloniki and driving through the country, a beautiful drive spending the night at Delphi in the temple of Apollo amongst the olive groves. They had spent one night with the gypsies in the north of Greece and Yanni had taken many photographs there. He watched the gypsies gallop on their horses. He watched the children with their matted hair and dirty faces fight and play. The drive through Europe was quite the adventure especially as they were still lads only 20 years old. Everything at that age was an adventure. In Athens they spent the night and the next day they went for a swim at Glyfada Beach. Yanni kept his camera in the car covered up behind the driver's seat when they went for a swim - when they came back the cameras and exposed rolls of film had been stolen - the many shots of the Swiss Alps, of Salzberg, Dubrovnik and the Gypsies and Delphi were lost forever. He remembered how upset he was at the loss of these pictures. Photographers have cameras to record images of life, like a painter has a brush or a writer a pen. The photo the image is a record of the experience and Yanni was very saddened by the loss of his recorded experiences. He didn't care so much about the cameras, but it was the memories that he lost, recorded on film that upset him more. A lot of the experiences were a one off, never to be repeated again. It left him empty like the death of a friend.

The next three months he didn't have to worry about looking after his camera only his passport and money. He lived in a cave in Mattala on the south coast of Crete and slept on the beaches of Mykonos, on Paradise Beach when there were only a couple of dozen hippies and travelers there. He lived in Santorini high up on the caldera overlooking the Volcano. He slept on black volcanic beaches that were caused by the erupting fiery earth that shot pumice stone high up into the air, so high that it landed on the continent of Africa a few hundred years ago. Yanni sat back in the chair at the airport chuckling to himself about his impetuous youth. He had had his moments and was proud to still be alive, thanks to the protecting arm of his father Zeus. He had calmed down since those days, indeed his body had told

290

him to. He was traveling with a strapped knee and a plastic eye. The previous November he had received cataract surgery on his right eye, not a good thing for a cameraman to be blind! He was only 44 years old at that time - 'very young,' the doctor had told him. Yanni may have stared at the sun too many times back in the early 70s. He couldn't remember, he never wore sunglasses maybe that's what happened. So that was Yanni in the third person. It was fun to be someone else once in a while.

After our stay in Naxos, which seemed to be the playground of the Germans we boarded a Ferry once again and landed on the island of Santorini that is one of the most beautiful places on Earth. It is thought by many to have been the ancient city of Atlantis and excavations have been going on there for years. It was the site of the biggest volcanic eruption in recorded history, which occurred 3,600 years ago at the height of the Minoan civilization. Supposedly the eruption caused a huge tsunami, which wiped out the Minoan civilization on Crete. A lot of the beaches are made up of black volcanic ash and rock. We rented a motor scooter there as we did on Naxos and managed not to fall off! I prefer to rent a motorbike, as they are a lot safer and easier to control as the wheels are larger and not back heavy like a scooter.

The Greek islands are notorious for scooter accidents as is Bali and other parts of the world that are overrun by tourists. From Santorini we sailed to Folegandros and then to the island of Sifnos where we stayed for a couple of weeks. We found some rooms behind a restaurant and rented one that was just fine, which consisted of two simple pine beds, and a marble bathroom with a shower. Sifnos is known for its pottery and there are little shops selling their wares all over the island. We had lots of cheese balls, which were delicious and I believe were made from manoura cheese a specialty of the island. There are hundreds of islands and each one has its own personality. The Greek islands are my favorite place in the whole world. So after Sifnos we took yet another crowded boat back to Piraeus and the day after flew back to England.

Back in the Big Apple

The trip to Greece was over and we were now back in New York City. It was a Monday morning and Sandra wrote her morning pages like she did every morning without fail. In an hour or so she will go off to work at an advertising agency as a part-time job while she is on hiatus from the Actors Studio. Last night they had their usual 'marry me' scenario "When are you going to marry me?" she asked me, I replied with the vacant stare of bewilderment and horror. The question was one of babies - she wanted to have a couple and I didn't. Here then lies the problem. Her body clock was ticking at 34 she had just turned it on 4th July the All-American girl from Hicksville, Ohio, sweet as a button, kind, loving and funny too. She was a one-off. She had two more years of school and at the end would leave her $50,000 in debt, this was the bone of contention from the night before - "That's great!" I said in a raised voice not a shout, but an agitated, can't believe you tone of voice. I didn't mean to be harsh with her, but maybe I came off that way.

We had had this conversation so many times before in one way or another but basically it always came down to kids or at least that was my excuse for not wanting to get married. The thought of getting married never really crossed my mind before. I didn't see the need to get married unless kids were involved. I wasn't going anywhere and had been faithful to Sandra. But now here I was with a pretty blue-eyed girl from Hicksville, Ohio whom I loved a lot, but didn't seem to fit into my little dream world very well. My world was a dream world–that wasn't relative to anything. I was now forty-five and possibly going through my midlife crisis. This wasn't unusual for me however to create a crisis from time to time - I had read all the books about keeping a balance in life, from the Autobiography of a Yogi to the Tao, to the Bhagavadgita and many of the Eastern philosophies. I had read books on how to free your spirit and unblock yourself so all your creativity can blossom - to get rid of what you haven't got, but

292

still quite frequently I would sink into the depths of depression where everything seemed hopeless and futile. A mood when nothing made any sense and what's the point? Then, not always then, but sometimes I would remember some of the teachings from the eastern books of wisdom like it is, and it isn't, all at the same time like we know everything and yet nothing. Man has always been searching for the meaning of life, but there is no meaning to life except to go forth and multiply - was that really the answer? Couples he knew with children seemed completely frazzled to him, they would say things like, "Of course we love Sammy or Zoe or Alex" or whoever "But we would never have another." "One is enough," so many of them would say. Invariably of course, they would have another one and be even more frazzled!

I walked around the apartment for the next hour scratching my head, scratching my chin looking out onto the little courtyard on 17th Street, and then decided to go out for a cup of coffee in Chelsea. It was a beautiful morning with clear blue skies. I loved just drifting around the streets of New York watching the people hail down taxicabs, watching them disappear into the hole in the ground catching a subway train, waiting for the bus, hanging out on street corners. The dudes in midtown with their cachet cases trying to sell jewelry, and then running off at the first sign of a cop. I enjoyed watching the rich people walk down Fifth Avenue with their poodles. I enjoyed 42nd Street with its sleaziness and pornographic cinemas, hawkers, junkies, guys with gold chains around their necks, the Upper East Side and its doctors and lawyers which I considered to be the most boring part of Manhattan. I was so glad I didn't live there when I came to New York. New York then to me was anywhere below 14th Street, to go above would only result in a nosebleed. The West Village, East Village, Soho, Tribeca, Battery Park was all good and trips to the West Side and Central Park were great, but home to me was always Downtown. I was a Downtown kind of guy. Soho had already changed by this point as I remembered the Soho of West Broadway when it was full of art galleries and warehouses and Tribeca smelled of spices and seemed quite desolate. It was where artists lived illegally in

293

commercial loft spaces and weekends were party time when one hopped from one loft party to the next. I sat for a while in Washington Square Park and watched the skateboarder's crash headfirst into trees or just slam onto the concrete. Chess players who were all searching for Bobby Fischer were playing under the dappled light of a hot July sun. The young kids with their guitars and drums singing in the square, the smell of reefer wafting in the breeze, old women walking their poodles, young men walking their girlfriends, and old men walking their Zimmer frames. It was all there a complete cross-section of life that was New York City to me, a place of extremes, but a good hodgepodge, a good cross-section of humanity was alive and well in The Big Apple.

During the mid-nineties when I was living in Laguna Beach with Sandra I was working as a director/cameraman for a production company in Dallas shooting Ci Ci's Pizza commercials, then for another company out of Detroit and another in Fort Lauderdale and a couple of other companies - one in Columbus Ohio and occasionally a job in New York. I also shot quite a few toy commercials in Vancouver and was traveling there about three times a year for about three years. I enjoyed the city and made some good friends there. After Sandra went off to New York I would visit every three months or so and stay for a while, until into the third year we seemed to have drifted apart. She had an affair with someone from her acting class, which I wasn't too happy about. It was a stupid idea of mine to have suggested her applying to the New School and after she got in I should have told her to stay in Laguna with me.

After three years I was bored with living in Laguna Beach on my own and decided to move to a tiny shoe-box of a place a couple of blocks from the beach in Santa Monica. My friend was moving back to New York and so his place that was rent controlled became available. It seemed there were a lot more like-minded people in Santa Monica that I could relate to, which was true. I remember when I packed up the house in Laguna and the place was empty, I had one more trip to make back to Santa Monica. I was sleeping in a sleeping bag for that last night and I cried as I realized I was leaving this lovely home with a spectacular view of the Pacific Ocean. My landlord wanted to sell the place for about $280,000. It would have been a stretch for me to buy on my own and I should have done it of course, but I was the 'would have, should have, could have, man.' The house went up in value to over one million dollars.

Wonder

He was the would have
Should have
Could have man.
And he wondered why he didn't,
And he wondered if he can.

And he knows he really should have,
And he would have, if he could,
But he really didn't do it,
And he knows he really should.

Now he sits at home and wonders
If he had of and he should of,
But he didn't do of course,
But he could have just done something
But was so filled with remorse.

But he's the would have, should have, could have man.

And wondering is his game,

And he really could have done it,

But Wonder was his name

It was the end of an affair and Sandra and I split up our furniture and belongings. She took my cast iron bed, as there was a built in bed that my friend had made in the cottage in Santa Monica. She took the table and chairs and I was left with the bookshelves and coffee table and some other odds and sods. I enjoyed living two blocks from the sea, but I missed the view and the space that I had in Laguna. I moved from about 2,400 sq. feet into a place of about 500 sq. feet - if that. I could walk to all the bars and restaurants around and had people that I could get a beer with. I still continued to work in Dallas, but I missed flying out of the little John Wayne airport in Orange County.

So life went on without Sandra and I met a lovely Colombian woman who was a nurse. I had just received a cataract operation from Jules Stein hospital that was part of UCLA. I friend of mine was driving me home and this nurse had to escort me off the premises, I suppose for insurance purposes. Whilst we were in the elevator together, with a patch over my eye, I was feeling like a pirate and I was very high from the drugs I had received. I asked this lovely woman her name and she told me it was Patricia. I asked her for her phone number and she was quite taken aback and refused, so I wrote down mine on a piece of paper and handed it to her there and then.

After three days or so Patricia called me. I was so happy. She told me that she had had a date with this jock at the weekend that didn't stop talking about himself, and bored her to tears and so decided to call me as she thought I was a little different. A jock I certainly wasn't! So we got together and she came over from work from UCLA and we went out for a drink. She told me that I wasn't her usual type, and that she usually dated fitter looking specimens then myself, but that she liked my personality despite my little beer belly that I had acquired over the years. I was no longer the Adonis that I thought I was in my early twenties as I was now only about four years from the big five - oh! We hit it off, she was a lovely Latina woman, her skin coffee colored and with an hourglass body. I made her laugh a lot and she would call me Juani and her English muffin, and I called her my little coffee bean.

We dated for almost five years, but I was leaving a lot for work in Vancouver. She came to visit me on a couple of occasions and Patricia enjoyed the city. It is a beautiful city, but rains too much in the winter and sometimes the sun hides for weeks at a time and people become depressed from sun depravation. It was at these times I would fly south back to my little cottage by the sea. I bought a sweet little apartment in Vancouver, down by English Bay and got my view back of the ocean and the mountains to the north. It was a corner apartment on the fifteenth floor, so I had north and west views and amazing sunsets, which were caused by the continuing changes in the weather as dark clouds could roll in creating godlike shafts of light at times and shades of violet and reds and orange would fill the sky like a huge abstract painting. Vancouver is in a rainforest that is why it is so green. I believe that British Columbia has the second biggest rainforest next to Brazil's in the world.

While I was living in Vancouver I shot a few low budget feature films. In fact the first film I shot there was called Christina's House, which I managed to get after being in Vancouver for only a couple of weeks. Another was a film called 11:11 and Ripper II which I went to the Czech Republic to film. In 2001 in February, I was the director of photography on a film called Hellraiser/Hellseeker the sixth film in the Hellraiser series, featuring Pinhead, and I was nominated for best cinematography for the Miramax dvd awards in Los Angeles.

Santa Monica

After packing up Laguna Beach I made a new home for myself in Santa Monica. I moved into a cottage built in about 1924 just two blocks from the beach. It was about one fifth of the size of the house in Laguna, but I was off on a new adventure. These little homes were originally built so I was told to serve the Hollywood crowd back in the twenties so that they could romp around on the beach at the weekends after driving down from Hollywood in their model T Fords. My particular place had quite a large kitchen and bathroom, considering the overall size. There were showers outside as well for showering off after a day at the beach that no longer worked.

In the twenty years that I have lived in the area I have seen some big changes and usually not for the better, too much gentrification, that in the end turns places into sterilized environments, devoid of their original charm. Nevertheless the beach is still two blocks away. One good improvement was the transformation of Third Street that used to be a funky street with second hand books stores and second hand clothing stores that turned into a re-vamped promenade. The Civic Auditorium was only a few blocks away and in the sixties played host to the Oscars. Many bands played there also in the past, including Hendrix, The Stones, Elton John, Dave Brubeck, Bowie, Bob Dylan, Joan Baez and many more. According to legend Beach Volley Ball was developed here in Santa Monica. It also had the nickname of Dogtown, but I think this was more an area closer to Venice beach where skateboarding was invented - a plague on pedestrians using sidewalks.

Lady Diana

I had only been living in Santa Monica a couple of months when I heard the tragic news of Princess Diana's death in a car crash. It happened on the night of August 31st, half an hour past midnight. She died as a result of injuries sustained in a car crash in The Pont de l'Alma road tunnel in Paris when a car that she was in, hit a pillar at over 65 miles an hour - the speed limit was way less! Dodi Fayed her boyfriend and Henri Paul (the driver) were pronounced dead at the scene. Lady Di was only 36 years old. Henri Paul, deputy head of security at The Ritz Hotel that was owned by Dodi's father was instructed to drive the couple in a '94 Mercedes. Trevor Rees-Jones, the bodyguard was the only survivor. Henri Paul the driver was on a concoction of anti- depressants. A tranquillizing anti-psychotic was also found in his body as well as the alcohol intake being well over the limits. No one was wearing seat belts, and it seemed like there was gross negligence all round.

During the four weeks following the funeral of Lady Diana, the suicide rate in England rose by 17%. The greatest increases being by women between the ages of 25 - 45 when the suicide rate increased by a staggering rate of over 45%. Dodi Fayed was an Egyptian and produced a number of films. He was a producer on Chariots of Fire. His father was Mohamed Al Fahed, a billionaire who bought the House of Fraser including Harrods in 1985 and is owned by the State of Qatar. He also owned Fulham football club. He claimed that the crash was as a result of a conspiracy and that MI6 was responsible. Later the charges were dropped.

I worked in Harrods at a place called The Way In, which was on the top floor. I was a photographer there for two or three years when I was twenty. It was a beautiful store where many members of the Royal Family would shop. Harrods' motto was 'All things for all people everywhere.' While I was working there someone put the motto to the test and ordered for a team of huskies and a sled to be delivered to an address in Kensington!

So the next few days after Lady Diana's untimely death were spent grieving and it seemed like the whole world grew a little darker. The funeral was on the 6th September, a week after the accident. The coffin was carried on a gun carriage through the streets of London where over a million people had gathered to show their last respects. People were in tears and others were literally wailing over the loss of their beloved Princess, as Diana seemed to have been loved by the whole world. Over two billion traced the event worldwide.

The funeral was held at Westminster Abbey and during the service Elton John sang a re-written version of 'Candle in the Wind' in tribute to his friend Lady Di. Celebrities and dignitaries and Kings and Queens and the great Nelson Mandela all attended the saddest ceremony in English history for years.

Earlier that year thirty-nine members of a religious UFO cult that called itself 'Heaven's Gate' participated in a mass suicide that was based in San Diego. They believed that an extra-terrestial spacecraft like the 'Mother Ship' was going to save their souls as they believed that Planet Earth was going to be wiped clean and rejuvenated and so the only way to survive was to leave the planet. So they committed suicide so that their souls could board the 'spacecraft.' They believed that this craft was trailing Hale's Comet. Eight of the members voluntarily underwent castration in Mexico including the cult leader Applewhite as a means of maintaining their ascetic lifestyle. That would certainly do the trick I thought! The members all took Phenobarbital mixed with apple- sauce (makes sense as the leader's name was Applewhite) and was washed down with vodka - delicious. (It reminded me of the Jim Jones cult in Guyana back in the late seventies). When the police found the bodies they were all dressed in identical black shirts and sweat pants and brand new black and white Nike athletic shoes! What great advertising for Nike I thought to myself as I realized that I might be living in one huge insane asylum!

Just a couple more notes on the year:

Versace was murdered in South Beach Florida. While on a more pleasant note the first book of 'Harry Potter' was published and 'Dolly' the sheep was successfully cloned in England. Also in the UK there was a total ban on handguns that made me think that politicians in England had a bit more sense than their counterparts in America (land of the brave and home of the free). While back in America again Timothy McVeigh was sentenced to death for his part in the Oklahoma City bombing. And in Hong Kong it was time for the Chinese take away as England gave back Hong Kong to China after it's ninety-nine year lease.

In this year Robert Mitcham died so to James Stewart, William Burroughs, Mother Theresa, Roy Lichtenstein, John Denver, Harold Robbins and poor Lady Diana Princess of Wales way before her time.

THE WALL AND THE WINDOW

The wall and the window have become my friends
People I knew have met their bitter end
So no more messages will I send.

The window I look at when I want to go outside
The wall I look at when I want to hide
The wall and the window, their time I divide.

The wall and the window have become my friends
I talk to the wall, which always listens
But the window changes with the weather
Should I wear shorts, or take my umbrella?

The wall and the window make up a house
Sometimes it's quiet, as quiet as a mouse
And sometimes it's stormier inside than out
When I try to figure what it's all about.

Santa Monica California

302

Abstract Painting

The bug finally hit me after years of wandering around museums and art galleries around the world and looking at the works of the masters. I decided it was time to pick up a paintbrush and paint - and paint I did like a man possessed. It was the most freeing experience that I had ever had. I was painting for twelve hours a day and more when I started, but eventually slowed down. Now fifteen years later I am the proud owner of over 600 works that are all in storage units that are shared between Vancouver and Santa Monica.

I sat in the kitchen looking at the abstract painting I had painted that hung over the gas stove. I enjoyed being my own curator and critic, biggest fan and student. I believed the tools and knowledge that was in the law lived inside of all of us - it was just a matter of opening it up with the right key. I had a dream the other night that I stood outside of my little cottage here in Santa Monica with a bunch of keys. I separated one key from the other and inserted them one by one into the lock on the front door. They all failed to open the door, I was locked outside of my own home, I couldn't even get in to where I lived. I think I was beginning to understand that there were other planes - that this material world was not the only one, and that the spirit world was within arms reach. I also noticed that thinking too much can contribute to the point of insanity - thoughts that just fly off into the sky. Creativity killed Van Gogh but at the same time kept him very much alive more alive than most men at his time I think. I understand some of his passion. But who could possibly understand what truly went on in that man's mind. It was love of what he felt, love for the ability to see beyond just what the eye sees, and understanding it. I felt like one of those little pawns that the Greek gods look down upon and move us here and there across oceans and valleys and mountains. Statements set adrift in their own little boats. The tick tock of the clock in the kitchen reminded me of my mother's house. She's dead now, so is my father and my sister and my cousin, six of my Aunts and quite a few old friends and even more people that I didn't know. I was happy with what I had done with my cottage. I had decorated the whole place, painted it white, put down a new floor in the kitchen and the bathroom. It was fun to dream and fantasize and I was really beginning to enjoy being alone. I had moments of loneliness, but not too many, I enjoyed my freedom, I enjoy and I still do enjoy supreme emptiness - enjoyed the pain and the sorrow, and love life. I appreciate being alive, although I must admit that sometimes I wished I were dead. That however could just pass as a romantic notion, because when you're dead you can't think anymore. The clock kept ticking. My mind kept thinking. My hopes kept hoping. Winter is approaching and I relished the idea. It was to be a time of great creativity and enlightenment. Hare Krishna had a drama, Rama Rama Hari Hari…

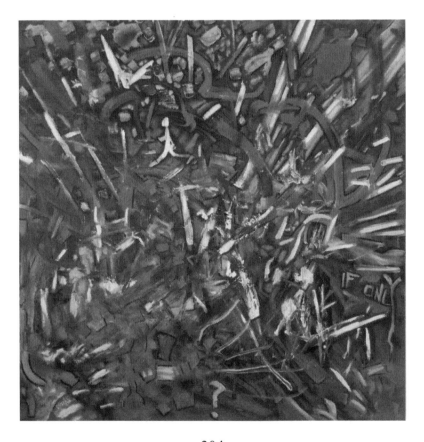

SANTA MONICA   LATER THAT MONTH...

It was another day.
I walked down the beach
Had a beer at the Water Front Café
Then walked back to my cottage on the Strand.

I passed a dog on the way and said,
"Hello dog" – he didn't answer,
Neither did his mistress –
It's OK – I didn't care for either of them really.

It was a perfect day
The sky was blue
With not a cloud in the sky,
But where were you?

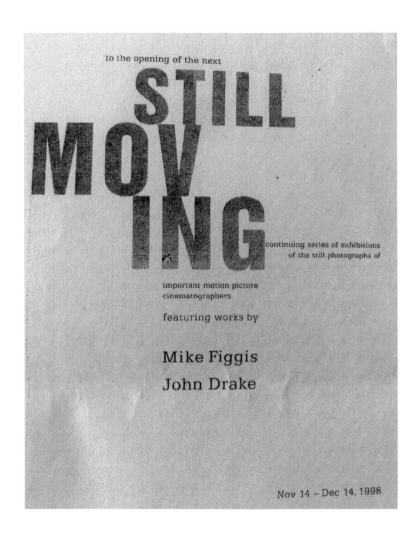

to the opening of the next

STILL MOVING

continuing series of exhibitions
of the still photographs of

important motion picture
cinematographers

featuring works by

Mike Figgis

John Drake

Nov 14 – Dec 14, 1998

*I had an opening on Melrose Avenue showing some of my travel
photographs along with Mike Figgis who directed 'Leaving Las Vegas'*

Detroit

I was in Detroit in pre - production for a commercial for a furniture company and shooting was to take place in a couple of days. I beeped in to my answering machine in the evening and there was a message from my mother saying that my poor sister probably only had a couple more days to live. She had been sick for a while with cancer. Originally she had breast cancer in her early forties, that was supposed to have cleared up, but it re-appeared when she was about fifty, but this time it had moved to her spine and her liver and was gradually taking over her body, this dreadful monster of a disease. My mother of course sounded quite distraught, but she was a strong woman and had seen my father pass away fifteen years before. I called my landlord to send my passport to me by Federal Express. I told him where it was in my apartment and I received it the next day. Of course I had to bail out of this job, which Andre understood. I hadn't thought about bringing my passport with me, as the last thing I heard was that my sister was in a quite stable condition. I left on Northwest Airlines to London, but somewhere past Newfoundland a woman on the plane got violently ill and the plane had to turn around to land in Sydney. The woman was taken off the plane but we were grounded for at least two hours whilst they were finding the woman's luggage. I felt bad for the woman of course, but why now? I said to myself - I was anxious to see my sister.

Finally we landed at Heathrow and my mother and brother-in-law were there to meet me and we drove straight to the hospital that was in London. My two nieces were already there at her bedside, and we all hugged each other on meeting. My sister was hooked up with all kinds of devices, oxygen tube in her nose and an intravenous drip in her arm. She was on heavy doses of morphine and it seemed like she was in a deep dream state ready to depart this world. All of us sat around her bed as I leaned into her and told her that her brother was here by her side. "Diane this is John, your brother" I said, as I got closer to her ear. I said it again, and told her how much I loved her - her eyelids flickered once, and her mouth slightly widened to a sad smile. I think she may have heard me somewhere in her altered state, between life and death. There was no talking as I held her hand in mine, I could only look at my poor sister, that I hadn't seen a lot of over the past years. My eyes started to tear up as I realized that I wouldn't be able to talk to her again. It was surreal - yesterday I was in Detroit and now here I was watching my sister die and there was nothing anyone could do about it. She lay there in her own cloudy universe, with barely a thread left connecting her to this earth. We left the hospital, and I drove us back to Epsom and nobody spoke a word. In the early hours of the next morning my dear sister died. I had flown across the Atlantic to say goodbye. Now once again I left my dear mother alone standing at the doorstop, waving goodbye, as she had done twenty-one years ago when I left after my father died. This time she had lost her daughter, and her son was leaving for America again. Once there was a family and now I felt terrible about leaving my mother once again.

In that same week Linda McCartney died, also from cancer.

Nothing is what it seems, and it seems like nothing is the same anymore. The world has changed so much since I was a kid running around the streets of London town. Now it seems like there is nowhere to go that feels like home anymore. I am adrift again in that life raft, bobbing up and down in a swirling sea waiting to be saved by a good soul. My life raft was sinking slowly but surely as I sat in the middle of an endless sea, surrounded by horizons in all directions, with not even a bird in sight to break the monotony and below a world of sharks waiting to indulge on my very being.

I began to wonder if there was any hope of being saved from my own personal purgatory as my mind drifted off to a sea of memories and happier times when I felt like I was in control of my own life. I was once the King of the Castle and now I was just a rascal as I sit alone adrift in my own nightmare that I alone had created. I wondered whom this person was that had made all these bad decisions in life as I floated off into oblivion and the edge of the world.

I was from another time and lately I felt like I was from another dimension as I began to wonder what was real and what was not. There was something I was looking for, but wasn't quite sure what it was. I was waiting for the Genie to come out of the bottle, but the only thing to come out of the bottle was drunkenness. I took another sip of tequila as I hid under my sombrero - the sun was baking hot as I nodded off to sleep in the shade of my sombrero as I dreamt of windmills on the island of Mykonos and beggars on the streets of India, as my Mother asked me for baksheesh with open palms. I caught a glimpse of hope in her jaundiced eyes and then she was gone - disappeared into a sea of beggars as the dust blew into my eyes. I heard the prayers to Allah and I thought about Speak and Burton and what it must have been like to travel in their day, and as I looked into the glimmering horizon a dust storm blinded me as I tried to blot out the sun with my hand. The desert turned into forests of rich green, olive green and lime and it was beautiful and so ended another day.

As a kid I listened to Beethoven's Pastoral Symphony No6, as it reminded me of the English countryside, even though it was composed by a German. I would lie on my bed at my parent's home and dream the hours away. Life was ahead of me and although I did love the English countryside I knew I was destined for lands far away.

Now I am in those lands far away, I drink myself into oblivion to forget. I had a beautiful home high in the hills in Laguna Beach overlooking the Pacific Ocean and a beautiful woman by my side and I gave it all away for something that didn't exist. I don't even know what I was looking for except a time before I was born. I would awake to find myself not where I wanted to be, although it wasn't always that way. I had become the most discontented man in the world and I had every right to be happy but I wasn't.

Words - I think of words, what else is left but words? Sometimes they don't come, so I pick up a paintbrush and paint the words that don't come, onto a canvass that become pure subconscious driven by emotion. Now when I have dreams, I'm not sure if they are mine or some convoluted contrived montage that I have concocted from TV and movies as I ask myself what is real anymore? Do we have any original thoughts or are they all stolen, possibly unintentionally from poets and writers from the past? I want my own mind back - where did it go - down the rabbit hole to visit Alice? Does an artist have to be tormented to be an artist? I suppose most people don't question the status quo. I am glad I grew up in a world without cell phones and computers. We have to enjoy life while we can, as we are not here for long. I need to repair my soul on this long and winding road that leads to only one place. The world is plastered in mediocrity. I am waiting at the door, sitting on the threshold, sitting in the darkness, looking around with no place to go.

I think about all the great sadness that there is in the world. I wish all the hatred would go away. I think of those who are born on the side of the streets in Bombay and Calcutta - and they die there, and that is their life and yet they have the spirit to smile at you and give you their last grain of rice if you asked for it. These are the living saints in this greedy materialistic world. These are truly God's children, no teachers, no education, just a spirit to live on regardless as they live on hope that their ashes will one day be set free to float down mother Ganges the holy river.

I have been haunted all my life by the ghost of a woman from a previous life. I have seen her over and over many times in dreams and in trances. I know exactly what she looks like and I have seen her many times walking in city streets and down country lanes, but I am old now, and the women I see are young in their twenties and thirties. Maybe they are all re-incarnations of my one and only love. Her hair is red and her face as white as ivory. She is very sophisticated in a natural way. The way of a country girl, simple yet intelligent, kind and loving with a wonderful sense of humor and a smile that would give a blind man back his sight. It is hard to describe in words the sense of loss that I have had my whole life.

It is because of these feelings that I know I have lived and loved with every part of my being. Sometimes when I am feeling very sad and lonely she comes to me and I am comforted immediately by her most wonderful smile - the smile like that of a young child, innocent, trusting and pure. Sometimes a woman may pass me in the street and the smell of her perfume surrounds me like a tornado and I know she has come back to say hello and to tell me never to forget her. I know she is from a time long ago, at least a hundred years into the weary past. I am sad that she is not with me, but I am happy that we did at one time meet.

Back to the Factory

The Woman I Once Met

In the winter time
I sit and drink old plum wine
Dressed so fine in silks and lace
I see your face.
Then realize it's just a dream
But surely once, it must have been
Sometime or other there was another
Not this year or the last
But from some long or distant past
I pray to God the dreams come true
For it's so difficult losing you
I have forgotten your beautiful face
And the time and the place
But I do know that you did exist
And sitting here so cold I wished
You'd appear for me just once again
Then maybe love would ease the pain

BACK IN THE BIG APPLE

I got a call to direct some toy commercials in New York starting the week of the 17th September, so I flew out from LA on about the 6th and stayed at a friend's place on the corner of Hudson and Perry St. My friend was in London (my home town) visiting her boyfriend there. The week of the 10th was to be spent in pre-production. It was good to be back in the Big Apple - the weather was perfect with sunny days with clear blue skies and a cool breeze with hints of Autumn in the air. It was not the New York that I remembered however. Bleecker Street had completely changed, the antique stores had gone because the rents were now too high and were replaced with high - end fashion stores that would show just one dress in the window, the price of it being enough to pay for the month's rent! The little diner had gone as well and just like Soho had lost its old world charm. New York was now only for the rich, and the lucky ones, those like my friend, who had been in their homes for the last 30 years that were still living in rent controlled or rent stabilized apartments. My friend was still only paying about $700 a month for a one - bedroom apartment and the person upstairs with the same space was paying $2,300 which they had to share with someone else so as to be able to afford the rent. This then was the changing face of New York. An old girlfriend of mine had to move out to Brooklyn, like so many other people because the rents were becoming astronomically high. She had been selling real estate for years to the Russians, people from the Middle East and India, where the prices of these loft spaces on the Hudson reached as high as two or three million and upwards for a view of New Jersey!

I got together with a few friends from the biz, that were all doing famously well, as they stuck it out in New York through the thick and thin. The White Horse Tavern was on my doorstep, just a block north on Hudson Street so I made that my local watering hole for the next few days. The Tavern had pretty much stayed the same, except the beers were probably twice the price that they were when I lived on Bethune St. in the Seventies.

314

The Bus Stop Café on the corner of Hudson and Bethune St, below where I used to live had been given a facelift and was now a polished greasy spoon diner, where the grease cost a lot more. My apartment above the diner was now renting (so I heard) for at least $1500, when I used to pay a walloping $175 a month! How things have changed. New York was still vibrant, energetic and noisy and the hustle and bustle was the same as it ever was - you just had to pay a lot more for the experience. The area around 42nd St had been turned into a mini Disney World and had lost all its sleazy charm that used to be full of hookers selling their wares, and pornographic bookshops and theatres. A place where dudes would be hanging out on the street corners selling dope and junkies would be sleeping in doorways. A smell of urine would occasionally waft through the air carried on the breeze, mixed with a delicate smell of marijuana. It was paradise for many, and an adventure for tourists into the abyss of human degradation and unadulterated sleaze into the depths of Dante's Inferno, but a lot more interesting than what it has been turned into.

I took the subway to Central Park that was the same as it ever was. The trees were the same but had grown since I last saw them, and couples still took the romantic carriage rides under the trees with the dappled sunlight caressing their faces, as love looked at each other, whilst skateboarders and cyclists flew by going as fast as they could to nowhere. I felt a little sad being back in New York, as there was a time when I felt a part of it, like a brick in an old building. Now I was here as a visitor looking at my favorite city in the world back then, and viewing it all though a new pair of glasses. The skyline was the same, unmistakable and powerful, with the twin towers at the base of the city and the Empire State and Chrysler building gleaming in the sunlight. The big yellow checker cabs were retired in 1999, but there were still hundreds of other ones, their colors breaking the grayness of the pot-holed streets destroyed by New York's harsh winters. I wandered like a lost tourist through the canyons of steel and glass, once again being seduced and mesmerized by the city's majesty and grandeur, as I shrunk in size in comparison to the mammoth buildings that surrounded me as I walked up Fifth Avenue, spying on the rich, as they rushed out of stores laden with expensive utensils for the kitchen, or clothes fit for a prince, as they frantically waved down cab after cab, as they flew by already filled with others that had shopped before them. They didn't seem particularly happy, but stressed. Mouths smothered in lipstick drooped, as if gravity was pulling them down. They rushed around as though they had a few days to live, not particularly appreciating the fine autumn climate. I was glad that I viewed life as a peasant, as I appreciated my life in small mercies and found the people I was looking at to be quite absurd in their frantic self-absorbed world. I began to realize that I had become softened by California's relatively easy life style, especially down at the beach, but did understand the New York state of mind also. I felt somewhere between the two worlds, not saying that I needed to live in the midwest!

I walked up to the park again the next day, and visited Strawberry Fields, and saw Alice in Wonderland and the Imagine dedication to John Lennon, as I remembered being at the wake with Abby the day after he was shot twenty one years before, and thought that John would be sixty-one years old had he still been alive today. I eventually made it back downtown to my safe haven in the village. I never felt comfortable venturing above Fourteenth Street when the nose bleeds would set in. I sighed a sigh of relief as I alighted into the sunlight out of the subway at Fourteenth and Eighth Avenue. I had forgotten about the subway experience, but I found people to be very depressed wearing gray complexions, and I compared it to the London Underground where people dare not make eye contact for fear of having to make conversation. The screeching noise of the trains in the subway sounded like an opera singer being strangled as the carriages sang to a halt tagged by gang members claiming their rights to the Big Apple, as the women with the bags on Fifth Avenue squeezed into those yellow cabs a hundred feet or so above the dark screaming world of Hades. I needed a beer and got one sitting on a wobbly wooden table outside of The White Horse Tavern. I wrote a poem about the place as I waited to meet my friend Ken who had come in from Pennsylvania to imbibe with me in a glass of hops and barley. The wooden tables reminded me of the times when I would sit with friends out in the English countryside gulping down pint after pint of best bitter, or a thick black hearty pint of Guinness, whilst crunching on some salt and vinegar crisps, that made one even thirstier for the next pint.

The White Horse Tavern Again

Twas in the White Horse Tavern
Where I met a man who wasn't there,
He wasn't there when I was here
Thirty years or more before,
The sky outside was turning grey
It never started out that way.

Dylan Thomas drank in here
As I devoured my second beer,
A picture of him on the wall,
I saw him from my old bar stool.
I recognized that man again -
I looked outside and saw the rain.

A pint of Guinness in my hand,
A long way from my own homeland,
I thought about that man I knew
Then realized he looked like you.

I wished that man would go away
But looked like he was here to stay,
I knew that things could be much worse
As I finished off this little verse.

318

Saturday 8th September.

Now it was the weekend when the invasion from across the rivers would happen, as people from New Jersey and the Boroughs went on a rampage, like hoard's of Vikings raping and pillaging everything in their path, while the inhabitants of Manhattan left, grabbing up their kids and belongings to escape to Looong Island or Upstate for some peace and tranquility, whilst the invading tribes from Europe and the Boroughs ate up The Big Apple taking mighty bites and spitting it out onto New York's crowded streets. There were lines outside of restaurants where people would wait in a queue to eventually be allowed in to experience the taste of an egg or two. I looked at it all as a kind of mad eating frenzy, the last supper before the Apocalypse and little did we know at that weekend of the 8th and 9th that indeed the Apocalypse was on its way!

It was now Monday morning and the hoards had left the city and people stood out on Hudson Street hailing cabs to take them to work in Midtown or wherever. I was up bright and early drinking a coffee and eating an egg or two at The Bus Stop Café as I watched the show go on through the window. The machine had cranked up again after the weekend and that New York energy buzzed like electricity on the streets. My feet started to tap under the table, as I too had to get out there, just to be a part of it. Later in the day I had a very informal meeting with the client, and towards the end of the week we would discuss the shooting of the up and coming commercials. I was going to be working again and making a bit of dosh. I felt good and positive about the prospect. In the evening I popped across the road to get a bite to eat and went back to my temporary home and watched some chat show or other.

Tuesday September 11th

For some reason I wasn't up so bright and early as I was making a slow start to the day and jumped in the shower at about eight-thirty. I looked out onto Hudson Street and the hubbub had already been long under way. It was a glorious morning as I felt a little cool breeze enter the apartment and couldn't wait to enjoy this day out on the street. I finished drying my hair with a towel, as I looked out of the window at the day ahead of me. I was dying for a coffee and finished dressing and by now it was about fifteen minutes to nine when I heard a plane fly over the apartment or close to. I realized that it was flying low as one never heard the sound of planes flying in Manhattan above all the other noise of the city. Planes flew over New York but they would be a few thousand feet above. This was a noise I had never heard before and in a second or two the noise was gone. This was New York where sirens and car horns and people yelling were an everyday occurrence, so I thought nothing of this alien sound. By now it was a few minutes before nine o' clock and I finally dragged myself out onto the street to experience this beautiful morning when I noticed a large crowd of people facing south and thought that maybe there was a movie being shot, when I looked up to see smoke pouring out of the North Tower. If this was a film then I thought this was a pretty spectacular stunt, but within seconds I realized this was no film being shot and that something dreadful had happened - a terrible accident. I walked over to Greenwich St, so as to get a clearer look at the Towers, and by now people were in a state of shock, women were screaming. Cars were parked and people had their radios turned up loud, so we could all hear on the news what was happening. It was like the radio show that Orson Welles put on about the Invasion of visitors from out of space, which was an episode of War of the Worlds that freaked everyone out back in 1938. But this was no Radio nor TV show. I stood standing there looking at the smoking Tower like everyone else, when out of nowhere another jetliner slammed into the other Tower this one from the South West that almost went all the way through. There are no words to really describe the next few minutes.

People stood dumbfounded mouths open, women and men were screaming - some of those people there with me on the street had friends or loved ones that were at work in those Towers. It was now about nine o' clock and about fifteen minutes since the first plane hit the North Tower. It was obvious that this was no freak accident - two planes within minutes of each other hitting the cities highest buildings.

Newscasters were now screaming on the radio stations that America was under a terrorist attack, as the crowds grew in the streets, all eyes facing south towards the Towers, now both in flames with thick smoke billowing out of the smashed windows breaking up the clear blue sky that had greeted New Yorkers just an hour before. It was a spectacle that no one wanted to see, but you stood there staring in awe, eyes wide open, and your mind not really understanding what your eyes were seeing. People were jumping from ninety stories onto the streets below to escape the inferno. Thank God I was too far away to see that. Sirens cracked through the crying of people the fire trucks screaming down the West Side Highway followed by ambulances and police cars. It seemed like the whole of the New York Fire Department and the NYPD were moving as fast as they could towards the burning Towers. It was now about 9.30am and someone yelled out that another plane had crashed into the Pentagon. The whole of America was under siege, being attacked by its own planes from the skies. Panic was beginning to set in with the crowd, as newscasters were reporting the series of events from car radios that were turned up high, so that all around could listen in. It seemed surreal, as we all stood mesmerized watching flames and smoke pour from the beautiful twin towers, whilst listening to other attacks elsewhere in the country.

At about 10am the South Tower that was the second tower to be hit fell to the ground about an hour after it was hit. In slow motion it descended its slow death to the ground as Lower Manhattan was shrouded in plumes of whirling gray and white smoke, which rose half way up the North Tower. A couple of minutes later - another news bulletin blared out from a tinny car radio that yet another plane had crashed into a field somewhere in Pennsylvania. People looked at each other in disbelief, stunned by this strange sequence of events that seemed so strategically well planned, like a well thought out film production, but this was no horror film- this was real life and people were being killed in New York, Pennsylvania and in Virginia and I wondered what would happen next. If I saw a huge mushroom cloud appear on the horizon next I would not have been too surprised as I felt resigned and helpless during this onslaught of terror, that had hit the hearts of everyone in America in the last hour and a half, and the finale of this devils opera was only another twenty five minutes away, when the North Tower plummeted to the ground to join his dead brother, as more dust and debris swirled and spun in gray clouds of smoke extinguishing from view everything around for blocks in all directions. From where I was standing all that could be seen was a huge cloud that swirled around replacing the towers that had disappeared like an evil magicians trick.

As the smoke settled down, the cityscape of New York was changed forever. It became mythology, as if the Titans had been struck down leaving an empty space, physically, spiritually and mentally, and I felt like I had lost a loved one. Thousands on that day had lost their loved ones as their husbands or wives, sons and daughters had innocently gone to work in the Towers like they had done every day, now never to return home. It had been merely an hour and a half since I stepped out onto a beautiful sunny day in The Big Apple and in that time the Apple had been poisoned. The strange spectacle was over as I watched the Towers both disappear and the crowds dispersed and people returned to the safety of their homes as though they had been to a rock concert. I turned on the TV like thousands of others and watched the replays, over and over, still not believing what I saw. My friend finally got through to me on the phone as the lines were jammed from London, and I told her all that I could.

In the afternoon I walked past St Vincent's Hospital and saw the billboards with hundreds of faces pinned to them of loved ones, and my heart sank as I tried to imagine that dreadful loss, and I burst into tears at the thought of it and the aftermath of what I had just experienced. I wanted to just hug everyone I saw. I walked around for a while in a daze until the late afternoon when I went back to the apartment to find out from the TV that World Trade Tower Seven had collapsed, which was a forty-seven story building that was close to the Towers - fortunately no one was killed. This building looked like it imploded on itself. So that was the final encore of disaster for the day as even more smoke swirled around Lower Manhattan as more people were evacuated from the area. Airports had been closed throughout the country during the day and one could not get in nor out of New York.

The smoke from the wreckage was blowing out towards Staten Island, but everyone was advised to keep their windows closed. The next couple of days were like a mourning period after a funeral, the Towers were gone and so too almost three- thousand people. The pictures of loved ones were added to the billboards outside of St. Vincent's Hospital as people hoped that the smiles from the photos were still alive somehow. In the evening a candlelight vigil was held in Union Square Park where shrines were dedicated to the lost loved ones, of brothers and sisters and mothers and fathers. People prayed that friends or lovers or relatives were still alive somehow, maybe some still buried alive under the rubble waiting for the sniffer dogs to search them out. The feeling in that square at night was not one of revenge or hatred, but of love, and people wanted peace in the world not this. There are reasons why things like this happen, but at this point in time people were too busy grieving. After three days or so the wind switched directions and started to blow that toxic smoke uptown. I called my friend out in the country and took a bus to escape from the sorrow and grieving that clouded the city as I felt like there was nothing I could do to really help. I didn't know of anyone who died on that day thank God.

Obviously my job was cancelled and I flew back to California the following week after a few days in the country.

I arrived in NYC at the birth of the towers in '76 as they were to have been completed as I was told for the celebration of the Bi- Centennial. I always looked at them as though they were two brothers standing steadfast keeping an eye on the rest of Manhattan as their mother the Empire State Building stood in Midtown a symbol of western culture and ideas. Twenty-five years later I saw the brothers   crumble when they collapsed like two young men dying in their prime at the age of twenty-five. The time of love and peace and innocence of the sixties and seventies was long gone, dissolved into history now a remnant from the last century as we now entered a new age of retaliation, the internet, pornography, self-indulgence, greed and religious wars. We had not evolved as humans but regressed, it was now a time for a rebirth of spirituality and a time to evolve into a state of higher thinking. The collapse of the Towers, and the rest of the carnage that happened on that day of September 11th 2001 will forever remain shrouded in mystery, just as lower Manhattan was shrouded in a choking grey dust on that beautiful sunny morning. As to what really happened and why, conspiracy theories abound, we perhaps will never know, much like the shroud of mystery that surrounded and still surrounds the Kennedy assassination that happened almost forty years before.

Now - in the year 2017 a huge question mark hangs over the world.
THE END

The Big Apple before September 11th 2001

A day that no one will forget...

Author Bio:

John Drake was born in London in the 1950's. He started his career in a photographic darkroom and went on to become a photographer in London. After much traveling throughout Europe and India he found himself in New York, after taking a freighter from England to Jamaica (these adventures can be found in his first Memoir called THE LAUGHING MAN on Amazon.com).

After settling in Manhattan (The Big Apple) he began a new career in the film business, and after a few years was working as a director of photography on feature films and commercials. In 1987 John moved to California where he worked as a director/cameraman for various companies in the United States and Europe.

Around 1998 he found a new love in painting, and after a couple of gallery openings of his work now has over 600 paintings to his name. In the same year he had a photo exhibit of his still photographs on Melrose Avenue in Los Angeles.

In 1999 John moved to Vancouver to continue working in film, but still keeps a place in Santa Monica. In 2004 he went to India to film a Bollywood production called 'My Faraway Bride.'

He still continues his nomadic gypsy lifestyle and lives in Mexico for half of the year, coming and going between Mexico, California and Vancouver.

In 2016 he compiled this memoir "Stories From The Big Apple and Beyond" from writings and diaries from his life in Manhattan and Woodstock during the Seventies and Eighties and also stories of his adventures traveling once again through India and South- East Asia. The story ends on 9/11 when there in New York for a job, John witnesses the attack on The World Trade Towers.

John Drake in the Santa Monica Mountains.

Made in the USA
San Bernardino, CA
07 April 2019